GUIDE
TO
PHOTOGRAPHS
AT THE
PENNSYLVANIA
STATE ARCHIVES

Linda A. Ries

Commonwealth of Pennsylvania
Pennsylvania Historical and Museum Commission
Harrisburg, 1993

THE PENNSYLVANIA HISTORICAL AND MUSEUM COMMISSION

To

The Memory Of

DOROTHY BRUSZO WEISER
1937-1991

A dedicated staff member and friend.

CONTENTS

NOTICE TO RESEARCHERS

Persons desiring more information on the research potential of particular photograph holdings or other records should inquire about unpublished box listings or inventories maintained in the Search Room of the State Archives, Box 1026, Harrisburg, PA 17108-1026. These inventories will provide a more complete folder-by-folder description. All collections of the State Archives are available for on-site research by the public. Requests by mail or telephone for research by staff are subject to a Search Fee. Reproductions from the collections are also available at a modest charge. Some holdings are specified as subject to U.S. Copyright laws or donor-imposed restrictions. In these cases it is the researcher's responsibility to obtain permission for use.

All photographs are black and white prints unless otherwise specified. "Cu. ft." stands for cubic feet.

The cover illustration is a 1906 photograph of the newly dedicated Capitol at Harrisburg, by William H. Rau (see page 65).

Introduction

This *Guide* describes the estimated 350,000 photographs among the holdings of the Division of Archives and Manuscripts (Pennsylvania State Archives) of the Pennsylvania Historical and Museum Commission. Most materials found at the State Archives are, of course, documentary in nature. These are arranged into record groups, i.e., records created by the Commonwealth of Pennsylvania's governing agencies and political subdivisions; and manuscript groups, or personal or private papers of individuals or businesses significant to Pennsylvania's history. Photographs are found within record and manuscript groups as well. Obviously, not all contain images, hence the reader will find gaps in the numerical sequence of this publication. Persons desiring more detailed information concerning the overall nature of the State Archives holdings should consult Frank M. Suran, *Guide to the Record Groups in the Pennsylvania State Archives* (Harrisburg: PHMC 1980) and Harry E. Whipkey, *Guide to the Manuscript Groups in the Pennsylvania State Archives* (Harrisburg: PHMC, 1976). There are also guides offering combined information from the above two on specialized subjects: Robert M. Dructor, *Guide to Genealogical Sources at the Pennsylvania State Archives* (Harrisburg: PHMC, 1981); Martha M. Simonetti, *Descriptive List of the Map Collection in the Pennsylvania State Archives* (Harrisburg: PHMC, 1976); and Frank M. Suran and Nancy L. P. Fortna, *Guide to County and Municipal Records on Microfilm in the Pennsylvania State Archives* (Harrisburg: PHMC, 1982).

The production of any guide requires the assistance of many persons. I would like to thank the staff members previously responsible for photograph collections, Dana Gisselman Beyer and James Arnold, who initially organized and prepared inventories for many of the holdings. Dr. Robert M. Dructor, Chief of the Division of Archives and Manuscripts and Harry E. Whipkey, Director of the Bureau of Archives and History, provided many constructive comments and suggestions. The manuscript, the first State Archives guide to be developed by computer, was processed by Angela M. Orsini and Dorothy B. Weiser, and proofed by James Arnold, John Shelly and Pat Appleby. The index was prepared by Richard Saylor, Pat Appleby, Hertha Williams and Barbara Hoyniak. The staff of the PHMC Division of Publications and Sales, including Douglas West, Diane Reed, Harold Myers, Jonathan Bream and Richard Kearns, handled the publication. I am indebted to all of you.

Linda A. Ries
Head, Processing Section
January, 1993

RECORD GROUPS

RG-6 Department of Forests and Waters #6984: "Carpenter squad of Pittsburgh boys, Civilian Conservation Corps, Pine Grove Furnace Camp, May 11, 1933" *(see p. 10).*

RG-1
RECORDS OF THE DEPARTMENT OF AGRICULTURE

The Department of Agriculture was created in 1895 to encourage the development of agriculture, horticulture, forestry and related industries. It is currently responsible for promoting the efficient marketing of farm products, controlling plant and animal diseases, and safeguarding the public against impure food, fertilizers and pesticides. Functions relating to forestry were transferred to the Department of Forestry in 1901 (See RG-6).

Bureau of Plant Industry

Photographic Negative File, 1905-1944, 13 cu. ft.

This series contains over 5,000 5x7 or 4x5 glass or film negatives created and used by the bureau for technical and publicity purposes. Each image, arranged numerically, is housed in a folder bearing a number and descriptive information. Plants and insects often bear their Latin taxonomic names. A contact print is occasionally filed with the negative. Subjects cover day-to-day activities of the bureau and other bureaus of the department, special events, animals, insects and plants.

Activities show staff at work at the Bureau of Animal Industry Labora-

RG-1 Department of Agriculture - Bureau of Plant Industry #2066d:
"Tobacco Planter in Operation, Lancaster, PA 1921."

tories at Summerdale; the Insect Collection Room at the Bureau of Plant Industry; exhibits at the Bureau of Zoology; egg testing at the Division of Poultry; treating potato wart, gummosis of cherry, peach tree borer, chestnut blight, tomato leaf wilt, white pine blister, and other plant diseases at experimental farms and orchards all over the state. Also included are formal portraits of Secretaries of Agriculture, 1895-1940, deputy secretaries, general staff and the Farm Show Commission. Special events cover staff at a 1919 Potato Conference and a 1922 Entomological Field Meeting in New York; a 1920 agricultural fair in Washington County; the 1922 dedication of the York Imperial Apple Marker near York; a 1926 Shade Tree Conference; the agriculture exhibits at the Pennsylvania Building of the 1926 United States Sesquicentennial Celebration, Philadelphia; the 1929 ground-breaking ceremonies for the State Farm Show Building, Harrisburg; various annual State Farm Shows including the 1938 cornerstone-laying ceremonies for the Farm Show Arena, Harrisburg; and various meetings of the American Association of Economic Entomologists.

Animals include domesticated and wild animals and birds, most native to Pennsylvania. Domesticated animals are shown at various farms throughout the state, especially the State College area. Animals include: black bears, cattle, chickens, deer, foxes, hogs, horses, mice, minks, muskrats, opossums, porcupines, rabbits, raccoons, rats, various reptiles, sheep, skunks, squirrels, weasels, woodchucks and others. Birds include: bitterns, coots, ducks, eagles, all types of finches, geese, gulls, herons, loons, mergansers, owls, quails, rails, turkeys, all types of warblers, woodpeckers and others.

Insects are either beneficial or harmful to farm and forest production. Many views are technical studies of an insect at various stages of development: egg, larva and adult. Most are devoted to bees and beekeeping, with views of various apiaries throughout the state. Other insects include: ants; aphids; beetles, especially Japanese beetles; peach tree borers; corn worms; cut worms; earwigs; flies and maggots; grasshoppers; ladybugs; lice; millipedes; mites; mosquitos; moths and tent caterpillars, especially gypsy moths; red bugs; scales; thrips; ticks; waterbugs and many others.

Plants are primarily vegetable, fruit and nut crops, shown at planting, cultivation, harvesting and processing. Examples are shown of healthy plants and those damaged by the above insects and typical diseases. Other problems include cankers, dry rot, fungus, rust, scabs, scale and smut. There are views of orchards in St. Thomas, North East, Exeter and other parts of the state. Fruits include many varieties of apples, blackberries, blueberries, cherries, elderberries, grapes, huckleberries, peaches, pears, plums, raspberries, strawberries, and tomatoes. Nuts include acorn, chestnut, hickory and pine. Vegetables include asparagus, barley, beans, brussel sprouts, buckwheat, cabbage, carrots, corn, chicory, clover, mushrooms, onions, peas, radishes, and wheat. Miscellaneous plants include azaleas, dodder, grass, mustard, nettles, poison ivy, rhododendron, roses, sorrel, tobacco, thistle, wound wort and many others.

Miscellaneous subjects include views of pruning and spraying trees in Capitol Park, Harrisburg; orchards owned by Governor William Sproul; farm machinery; greenhouses at Langhorne; flour mills in Annville, Chambersburg, Codorus, Durham, Highspire, Muncy and Paoli; the town of Somerville, N.J., during a 1920 gypsy moth infestation; the Heinz Tomato Canning Factory, Chambersburg; and "war gardens" cultivated by anthracite coal miners in Highland, Jeddo and Weatherly, and bituminous miners in Fayette County.

Lantern Slide File, 1905-1944, 7 cu. ft.

This series contains approximately 3,500 glass lantern slides primarily created from the above negative file for educational and study purposes. Most bear descriptive information and the number of the negative from which each was taken. Others are illustrations taken from books, maps, charts or graphs. There are also title slides prepared by staff for use in lectures. A few were purchased from commercial photographic firms such as Williams, Brown & Earle Co., Philadelphia; the Edmondson Co., Cleveland, and from Mrs. M.V. Slingerlund. Though originally arranged by subject, this order has been lost, and the file is presently unorganized. See the above negative file for subjects.

Reports and Related Records, 1917-1961, 2.5 cu. ft.

This series contains annual and biennial reports, memoranda and correspondence of the bureau. Occasionally contact prints of the above negative file are found among the records or printed in the reports. The photograph file is periodically referred to in these records.

Bureau of Markets

Lantern Slide File, ca. 1920, 50 items

The file consists of lantern slides of interior and exterior views of public markets in Pennsylvania, ca. 1920. The slides, in a slotted wooden container, are arranged as for a lecture. There is no index to the lecture, and most markets are unidentified. Identified items include the Farmers' Market, Lancaster; Broad Street Market, Harrisburg, and the South Side and Diamond Markets, Pittsburgh.

RG-5
RECORDS OF THE CONSTITUTIONAL CONVENTIONS

Pennsylvania has held five constitutional conventions, in 1776, 1789, 1837, 1872 and 1967, all in response to demands for sweeping changes to the existing document. There are no illustrative materials in this record group for the first four conventions.

The Constitutional Convention of 1967-1968

Records of the Preparatory Committee, 3.5 cu. ft.

Includes nineteen prints, usually 8x10, of portraits of Committees on Local Government, Rules, Legislative Apportionment, Judiciary, etc.; formal and informal portraits of convention delegates such as William Scranton, James Michener, Robert P. Casey, Raymond Broderick, Richard Thornburgh, Thomas Fagan, and others.

Records of the Information Office, 3.5 cu. ft.

Includes an 800 ft., 16mm color motion picture film, "A Living Constitution," telling the story of the convention's proceedings. Produced by Stuart Finley of Falls Church, Virginia.

RG-6
RECORDS OF THE DEPARTMENT OF FORESTS AND WATERS

The Department of Forests and Waters was created in 1923 to consolidate the Department of Forestry, the Water Supply Commission and the Bureau of Topographic and Geologic Survey. The Department of Forestry was originally established in 1895 as the Division of Forestry in the Department of Agriculture and became separate in 1901. It was responsible for the acquisition and management of state forest lands, the development of state parks, the protection and improvement of the Commonwealth's water supply, and other related duties. The Department of Forests and Waters was absorbed by the Department of Environmental Resources in 1971.

Water Supply Commission

Records of the Water Resources Inventory Report, 1913-1920, 14 cu. ft.

The State Legislature passed the Inventory Act of 1913 to create a systematic inventory of the Commonwealth's water resources in order to better determine locations for reservoirs and dams, learn ways to minimize floods, increase navigation, etc. It resulted in the ten-part *Water Resources Inventory Report*, published by the State Printer in 1916. Records include correspondence, maps, charts, field notes, photographs and typewritten drafts of the final report. Photographs are nearly 300 prints of varying size either taken by staff or obtained from other sources and glued to pages of the final draft. Those collected but not used in the draft are interfiled with the appropriate section. All items are identified on the reverse, often giving the date and photographer. Some are air-brushed. Prints are not found in Parts I, V and VI.

Part II. *Turtle Creek Investigation,* 1913-1916, contains 104 views taken between 1907-1914 of factories, railyards and homes in East Pittsburgh, Harrison City, Pitcairn, Trafford, Turtle Creek and Wilmerding. Notable items include views of the Edgar Thomson Open Hearth Steel Works, the Westinghouse Air Brake Company, and the Turtle Creek Floods of 1907 and 1911. Most views are 3 x 5 1/2 contact prints by staff taken in the summer of 1914. A few are by Henry Sonnenberg, a Turtle Creek photographer.

Part III. *Gazetteer of Streams,* 1914-1916, contains nineteen views of streams throughout the Commonwealth, including views of the Analomink, Broadhead and Pennypack Creeks and the Lehigh, Delaware (at Narrowsville), Schuylkill and Susquehanna (at Rockville) Rivers, by James Bartlett Rich, a Philadelphia photographer. Views by unidentified photographers include the Beaver, Monongahela, Raystown, Shenango, Youghiogheny and Susquehanna (North and West Branch) Rivers. Also included is a view of the Allegheny at New Kensington, by the U.S. Engineer's Office, Pittsburgh.

Part IV. *Gazetteer of Lakes and Ponds,* 1916, contains sixteen views of lakes and ponds in Crawford (especially Conneaut Lake), Lackawanna, Monroe, Pike, Susquehanna and Wyoming Counties by staff photographers.

Part VII. *Water Power,* 1913-1916, contains nearly 100 views of dams, waterfalls and power plants in the Delaware and Susquehanna River basins, taken by staff during 1914. Delaware Basin sites include Kalbach Company plants on Tulpehocken Creek; the Philadelphia Suburban Gas and Electric Company at Cromby; the Wilson Hauser and White Haven Water Company on the Lehigh River; the Pennsylvania Utilities Company at Easton; the Dexter/Lambert Silk Mill and Paupack Electric Company at Hawley; and smaller plants and dams at Birdsboro, Norristown, Fairmount,

Womelsdorf, Manayunk, Mauch Chunk, Stroudsburg, Phoenixville and New Hope. Susquehanna Basin sites include the Lancaster Light, Heat and Power Company; Eagles Mere Light Company; the Pennsylvania Water and Power Company at Holtwood; Wrightsville Light and Power Company; York Haven Water and Power Company; and smaller plants and dams at Belleville, Boalsburg, Boiling Springs, Carlisle, Cypher, Grantham, Fishing Creek, Hummelstown, Huntingdon, Middle Creek, Middleburg, Mifflinburg, Millersburg, Orangeville, Raystown, Reynoldsdale, Selinsgrove, Shippensburg, Strasburg, Tunkhannock, Warrior Ridge and Yeagertown. Also included are power plants of paper mills at Mount Holly Springs and York Haven.

Part VIII. *Floods*, 1916, contains seventeen views of floods in Huntingdon, Lewistown and Williamsport, 1889; Easton, 1903; Shenango, Tarentum, Warren and Wilkes-Barre, 1913; and Dunmore, Scranton and Westmoor, 1914, by unidentified photographers.

Part IX. *Navigation*, 1912-1916, contains eighty-four scenic views along the Delaware, Lehigh and Schuylkill Canals, most by James Bartlett Rich. Other items include the Tidewater Canal at Wrightsville, and dams on the Allegheny and Monongahela Rivers taken by the U.S. Engineer's Office and other photographers.

RG-6 Department of Forests and Waters Photograph File #334: "Group of Bark Peelers" ca. 1890 by William T. Clarke, probably Potter County.

Part X. *Culm in the Streams of the Anthracite Region,* 1916, contains eleven views by staff of coal slush and culm contaminating Mahanoy and Shenandoah Creeks, the Schuylkill River and other streams in the Anthracite Region.

Chief Engineer's Office Records, 1921-1963, 5 cu. ft.

The series contains records pertaining to the acquisition of land by the Commonwealth for the Pymatuning Reservoir Project. Areas in Crawford County, Pennsylvania, and eastern Ohio were flooded in the 1930s to create the multi-use Pymatuning Lake. Records include land deeds, reports, insurance appraisals and surveys, arranged numerically by file number. Occasionally interfiled are photographs of a property and any pertinent buildings thereon, usually farmhouses, barns, etc. These are roughly 3x5 contact prints, sometimes with matching negatives. Most appear to have been taken during the 1930s by G.S. Beal, possibly an insurance appraiser. Many contain identification as to subject and date photographed.

Bureau of Parks

General Correspondence, 1922-1941, 9 cu. ft.

Among these records is the "Historical Report on Fort Necessity, Jumonville's Grave, and Braddock's Trail," prepared by Roy Edgar Appelman for the National Park Service, August 21, 1935, which includes nine 2 3/4 x 5 photographic prints showing existing features at Fort Necessity State Park. Also included are eight similar prints taken November 20, 1936, showing Emergency Conservation Workers constructing paths, planting trees, etc., around the park.

Bureau of Forest Management

General Correspondence, 1920-1930, 1 cu. ft.

This series consists mainly of survey forms of buildings on state forest lands, primarily rangers' homes and outbuildings. Occasionally there are photographic prints of the building interfiled with the survey form. This file is unorganized.

Public Relations Office

Photograph File, ca. 1889-ca. 1960, 20.5 cu. ft.

The file contains over 2,700 negatives and approximately 8,000 matching prints generated by staff for education and publicity purposes. All negatives are glass, either 5x7 or 6 1/2 x 8 1/2, arranged numerically and accompanied by a contact print mounted on heavy board containing captions and negative numbers. The prints are arranged by subject. More prints than negatives attest to the fact that most original negatives were of nitrate base and have not survived.

Photography has been closely associated with the agency's work since its inception as the Division of Forestry under the Department of Agriculture. Many images were taken by forest rangers as part of their duties. Some later became high-ranking agency officials, such as Joseph Illick, George Wirt, Henry Clepper, and others. Later images of the 1930s and 1940s were taken by staff photographers, especially David S. Nace. Integrated with these are the private photograph collections of Dr. Joseph T. Rothrock and William T. Clarke, some of which predate the Division of Forestry. Rothrock was known as the "Father of Pennsylvania Forestry." Many of his photographs include those taken for *Forest Leaves* (now *Pennsylvania Forests*, the journal of the Pennsylvania Forestry Association), and views of Mont Alto Sanitarium, which he was instrumental in creating. William T. Clarke was a commercial photographer operating in Galeton in the late nineteenth century. He took many images of the Pennsylvania lumbering industry and community life therein.

The photographs were apparently arranged in their present form sometime in the 1920s and added to for years afterward, especially in the 1930s and 1940s. There are few items after 1950. Original large subject categories include:

Arbor Day exercises in New Cumberland, 1924, and at Slippery Rock Normal School, 1925.

"Big Trees" that are representative examples of Pennsylvania oak, elm, tulip, poplar, hemlock, white pine, etc., which have lived several hundred years.

Forestry Buildings, especially forest rangers' homes with associated outbuildings, picnic pavilions in various state parks, fire observers' cabins, the chapel and public school at Mont Alto, James Buchanan's birthplace, iron furnaces at Mont Alto and Caledonia, Laurelton State Village, the Jacob Nolde Estate, Civilian Conservation Corps buildings, the General Refractories Company at Karthaus, the Clarks Ferry Bridge, lock houses along the Delaware Canal and miscellaneous gristmills, country churches and other buildings.

Camps and Camp Sites, including those for forest rangers, Boy Scouts, the general public, and private hunting and fishing camps.

Demonstration Forests at Caledonia, Lebo, Sigel Millstone, and elsewhere.

Forest Destruction caused by chestnut blight, deer, erosion, floods, fungi, insects, humans, rabbits, snow and ice, wind, etc.

Emergency Conservation Work showing Civilian Conservation Corps members living and working at many camps throughout the state.

Farm Woodlots showing the use of forests as parts of farms throughout the state.

Floods and Flood Control along the Delaware Canal and elsewhere.

Forest Animals such as bear, beaver, bison, deer, elk, fish (trout farms), grouse, snakes, turtles and others.

Forest Conditions showing stand composition, water supply, natural regeneration, original stands, and miscellaneous views.

Forest Officials, with formal and informal portraits of members of the Forestry Commission, including Joseph T. Rothrock, S.B. Elliott, Robert S. Conklin, George Wirt, Mira L. Dock, Henry W. Shoemaker, and other agency officials. Also shown are group portraits at annual conferences of the Pennsylvania Forestry Association, the Pennsylvania Forest Research Institute, the State Foresters' Conventions, the Society of American Foresters, and Governor Arthur James's visit to Ricketts Glen State Park, 1941.

Forest Parks and Public Camps, including Bear Valley Public Camp, Buchanan State Forest; Big Spring Public Camp; Black Moshannon State Park; Blue Hole Spring in Forbes State Forest; Bucktail State Park; Bushy Run Battlefield; Caledonia State Park; Cherry Spring Station, Cherry Springs State Park, Childs State Park; Clear Creek Public Camp; Colerain State Park; Cook Forest State Park; Conrad Weiser Park; Cowan's Gap Park; Drake Well Park; S.B. Elliott Public Camp; Pennsylvania State Park (Presque Isle); Fort Necessity Park, including dedicatory exercises, July 4, 1932; Governor Printz Park; Greenwood Public Camp; Halfway Recreation Area; Leonard Harrison State Park; Hemlock State Park; Voneida State Park (Hairy Johns); Hickory Run Park; Hopewell Tower Park (Hopewell Village); Kettle Creek Park in Sproul Forest; Kooser Lake Park; Joyce Kilmer Park and Krumrine Public Camp in Bald Eagle Forest; Laurel Dam in Michaux Forest; Mont Alto State Park; John Morton Birthplace; Ole Bull Public Camp; Parker Dam State Park, including dam construction, 1939; Penn-Roosevelt Dam; Pine Grove Furnace Park; Poe Valley Lake; Promised Land Public Camp and Lake; Pymatuning Dam State Park, including opening day for fishermen, July 1, 1937; Ricketts Glen Park; Sizerville Park in Elk Forest; Roosevelt State Park; Sideling Hill Public Camp in Buchanan State Forest; Snyder-Middleswarth State Park; Stony Batter Park in Buchanan State Forest; Ralph Stover State Park (Burnt Mill); Valley Forge State Park; Washington Crossing State Park; and Worlds End State Park.

Forest People, including portraits of Andre Michaux, Alan Seeger, Joyce Kilmer, and various river raftsmen, snake-catchers, tar-burners, and others.

Forest Recreation, including the general public fishing, golfing, hiking, hunting, picnicking and swimming in the parks listed above, and outings with private clubs or organizations, including Girl and Boy Scouts, Young Men's Christian Association, Pennsylvania Alpine Club, and the Pennsylvania Forestry Association. Also included are views of waterfalls in Childs Park.

Forest Schools, especially views of Mont Alto State Forest School and Yale Forest School (Pike County); the Royal Forestry School in Italy; and the Nancy Forest School in France, where Gifford Pinchot studied.

"Important Tree Study Places," such as the A.E. Ball property, Mercer County; D.P. Drake property, Monroe County; Pierre du Pont Estate (Longwood); Gettysburg Battlefield; Lehigh University Campus; Marshall Arboretum and Westtown School, Chester County; H.Y. Miller Farm, Warren County; Mont Alto State Forest School; Nolde Estate, Berks County; Sligo, Clarion County, and the York Water Company Property, York County.

Lumbering Operations in Clinton, Lycoming, McKean, Sullivan and Potter Counties showing sawing, bark peeling, log loading and hauling by cart or railway; floating logs down the West Branch of the Susquehanna near Williamsport by the Central Pennsylvania Lumber Company, and other activities; devastated forests due to heavy logging; and views of life in logging camps.

Lumbering Towns, including Cameron, Driftwood and Emporium, Cameron County; Bitumen, Clinton County; Straight, Elk County; Betula, Gardeau and Norwich, McKean County; Austin, Cross Fork, Costello, Hull, Keating Summit, Logue, Lyman Run, Mina, Nine Mile, Roulette and Wharton, Potter County; and Leetonia, Tioga County.

Miscellaneous, including apple cider presses in Perry County; collecting maple syrup in various areas; a Raftsman's and Riverman's Reunion in McElhattan, 1928; the Mount Holly Forest Fire Association Annual Picnic, 1931; the Dauphin County Firemen's Association Parade, 1932; workers receiving unemployment relief, 1932, by gathering firewood, etc.; gypsy basketmakers; different examples of wood fencing; views of home and community life in coal mining and lumbering regions; ox teams; Allentown streets decorated with evergreen boughs, 1927-1929; Copperas and Ganister Rocks, Huntingdon County; idle farmlands in Lawrence, Crawford and Franklin Counties; various forest rangers' homes; gathering Christmas greens and shipping Christmas trees; site of Ole Bull Castle; copies of views of Pine Grove Furnace, ca. 1883; and anthracite mining and bituminous coal strip mining.

Monuments and Markers, including dedication ceremonies for the "Road of Remembrance," Wrightsville, 1922; birthplace and grave markers for President James Buchanan; the York Imperial Apple marker, York; Joseph T. Rothrock's grave in Chester; monument to Mary Jemison (the White Squaw), Adams County; markers honoring H.A. Smith in Venango County, George Wirt at Mont Alto, S.B. Elliott in Moshannon State Forest; markers at Fort Necessity and Braddock's Grave; Perry Victory Memorial at Presque Isle; 1930 dedication ceremonies of a marker commemorating the first purchase of State Forest Land at Young Womans Creek, Clinton County; 1936 dedication ceremonies of a marker honoring S.T. Moore at Greenwood Furnace; Mason and Dixon stone boundary markers; marker on the summit of Negro Mountain; and cemeteries in Perry, Huntingdon, Northampton, Bedford and Bucks Counties.

Tree Nursery Operations by the Department at Clearfield, Mont Alto, Milton, and Greenwood; at state prisons at Huntingdon, Rockview, and Graterford; and others including Antietam Nursery, Reading; Wernersville State Hospital; Overbrook Nursery, Philadelphia; Penn Nursery, Centre County; and the Clearfield Bituminous Coal Corporation, Indiana County.

Reforestation of Pennsylvania, ca. 1909-1930, shows planting trees in devastated and denuded areas due to forest fires, heavy timbering, mining, etc.; how trees are planted; types of trees planted; tools used to plant them; and life in planting camps.

Ornamental Tree Planting along streets and rural roads, including Front Street, Harrisburg; various streets in West Chester; near Echo Lake, Monroe County; along the Lincoln Highway and Route 1 near Halifax.

Sawmills, notably those of the Central Pennsylvania Lumber Company, the Wheeler and Dusenbury Company, the Clearfield Bituminous Coal Corporation, E.C. King Sawmill in Cambria County, and smaller mills in Austin, Costello, Gardeau, Sizerville, Leetonia, Hull, Norwich, Keating Summit, Roulette and Cross Fork. Also included are up-and-down and portable mills in Berks, Cameron, Centre, Franklin, Huntingdon and Perry Counties.

Wood-using Industries and Wood Products include the following paper mills: Glatfelter Pulp and Paper Company, York County; New York and Pennsylvania Paper Company, Elk County; West Virginia Paper and Pulp Company, Blair County; Hammermill Paper Company, Erie; and an unidentified paper mill at Austin; chemical companies such as the Gray Chemical Company and the Keystone Chemical Company, McKean County; Tionesta Valley Chemical Company, Forest County; the Gaffney Brothers Wood Products Plant, Potter County; and miscellaneous companies such as the Norwich Lumber Company and the Wheeler and Dusenbury Company in northern Pennsylvania; the Costello Tannery; the Elk Tanning Company, Sullivan County; Edwin Bell Stave Mill, Franklin County; Columbia Wagon Works, Lancaster County; and a locust pin mill in Bedford County. Other items include charcoal-making, and activities at various mills producing keg staves, pins, fruit and vegetable baskets, shingles, tanbark, etc.

Small Subject Categories include: chestnut tree culturing; views of European forests, especially in Germany and Switzerland; exhibits staged by the Department at the Pennsylvania Farm Show, county fairs, and elsewhere; experiments in forest conversion; forest fires, fire fighting equipment, fire towers and fire lines; forest mensuration and weather instruments; forest growth studies at Mont Alto and other forests; patients at Mont Alto Sanitarium; box huckleberry studies, including views of immigrant berry pickers; boundary and division lines for state forest property and the construction of the boundary markers; maps of state forests and statistical charts on forest fires, forest growth, etc.; tree grafting; tree plantations; state forest road construction; experimental and sample tree plots; seed supply stations; road signs for state forest boundaries, trails, picnic areas, fire prevention, etc.; surveying crews; state forest trails in Cameron, Bedford, Franklin, Lancaster, Perry, Pike and other counties; tree bark; tree surgery; unique (freak) trees; and willow tree culturing.

Motion Picture Films, ca. 1930-1950, 41 reels

These are 16mm black and white and color films produced by the Department of Forests and Waters to document and publicize its various programs. Most are 400 ft. silent black and white films showing departmental activities such as "Gypsy Moth Control," "The Story of a Pine Seed," and "Tree Trimming." Of note here are two films showing unemployment relief workers cutting firewood and building roads at Birch Run Dam, and five films showing Civilian Conservation Corps activities around the state. Items for public education include "The Maple Sugar Industry in Pennsylvania," "Trees for Tomorrow," and "The Life of a Seedling." Two films concerning forest fires were produced by federal agencies: "Then It Happened," by the U.S. Department of Agriculture; and "The Enemy Fire," by the U.S. Office of Civilian Defense.

RG-9
RECORDS OF THE GENERAL STATE AUTHORITY

The General State Authority was created in 1935 as an independent public corporation, as the Commonwealth of Pennsylvania could not legally take advantage of the federal grant and loan offers from the Public Works Administration. The Authority had responsibility for negotiating funds needed to build, expand and modernize state facilities. The Department of General Services, created in 1975, replaced the General State Authority.

Blueprints and Photographs, 1937-1939, 5 cu. ft.

This series contains 8x10 prints of construction, expansion or modernization of various Commonwealth-owned properties. The prints are arranged by docket number and each is labeled with the job and docket number, name of facility, location, date, name of contractor and status of construction. Blueprints are some-times interfiled with the prints. No original negatives are present. Local commercial photographers were often hired, and their identification occasionally is found on the print. Subjects are almost all exterior shots of construction progress at Pennsylvania National Guard Armories, hospitals, teachers colleges, prisons and miscellaneous state buildings.

Armories include those at Altoona, Canonsburg, Clearfield, Coraopolis, Gettysburg, Hamburg, Harrisburg, Huntingdon, Lancaster, Lewistown, Ligonier, Philadelphia, Tunkhannock, Waynesboro and Williamsport.

Hospitals include those at Allentown, Ashland, Blossburg, Coaldale, Connellsville, Danville, Fairview, Hazleton, Locust Mountain, Nanticoke, Norristown, Philipsburg, Scranton, Torrance, Warren, and Wernersville; the Western Pennsylvania Tuberculosis Hospital at Butler, and the Western Pennsylvania Psychiatric Hospital at Pittsburgh.

Teachers Colleges include those at Bloomsburg, California, Clarion, East Stroudsburg, Edinboro, Indiana, Kutztown, Lock Haven, Mansfield, Shippensburg, Slippery Rock and West Chester.

Prisons/Industrial Homes and Schools include the Eastern State Penitentiary, Huntingdon Industrial School, Lawn Maximum Security Prison, the Industrial School at Pennhurst, Polk State School and the Industrial Reformatory at Huntingdon.

RG-10
RECORDS OF THE OFFICE OF THE GOVERNOR

As chief executive officer of the Commonwealth, the Governor is responsible for directing and supervising the activities of administrative departments, boards and commissions under his authority to ensure the faithful execution of the laws of the Commonwealth. He is also commander-in-chief of the state's military force except when called into federal service.

Office of the Secretary of Administration

Secretary's Correspondence, 1971-1979, 23 cu. ft.

Includes ten 8x10 prints of a PUSH Conference (People United to Save Humanity), ca. 1976, featuring the Reverend Jesse Jackson as speaker.

Council of National Defense and the Committee of Public Safety (World War I)

General File, 1917-1920, 2 cu. ft.

Includes eight glass lantern and film slides by the Council to encourage military recruitment; and prints of varying size of the Junior Red Cross at Allegheny County schools and the Senior Red Cross at Allentown and Carlisle, showing volunteers wrapping bandages, selling bonds, tending war gardens, parades, etc.; forty-six items on activities of the Women's Land Army in America in eastern Pennsylvania and Pittsburgh, notably the Canning Unit; miscellaneous items on the "Suffrage Service Hut" maintained for soldiers by the Eastern Franchise Federation and the Recreation Room of the Jewish Welfare Board, both in Pittsburgh, 1918.

RG-10 Office of the Governor--Council of National Defense...General File: "Vice Chairmen and Surgical Dressings Department of the Allentown Chapter, American Red Cross, Fourth Liberty Loan Parade, September 1918, Allentown."

Also included are the remains of an album, "History of Curb Markets Established by the U.S. Food Administration, 1917-1918," containing twenty-two prints with captions of markets in the following municipalities: Allentown, Beaver, Bethlehem, Bradford, Bristol, Chambersburg, Coatesville, Connellsville, Erie, Franklin, Harrisburg, Hazleton, Lehighton, Palmerton, Philadelphia, Pittsburgh, Plymouth and Shippensburg.

Pennsylvania Selective Service Headquarters

General File, 1940-1946, 4 cu. ft.
Includes an album entitled "The American Red Cross in Pennsylvania, 1942-1945, a report to the Honorable Edward M. Martin," with prints, usually 5x7, showing Red Cross volunteers and nurses at home and abroad assisting in the war effort; and thirteen 8x10 loose prints of activities of the Pennsylvania Reserve Defense Corps, showing Governor Arthur James with soldiers.

Commission on the Status of Women

History File, 1972-1975, 3 cu. ft
Interfiled among these records are occasional 8x10 photographs of members of the commission at various activities, most notably with Governor Milton Shapp signing a proclamation for Equal Rights Day, August 26, 1972.

RG-11
RECORDS OF THE DEPARTMENT OF HEALTH

Created in 1905, the Department is responsible for enforcing statutes and regulations pertaining to public health matters. These include drug control, maternal and child health programs, dental health, crippled child services, health education and disease suppression.

Division of Graphics Photograph File, 1944-1978, 32 cu. ft.

This series contains approximately 11,500 original negatives and matching prints by staff photographers. They record department activities for education and publicity purposes. Some work for other state agencies is included. Negatives made before 1970 are 4x5 film with accompanying 8x10 prints mounted on heavy board containing captions and negative numbers. Negatives produced after 1970 are 70mm film with contact print sheets. Some color items appear after 1974. Captions often give dates, location, subject and negative number. The original photographers' log (two volumes) filed with the series numerically, contains the above information and often the photographer's name.

The photographs were either taken in the Health Department's studio in Harrisburg, or in the field at various clinics, such as Cresson, Elizabethtown, Mont Alto, Norristown, Danville, Harrisburg, Warren, Philadelphia, and other locales pertaining to the Department's functions.

Subjects include: administrative work of the Secretary of Health; social activities such as conferences, workshops, parties, softball and bowling teams, etc.; air and stream pollution abatement, control, compliance, and monitoring with before and after scenes of factory smokestacks, waste drains, etc.; members and activities of the Air Pollution Commission; air raid tests and civil defense; alcoholism studies and rehabilitation; ambulance training; behavioral science; interior and exterior views of Department of Health Buildings and facilities all over the state; cardiology programs; cerebral palsy treatment; child health care; chronic diseases; communicable diseases; community environmental services; culm bank fires at Johnstown, Scranton, Centralia and other places; cystic fibrosis treatment; dairy farm and creamery sanitation; dental health; disaster medicine; drug and narcotic abuse and control; environmental protection; epidemiology; public health exhibits at the Pennsylvania Farm Show and elsewhere; field services and clinics; fish kills; food protection and sanitation; garbage dumps and cleanups; Governors Duff, Fine, Leader, Lawrence, Scranton, Shafer and Shapp signing health legislation and participating at conferences, field reviews, etc.; home safety; home and institutional environments; industrial waste; hygiene; department laboratories; maternal health; medical social work; medicare services; migrant labor health services (primarily for Blacks and Puerto Ricans); mine drainage; mine safety; nutrition; nuclear waste; occupational health; physical therapy and prosthesis; polio therapy and vaccinations; portraits of department personnel; public health education; public health nursing; rabies clinics; radiology; recreational sanitation and safety; respiratory diseases; rheumatic fever; sanitary engineering; landfills; Sanitary Water Board activities; Secretary of Health activities; scenic views of clean streams; sewage disposal; tobacco smoking; solid waste management; strip mining; tuberculosis clinics and treatment; vector and insect control; venereal disease studies and treatment; veterinary clinics; water quality and supply; and x-rays.

Notable events include Department of Health participation at: the inaugurations of Governors Duff and Fine; flood disaster cleanup in Bucks and Monroe Counties, 1955, and in Elizabethtown following Hurricane Agnes in 1972; Boy Scout Jamborees at Valley Forge in 1957 and 1964 and various state camporees; the National Campers and Hikers Association Annual Camp at Prince Gallitzen State Park, 1967; operating field clinics during the Hong Kong Flu epidemic, 1969; and the annual Pennsylvania Health Conference held at State College and other towns, 1952-1977.

Office of the Secretary of Health

General Correspondence, 1939-1955, 2 cu. ft.
Contains letters between the Health Department and the Washington, D.C., photographic firm of Harris & Ewing regarding the making of portraits of the Secretaries of Health.

Portraits, 1905-1971, 14 items
Framed 16x20 portraits of the Secretaries of Health, some by Harris & Ewing (see above) or department photographers.

Sanitary Water Board

Office of Legal Counsel, Hearings and Opinions, 1953-1962, 14.5 cu. ft.
Records contain case files of information compiled against violators of state laws pertaining to water quality. Occasionally filed with the records are 8x10 prints of the site of the violation.

State Hospital for Crippled Children—Elizabethtown

Photograph Albums, 1942-1947, 1961-1965, 5 volumes
Four albums contain snapshots taken and compiled by staff members, showing patients in their wards; day-to-day activities; special events such as Easter, Halloween, and Christmas parties, "circus days" and picnics; and visits by the Shrine Circus in 1961 and 1964. One album was compiled by patient Betty Salada to record her stay. Also interleaved are newsclippings pertaining to hospital events, and editions of the newsletter *Our World*.

RG-12
RECORDS OF THE DEPARTMENT OF HIGHWAYS

When created in 1903, the Department administered state grants for road improvements by local communities. Reorganized in 1911, with duties expanded, it assumed responsibility for creating and maintaining a system of highways solely operated by the state. Later, additional responsibilities included supervisory powers over all roads funded in whole or part by the state, and the licensing of motor vehicles. Abolished in 1970, Highways was replaced by the Department of Transportation.

Bureau of Public Information

Photograph files, 1907-1973, over 62,000 items

These files are several distinct groupings of photographs encompassing the history and scope of the Department from its beginnings to its abolishment. The photographs were usually taken for recording or technical purposes, but after 1920 images were also taken for publicity, public education, etc. The Photograph Unit of the Department by the 1950s expanded to the point where photography work was also done for other state agencies unable to maintain their own photographers. The unit is known today as Commonwealth Media Services, part of the Department of General Services.

The Application File, 1907-1910, consists of 892 glass and film negatives, some with matching contact prints. The Highway Act of 1905 enabled county officials to apply to the state for assistance in repairing and rebuilding roads. The road in need of service was given a grant application number. The photographs show these roads before, sometimes during and after improvement, often taken from the same survey point. The negatives are arranged numerically, accompanied by contact prints mounted in four volumes arranged alphabetically by county. There is a log book with the file, containing numerical entries, often giving the date, location and other pertinent information. Though the log numbers 990 entries, only 892 negatives are present.

Roads in the following counties are included: Adams, Armstrong, Bedford, Blair, Bradford, Bucks, Butler, Cambria, Cameron, Centre, Chester, Clarion, Clearfield, Clinton, Crawford, Cumberland, Dauphin, Delaware, Elk, Erie, Forest, Franklin, Greene, Huntingdon, Indiana, Jefferson, Lancaster, Lebanon, Lehigh, Luzerne, Lycoming, McKean, Mercer, Monroe, Montour, Northumberland, Perry, Schuylkill, Sullivan, Tioga, Venango, Warren, Westmoreland and York.

The 5x7 File, 1913-1932, consists of approximately 11,000 contact prints from glass and film negatives. Following the reorganization of the Department in 1911, a new photograph file was created, known as the 5x7 file to differentiate it from later files containing other size negatives. Only a few images on glass from this file survive; others on nitrate base have deteriorated or have been destroyed. Prints are arranged by negative number and are mounted on a card containing descriptive information. Not all prints are present. Two logbooks with entries for negative number, subject, date, photographer and other descriptive information are present, along with a card file subject index arranged by county.

Subjects are primarily state highway work in all sixty-seven counties, usually before, during and after views taken from the same surveying point. Topics cover automobile accidents; bridges, including covered bridges, canal and railroad bridges, and others; road work equipment; the state motor police; types of road surfaces; snow and ice removal; district engineer offices; railroad grade crossings; directional signs and markers; quarries; toll houses; and other subjects relating to road work. Notable items show a 1915 flood in Erie; "Good Roads Day" ceremonies, 1915-1917, including Governor Martin Brumbaugh and highway officials touring Dauphin and Perry Counties, May 25, 1916; views of Prince Gallitzen Spring; Dingmans Falls; the Lehigh Canal in Bucks County; toll gates along the National Road; piers at the Erie waterfront; roadside monuments commemorating Fort Granville, Buchanan Birthplace, the Portage Railroad, the "Lost Children of the Alleghenies"; views of the Capitol Complex, Harrisburg; and many others.

The Main File, 1924-1970, consists mostly of 8x10 negatives numbering over 37,000 items with matching contact prints. Prints are arranged by subject, mounted on cards containing descriptive information including negative number, subject, location, photographer, etc. There are six logbooks listing negatives numerically, with similar descriptive information. The file continued after 1970 under the Department of Transportation (see RG- 52). Subjects include:

Buildings, especially the state government buildings of the Capitol Complex in Harrisburg, including the Education Building, Capitol, Northwest Office Building and construction of the Labor and Industry and North Office Buildings in 1928. Also included are the Farm Show Building and Harrisburg Arsenal. Other photographs show some county courthouses, gas stations, and historic structures around the state, including Albert Gallatin's "Friendship Hill," the Accomac Hotel in Wrightsville and the Elmwood Hotel in Conneaut.

Highway bridges for all sixty-seven counties, including covered bridges.

Highways, with scale models of proposed construction; views in all counties of construction in progress, climbing lanes, highway flooding, garages, grade crossings, guard rails, interchanges, intersections, maintenance, road breaks and faults, roadside planting of trees and shrubs, roadside rests, rock slides, road tests and laboratory experiments, road surfaces, safety, directional signs, snow fences, snow plows, snow removal, road stabilization, surveying crews, two-, three-, and four-lane highways, township roads, traffic congestion, tunnels and underpasses. Notable items include department staff activities and demonstrations, construction of the

Penn-Lincoln Parkway in Pittsburgh, 1948-1951; the Schuylkill Expressway and Penrose Avenue Bridge in Philadelphia, 1948-1952; and remains of the South Penn Railroad Tunnels used for the Pennsylvania Turnpike, and U.S. Army Officers at Ft. Howard, Md.

Historical topics, with the Emsworth Locks on the Ohio River; the Delaware Canal, the Lehigh Canal, the Philadelphia and Reading Canal and the Pennsylvania Canal at Sunbury, Columbia, Harrisburg and Dauphin; Gettysburg Battlefield; Valley Forge; Fort Necessity; Daniel Boone Homestead; Pennsbury Manor; the Fort Pitt Blockhouse; Conrad Weiser Park; Washington Crossing Park; Drake Well; Searight's Tollhouse; Sally Ann Furnace; Ephrata Cloister; Buchanan Birthplace; Girty's Notch; home of the Cornplanter Indians; fossils; and others.

Industry, with steel mills in Coatesville, Homestead and Steelton; cement works in Lehigh and Northampton Counties; sand quarries near Huntingdon; a slate quarry near Easton; coal mines near Ashland, Frackville, Girty's Notch, Mauch Chunk, Tamaqua, Tremont, and Somerset; oil refineries near Butler, Farmers Valley, Franklin, Rexford, Washington and Waynesburg, and a Gulf Oil Refinery near Philadelphia; iron production at Coventry Forge, Mont Alto Furnace and Sally Ann Furnace; the Bethlehem Steel Chemical Plant in Cambria County; and ruins of beehive coke ovens.

Monuments and statues, including those commemorating the Appalachian Trail, the Barnard Statues at the State Capitol, Brandywine Battlefield, General Braddock Grave, James Buchanan Grave, Confederate soldiers in Fulton County, Conrad Weiser, Chief Cornplanter, Thomas Cresap, Gettysburg Battlefield, Mary Jemison, the Kittanning Trail, the Kresge Family, Minquas Path (the Great Trail), the Paoli Massacre, Molly Pitcher Grave, Oliver Hazard Perry, Robert E. Peary, the Portage Railroad, Sally Ann Furnace, the Tulpehocken Pioneers, Valley Forge, George Washington at Braddock's Field, Washington Crossing, the Wyoming Massacre, and others.

The State Museum at Harrisburg showing artifacts and documents pertaining to Indians, transportation, natural history, the William Penn Charter, etc.; and Works Progress Administration Museum Extension Project workers with artifacts and making lantern slides.

The Rural Roads Program of Governor Gifford Pinchot, including Pinchot inaugurating the program in York County, July 23, 1931.

Scenic views of flowers and blossoms, especially apple blossoms in Adams County, mountain laurel in Monroe, Pike and Potter Counties, dogwood at Valley Forge and other places, and roses at Hershey Rose Gardens; cities and towns, especially Cooksburg, Dubois, Erie, Foster, Harrisburg, Johnstown, Logans Ferry, Mauch Chunk, Nanticoke, Nesquehoning, Newell, Philadelphia, Philipsburg, Pittsburgh and

Punxsatawney; dams, including Pymatuning Dam, Roosevelt Dam, Safe Harbor Dam, Tionesta Dam, a dam near Good Hope Mills, ruins of the Austin Dam, and various smaller dams in Monroe, Sullivan and York Counties; springs and fountains including Arch Spring, Brown Spring, Chestnut Spring, Prince Gallitzen Spring, springs near Clarion, Nebraska and Port Matilda, and fountains at Longwood Gardens; harvesting peaches in Berks County, corn in Cumberland, Dauphin and Perry Counties, tobacco in Lancaster County and wheat in Chester, Clearfield, Cumberland, Dauphin, Franklin, Indiana, Lancaster, McKean, Mifflin, Perry and Westmoreland Counties; lakes, including Boiling Springs Lake, Chehocton Lake, Conneaut Lake, Conowago Lake, Corey Lake, Eagles Mere Lake (showing hotels), Edinboro Lake, Lake Erie (with Flagship Niagara), Italian Lake, Minausin Lake, Lake Pocono, Poyntelle Lake, Promised Land Lake, Pymatuning Lake, Skytop Lake, Subala Lake, Tionesta Lake, Lake Wallenpaupack, Williams Lake, Winola Lake, lakes at Highland Park in Pittsburgh, Sally Ann Furnace, Parkesburg, Doubling Gap, Good Hope Mills, and reservoirs near Hollidaysburg; state parks, including Caledonia, Cherry Springs, Colerain, Cook Forest, Samuel B. Elliott, Greenwood Furnace, Halfway, Hemlock, Kettle Creek, Presque Isle, Promised Land, Ole Bull, Ravensburg, and Worlds End; public and private parks including Capitol Park, Childs Park, Clairton Borough Swimming Pool, Conrad Weiser Park, Drake Well Park, Hershey Park, Highland Park, Longwood Gardens and Wildwood Park; rivers and creeks including the Allegheny River, Little Antietam Creek, Beaver River, Bixler Run, Brandywine Creek, Bush Creek, Clarion River, Conemaugh River, Conodoguinet Creek, Custer Swamp, Delaware River and Water Gap, French Creek, Juniata River, Kishacoquillas Creek, Lehigh River, Loyalhanna Creek, Lycoming Creek, Mahantango Creek, Mahoning Creek, Marsh Creek, Monongahela River, Little Moshannon Creek, Neshaminy Creek, Penns Creek, Pine Creek, Raystown Creek, Roaring Brook, Rocky Mountain Creek, Schuylkill River, Shenango River, Shermans Creek, Sinnemahoning Creek, Slippery Rock Creek, Sugar Creek, the North and West Branches of the Susquehanna, Swatara Creek, Tioga River, Tulpehocken Creek, Yellow Breeches Creek, Youghiogheny River and Wissahickon Creek.

Miscellaneous scenic views in all sixty-seven counties with Wyalusing Rocks, Table Rocks, Charles Schwab Home, Snow Shoe Mountain, Bellefonte Police Barracks, Penns Valley, Bald Eagle Valley, Valley Forge, Cooksburg, the Cumberland Valley, Jack's Narrows, the Susquehanna Trail, the Roosevelt Highway, the Lincoln Highway, Wissahickon Drive, Girty's Notch, Gibson's Rock, Ticklish Rock, Pine Creek Gorge, white tail deer and forest fires.

Snow scenes along highways in Bedford, Berks, Blair, Cambria, Chester, Clearfield, Columbia, Crawford, Cumberland, Dauphin (includes Capitol

Building), Elk, Erie, Franklin, Fulton, Huntingdon, Juniata, Lackawanna, Lancaster, Luzerne, McKean, Mifflin, Monroe, Perry, Potter, Somerset, Sullivan, Tioga, Union, Westmoreland and York Counties.

Waterfalls, including Bushkill Falls, Childs Park Falls, Dingmans Falls, Indian Ladder Falls, falls near Leonard Harrison State Park, Kitchen Creek Falls, Raymondskill Falls, Ricketts Glen Falls, Sawkill Falls, Shohola Falls, Swiftwater Falls and Winona Falls.

The Lantern Slide File, 1907-1939, consists of over 1,400 glass slides made from the Application File, 5x7 File, Main File, and other sources. Subjects cover many of the same topics listed in the above files and include charts and graphs for lecture purposes. The slides, arranged numerically, are accompanied by a logbook containing descriptive information. Some are hand colored.

Motion Picture Films, ca. 1940-ca. 1958, consists of seventy-one 16mm Kodachrome films showing highway construction, road tests and experiments, and other highway activities. Most films are 100-400 ft. in length. Notable topics cover construction of the Schuylkill Expressway, Penn-Lincoln Parkway and Harvey Taylor Bridge, ca. 1950; "A Trip over the Pennsylvania Turnpike," 1940; skid tests, paint tests, snow removal, scenic highways, the State Capitol, Fort Indiantown Gap, Highway Department annual picnics and others.

The Construction File, 1933-1961, consists of over 2,500 8x10 negatives of highway construction primarily in Allegheny and Philadelphia Counties, 1944-1960. The negatives are arranged by county and thereunder by legislative route number. Other counties include Armstrong, Beaver, Bedford, Berks, Bucks, Butler, Cambria, Carbon, Chester, Clearfield, Columbia, Crawford, Cumberland, Dauphin, Delaware, Erie, Fayette, Franklin, Huntingdon, Indiana, Jefferson, Lackawanna, Lancaster, Lawrence, Lebanon, Lehigh, Luzerne, Lycoming, Montgomery, Northampton, Northumberland and Perry.

The Portrait File, 1928-ca. 1951 and 1955-1962, consists of 350 formal portraits of state government officials. The photographs are arranged alphabetically by name and are usually 4x5 and 8x10 negatives, with some matching prints. Subjects include Governors John S. Fisher, Edward M. Martin, John C. Bell, James Duff, John S. Fine and George M. Leader, often signing legislation or posing with their cabinets, wives and families. Also included are Adjutants General, Attorneys General, Lieutenant Governors and Secretaries of Agriculture, Banking, Budget, Commerce, Commonwealth, Forests and Waters, Health, Highways, Internal Affairs, Labor and Industry, Police, Property and Supplies, Revenue, Welfare and other agencies. Notable persons include: Attorney General Anne X. Alpern; Secretary of Budget Andrew W. Bradley; Lieutenant Governor Roy E. Furman;

Secretary of Forests and Waters Maurice K. Goddard; and Secretary of Public Assistance Ruth Grigg Horting.

The Kodachrome File, 1940-1954, consists of 528 4x5 and 8x10 Kodachrome transparencies of highway construction and scenic views. Topics cover road work in Adams, Allegheny, Bedford, Berks, Blair, Butler, Chester, Dauphin, Delaware, Franklin, Huntingdon, Lancaster, Lebanon, Lycoming, Montgomery, Philadelphia and York Counties; scenic views of farms in Butler, Berks and Lancaster Counties; the Rockville Bridge; Crooked Creek Dam; Conrad Weiser Homestead; Cornwall Ore Mine; Fort Necessity; Ephrata Cloister; Pennsbury Manor; and the Harrisburg skyline. Notable items include construction of the Squirrel Hill Tunnels and Penn-Lincoln Parkway in Pittsburgh, the Schuylkill Expressway and Penrose Avenue Bridge in Philadelphia, and the Harvey Taylor Bridge in Harrisburg.

The Governor's File, 1950-1969, consists of over 6,500 negatives taken for the Office of the Governor. The images loosely follow in chronological order the administrations of John S. Fine, 1950-1954; George M. Leader, 1955-1959; David L. Lawrence, 1959-1963; William W. Scranton, 1963-1967; and Raymond P. Shafer, 1967-1968. The negatives are generally 4x5,

RG-12 Department of Highways, Main File #24616: "Looking NE at viaducts from slag pile." Construction of Penn-Lincoln Parkway near Squirrel Hill Tunnels, Pittsburgh, November 11, 1948 (see p. 22).

arranged numerically with an occasional matching print present. Negatives for John Fine and part of George Leader's administration were originally taken by the Department of Commerce and later transferred to the Department of Highways.

Subjects cover the daily activities of the governor at his office in the State Capitol, Harrisburg. These are usually formal and candid shots taken during a "Photo Hour," when he would greet guests, present awards, sign legislation and proclamations, etc., for publicity purposes. Also present are views of inauguration ceremonies, speeches, celebrating holidays with family members, crowning agricultural queens, dedication ceremonies for

RG-13 Pennsylvania Historical and Museum Commission (Pennsylvania Historical Commission)--Administrative Files of the Commission's Research Assistants: "2 ¹/₂ ton, 6x6 Cargo Trucks in Parking Lot at Gate 1," Letterkenny Army Depot, May 1946 (see p. 32).

state parks, highways, buildings, etc., Christmas tree-lighting ceremonies, the State Farm Show, and visiting economically distressed or disaster areas. Views of the lieutenant governor, state senators and representatives are also present.

Notable persons include department officials such as Attorney General

Anne X. Alpern, Secretary of Internal Affairs Genevieve Blatt, Secretary of Property and Supplies Andrew W. Bradley, Secretary of Forests and Waters Maurice K. Goddard, Secretary of Public Welfare Ruth Grigg Horting, and others; and personalities such as Governor Leader with John L. Lewis, the Mousketeers and Jonas Salk, Governor Lawrence with President John Kennedy and Governor Scranton with former President Dwight Eisenhower. Community and charity organizations meeting with the governor include the American Legion, Boy and Girl Scouts, B'nai B'rith, Civil Air Patrol, DeMolay, Easter Seals, 4-H, Future Farmers of America, Gold Star Mothers, Kiwanis Club, March of Dimes, Muscular Dystrophy Association, the Red Cross, Rotary Club, United Fund, Veterans of Foreign Wars, the Young Men's Christian Association, and many others.

The Miscellaneous File, 1955-1962, consists of approximately 800 4x5 negatives with occasional matching 8x10 prints of miscellaneous activities of the Department of Highways. The file is arranged chronologically and includes group portraits of staff members; office parties; copies of charts and graphs; Pennsylvania Turnpike and other highway scenes; road maintenance equipment, accidents and others. Many center around the activities of Secretaries of Highways Joseph Lawler and Park Martin including meetings with other highway officials. Governor George M. Leader, former President Harry S Truman and others are pictured at highway ribbon cutting ceremonies; dedication of Fort Pitt Tunnels, 1960, and other events. Though the file numbers to 800, some items are missing.

RG-13
RECORDS OF THE PENNSYLVANIA HISTORICAL AND MUSEUM COMMISSION

The Pennsylvania Historical and Museum Commission was created in 1945 to consolidate the functions of the Pennsylvania Historical Commission, the State Museum, and the State Archives. The Historical Commission had functioned as an independent agency since 1913. In the 1930s and 1940s it oversaw several Works Progress Administration projects in Pennsylvania, including the Federal Writers Project, the Frontier Forts and Trails Survey, the Museum Extension Project, the Historical Records Survey, and others. The State Archives, established in 1903, and the State Museum, established in 1905, functioned under the aegis of the State Library. The PHMC is responsible for preserving the Commonwealth's historical resources. It administers the state archival program, operates and maintains museums, historical sites and properties and assists local government agencies and historical societies in all historical matters.

Office of the Executive Director

Administrative and Correspondence Files of the Executive Director, 1945-1971, 10.5 cu. ft.

Among the files of Donald A. Cadzow are seven 2 1/2 x 4 1/4 prints showing the entrance sign to Pennsbury Manor and dredging operations of the riverbed nearby, 1950. Among the files of Sylvester K. Stevens's Civil War Centennial Commission are seven 8x10 prints of a September, 1962, ceremony in the Capitol Rotunda, Harrisburg, honoring Pennsylvanians who fought at Antietam. Shown giving speeches are Stevens and Governor David Lawrence.

Administrative and Correspondence Files of the Commission Chairman, 1956-1961, 3 cu. ft.

Frank Melvin was chairman of the PHMC Philadelphia Office. Among his records are 5x7 prints of Old Economy Village taken by Charles E. Stotz,

RG-13 Pennsylvania Historical and Museum Commission-Federal Writers Project Records, Job #11: "Change of Shift at the Aliquippa Steel Plant, Pennsylvania," from Farm Security Administration, Arthur Rothstein, photographer, ca. 1935 (see p. 34).

Jr., July 21, 1938, and a pamphlet "Some Notes, Pictures and Documents relating to the Harmony Society...," by J. M. Tate, Jr., 1925 (See MG-354); and two miscellaneous views of the property. Also included are six 8x10 publicity prints of Melvin and other commissioners, 1956-1959, taking the oath of office, accepting the deed to Hope Lodge, and with Governor George Leader signing the "Germantown Colonial Compound" Act, April 12, 1956.

Bureau of Archives and History

Administrative and Correspondence Files of the State Archivist, 1945-1975, 5 cu. ft.

Among the files of State Archivist Henry Howard Eddy are eight 8x10 prints of archives cataloging and storage facilities in the Forum Building, Harrisburg, 1947. Among the files of State Archivist Harry E. Whipkey are sixty-five black and white and color prints by staff of varying size relating to the salvaging and cleanup of documents following Hurricane Agnes in 1972. Views show the archives staff assisting at the archives facility in Harrisburg, the Fort Pitt Museum in Pittsburgh, and the Wyoming Historical and Geological Society in Wilkes-Barre. A few matching negatives are present.

Administrative and Correspondence Files of the State Historian and Staff Historians, 1945-1975, 5 cu. ft.

Included in the files of Autumn Leonard, Associate Historian, are seven 8x10 prints of the October 19, 1949, dedication of flags to the War Trophy Hall of the State Museum. Shown giving speeches are ex-Governor Edward Martin and Lieutenant Governor Daniel Strickler. Also present is an 8x10 publicity view of PHMC staff members posing with a statue of George Washington at Fort LeBoeuf, 1945.

Minutes, Reports, Correspondence and Related Records of the Pennsylvania Federation of Junior Historians, 1954-1976, 6 cu. ft.

Among these records are 250 8x10 prints of activities of the PFJH, ca. 1965-1975. Most are by PHMC photographer Terry Musgrave. Items show members visiting the State Museum, the Mobile Museum and other PHMC properties; participating in William Penn's birthday celebration, the Commonwealth History Fair and other events, and annual meetings at Seven Springs Resort, Mount Airy Lodge, and other places; and posing with Governors Raymond Shafer and Milton Shapp, Executive Director Sylvester K. Stevens and others. Many prints are duplicates and most are unidentified.

Reports, Correspondence and Research Files Relating to the War History Program, 1938-1947, 36 cu. ft.

The War History Program researched and collected information to document Pennsylvania's involvement in World War II. Included in part 5, "Industry's Contribution to War Production," are eighty 8x10 prints obtained from various industries showing how they assisted the war effort. A few show women workers. Subjects include armored vehicles and their production at the Autocar Company, Ardmore and Autocar employees at war bond rallies, and the "Ordnance for Victory Show," 1943, sponsored by John Wanamaker's; the Dravo Corporation launching a naval transport at Neville Island; making boxes for aircraft wing tanks at the Free Corrugated Box Company; and armored steel plate production at the Disston and Sons Company.

Bureau of Historic Sites and Properties

Administrative Files of the Bureau Director, 1956-1978, 13 cu. ft.

Included are eight 8x10 prints of Cornwall Iron Furnace, 1961, by staff photographers; five 4x5 and 5x7 prints of Ephrata Cloister taken October 21, 1900, by an unidentified photographer; forty-five 5x7 prints of artifacts on display at Pennsbury Manor, ca. 1944; and approximately 100 35mm negatives of activities at Valley Forge, 1974.

State Museum of Pennsylvania
Natural History Section Photograph File, 1911-1922, 2 cu. ft.

The file consists of 240 4x5 and 6 1/2 x 8 1/2 lumiere autochrome plates of specimens in the collections of the Natural History Section made by Boyd P. Rothrock, Curator of the State Museum. Original envelopes bear detailed identification in Rothrock's handwriting and often include time of day and type of exposure. Notable specimens include bass, brown trout, pike, walleye, mallard ducks, snakes, lilies, geraniums and views of the flower beds in Capitol Park, Harrisburg.

Also included is an unprocessed file of approximately 100 4x5 glass and film negatives containing many of the subjects listed above.

Curator's Photograph File, 1914-1929, 2.5 cu. ft.

This file consists primarily of 4x5 and 6 1/2 x 8 1/2 glass negatives taken by Curator Boyd P. Rothrock, with assistance from photographer Edward Manser. The images are views of the Museum storage and exhibit areas and collection specimens. All items are numbered and labeled in detail by Rothrock, often giving the time of day and type of exposure. Also included is Rothrock's 3x5 card subject index. The file is incomplete and unprocessed. Subjects include views of Museum exhibit areas, 1921; the Museum, State Library and Archives taken for the 1926 U.S. Sesquicentennial Celebration; Flag Day Parade, June 14, 1914, to place state battle flags in the Capitol Rotunda; Capitol Park Extension work, 1917; the Susquehanna River coal industry; Rothermel's "Battle of Gettysburg" series of paintings and others. Notable items include a view of the Capitol, ca. 1870, autochromes of the Revolutionary War "Rattlesnake Flag" of John Proctor's Westmoreland County battalion, and a folder of receipts, 1916, from William H. Rau to the Museum for photography work.

Also included is a series of 236 glass lantern slides, some hand colored, arranged in three wooden boxes. Two of these were originally owned by Joseph T. Rothrock (see RG-6). They deal with natural and scenic views of Maine, Florida, Georgia and other states, and views on battleships by William H. Rau, especially the *Maine* and others stationed in Cuba, 1898. The third box contains slides by various photography studios of historic sites in the Philadelphia area.

Pennsylvania Historical Commission

Administrative and Correspondence Files of the Chairman and Executive Secretary, 1927-1945, 15 cu. ft.

Among the files of Frank Melvin, Chairman, are seventeen 8x10 prints of Pennsbury Manor by Philip Wallace, 1939, and four 5x7 prints of groundbreaking ceremonies at Pennsbury, 1938. Shown are Governor George Earle, Frank Melvin and others. Among the files of Myrtle Keeny, Acting Secretary, are thirty-four 5x7 prints showing staff of the Works Progress Administration Museum Extension Project making plaster-of-paris models of Independence Hall, ca. 1938. Among the files of Donald Cadzow, Executive Secretary, are 172 "snapshot" prints, approximately 2 1/2 x 4 1/4, of archaeological excavations conducted by Cadzow between 1933 and 1939 at Pennsbury Manor, John Morton Homestead and Governor Printz Park, and a 16mm 1,000 ft. motion picture film by Cadzow showing the above excavations plus views of Old Economy Village and the launching of the reconstructed Flagship Niagara.

Administrative and Correspondence Files of the Staff Archaeologist and Anthropologist, 1929-1945, 5.5 cu. ft.

Included in the files of Donald Cadzow, staff archaeologist, are manuscripts of W.P.A. Museum Extension Project pamphlets designed to assist Museum personnel in public education. Occasionally filed with these manuscripts are 5x7 prints of products of the project, such as scale models of historical buildings, etc.

Administrative Files of the Commission's Research Assistants, 1942-1946, 2 cu. ft.

The research assistants to the Executive Director were the forerunners of the Public Information Office. They collected, researched and publicized information on Pennsylvania's contribution to World War II. Included are newsclippings, reports, correspondence, etc., especially for the Commission's education programs on "Pennsylvania: Keystone of Democracy" and the War History Program. Among records collected for the War History Program are 280 8x10 prints showing Pennsylvania military installations, factories mobilized for war production, including the employment of women workers and Pennsylvania soldiers and equipment in the European and Pacific Theaters of Operation. Most items are identified and credited on the reverse to a military branch or industry.

Subjects include: training medics at the Medical Field Service School, Carlisle Barracks; producing weapons at the Cherokee Ordnance Works, Cressona Ordnance Plant and Frankford Arsenal; processing recruits at the New Cumberland Army Reception Center; activities at Indiantown Gap Military Reservation, Letterkenny Army Depot, Middletown Air Depot (Olmsted Field), and Tobyhanna.

Military Reservation; the Naval Aircraft Factory and the U.S. Marine Depot in Philadelphia; preparing clothing and supplies at the Philadelphia Quartermaster Depot; the American Red Cross and American Friends Service Committee activities; various ships under construction at the Philadelphia Navy Yards; land-sea transports being built at Neville Island; soldier rehabilitation at Valley Forge General Hospital manufacturing war materials at the U.S. Rubber Company, Bethlehem Steel Company, and U.S. Steel Company factories in the Pittsburgh area, the National Tube Company, Pittsburgh Forgings Company, H. K. Porter Company, Autocar Company of Ardmore, Aluminum Company of America (Alcoa) at Canonsburg, and the Read Machinery Company, York; and Pennsylvania soldiers, especially of the 28th Division, fighting in Europe and the Pacific.

Works Progress Administration

Frontier Forts and Trails Survey, Photograph (Erie Survey) File, 1940-1941, 5 cu. ft.

The Frontier Forts and Trails Survey collected information pertaining to the colonial period in western and northwestern Pennsylvania. Records consist of copies of historical manuscripts, letters, maps, etc. collected by W.P.A. employees from a variety of sources. The photographs are over 1,300 5x7 and 8x10 prints relating primarily to W.P.A. archaeological excavations in the Erie Triangle area. Also included are views of historic sites, copies of documents, maps, portraits of French and Indian and

Revolutionary War soldiers, etc. Each negative has a matching print and is coded and identified on the envelope.

Subjects include views of archaeological excavations at the following sites: Buckaloons, Fort Presque Isle, East 28th Street in Erie, Wesleyville, Fort LeBoeuf, Goddard, Wintergreen Gorge, Herrington, McFate, Custologas Town, Heydrick Farm, Shaws Landing and others; views of Indians living on the Cornplanter Reservation, including ceremonies adopting Governor Arthur James as a Seneca Indian, 1941; the Lehigh Canal near New Hope and Washington Crossing; buildings at Old Economy Village, Pennsbury Manor, Daniel Boone Homestead, Drake Well and other historical properties; the remains of the "French Trail" between Waterford and Erie; the Eagle Hotel, Erie; welcoming the plane inaugurating regular airmail service to the City of Erie, ca. 1940; offices and staff of the FFT Survey at the old Customs House, Erie, including members of the W.P.A. Museum Extension Project with models of Fort Machault, Fort LeBoeuf, Fort Duquesne, Fort Venango, Fort Presque Isle and others; copies of portraits, correspondence and manuscripts of Henry Bouquet, Chaussegros DeLery and others; and views of the reconstructed Flagship *Niagara*.

Items taken for the Pennsylvania Historical Survey include views of public school buildings in Sunbury; furniture on display at Pennsbury Manor; records storage areas in the Berks County Courthouse; and additional views of the reconstructed *Niagara* and Governor James's Seneca adoption.

Federal Writers Project Records, 1935-1943, 27.5 cu. ft.

These records pertain to Pennsylvania's involvement with the project, most notably the American Guide Series. The project was designed to employ white collar workers debilitated by the Great Depression and publish comprehensive guides to each state. Project workers in Pennsylvania published *Pennsylvania: A Guide to the Keystone State* (1940), *Philadelphia: A Guide to the Nation's Birthplace* (1937) and many guides to individual counties or historical subjects. Records consist primarily of field notes, manuscripts and photographs taken or collected for a particular guide, which are arranged by job (individual project) number. Not all manuscripts and photographs prepared were eventually published.

Most images date between 1935 and 1940 and are interfiled with various projects. Most were taken by Frederick W. Ritter, a professional photographer employed by the F.W.P. Many were also collected from local newspapers, freelance photographers, chambers of commerce, private businesses, and state agencies such as the Departments of Forests and Waters, Highways, and Commerce. Some, provided by the U.S. Farm Security Administration, were taken by Walker Evans, Carl Mydans, Arthur Rothstein, Ben

Shahn and others. Most images are identified on the reverse by subject, date and photographer.

Job #10, an unpublished guide to Pittsburgh, contains approximately 280 mostly 8x10 prints arranged by subject. Images show coal barges; bridges; churches; historic and public buildings; hospitals; the William Penn Hotel; the Carnegie Institute and Library Main Branch; high schools; the University of Pittsburgh and other colleges; industries including the H.J. Heinz Company, Pittsburgh Plate Glass Company, Carnegie-Illinois Steel Corporation at Duquesne, steel mills at Homestead, Etna and Rankin, and the atom smasher at the Westinghouse Electric and Manufacturing Company; statues and memorials in city parks and elsewhere; parks including North, South, East and West Parks; Frick Park; Schenley Park; Forbes Field; downtown street views; panoramic city views; the first motion picture projector used in Pittsburgh, and others.

Job #11, was *Pennsylvania: A Guide to the Keystone State*. Files include over 3,100 mostly 8x10 prints arranged alphabetically by county. Large numbers of images are in the following counties: *Adams*: Gettysburg Battlefield and Cemetery, including activities at the 75th Anniversary, July 1938; churches, wildlife and scenic views. *Allegheny*: Pittsburgh coal barges, bridges, industries, parks, the University of Pittsburgh and miscellaneous views. *Beaver*: Old Economy Village and housing conditions for steelworkers. *Berks*: agriculture, bridges, churches, historic buildings, industries, monuments, parks, schools, fire companies of Reading and the Horse Shoe Trail. *Bradford*: the site of French Azilum, LaPorte House, monuments to the Sullivan Expedition, David Wilmot, the Wyalusing Moravian settlement, and Wyalusing Rocks. *Cambria*: the Johnstown Floods of 1889 (copies) and 1936, industry, the 1938 Conemaugh River Flood Control Project by the U.S. Army Corps of Engineers, and miscellaneous views. *Chester*: agriculture, bridges, buildings, Longwood Gardens, the Horse Shoe Trail, and Valley Forge. *Clinton*: primarily views of Lock Haven including the airport, bridges, buildings, floods of 1918 and 1936, historic sites, industries, markets, tobacco farming and others. *Dauphin*: primarily views of Harrisburg and Hershey, including the State Capitol, Farm Show Building, Hershey Hotel, Hershey Community Theatre, Hershey Arena, Chocolate Factory, etc.; Susquehanna River bridges and scenic views; the 1936 flood; Bethlehem Steel mills at Steelton; the Horse Shoe Trail and the 1938 encampment at Indiantown Gap Military Reservation. *Delaware*: bridges, historic and public buildings, churches; the Hedgerow Theatre; public housing; the ship building and oil refining industries, and others. *Erie*: historic and public buildings; churches; vineyards; industry including the City Iron Works, Erie Casket Company, Zuck and Sons Greenhouses, shipping and iron ore docks, and others; recreation on Lake Erie; Perry and Gridley monuments;

Flagship *Niagara*, S.S. *Wolverine*, and others. *Franklin*: schools, including Penn Hall School, Mercersburg Academy, Mont Alto Sanitarium; Buchanan and Caledonia State Parks, Michaux State Forest; the Kittatinny Tunnel and scenic views. *Lackawanna*: churches, collieries, historic and public buildings, schools, general views of Scranton, and Archbald Pothole. *Lancaster*: agriculture, including tobacco farming; Amish; churches; historic and public buildings, including the Central Market; industry, especially the Armstrong Linoleum Plant; Ephrata Cloister; general views of Lancaster City; and others. *Lehigh*: agriculture; historic and public buildings, including the Lehigh Valley Farmers' Market, Moravian Archives, etc.; industries, including Trexler Trout Hatchery, Musser Nursery, and textile mills; recreation in Trexler Memorial Park and Dorney Park, general views of Allentown, and others. *Lycoming*: agriculture; historic and public buildings including Fort Muncy; recreation at Goose Island, Cedar Pines Camp; scenic views of Pine Creek Gorge, Susquehanna Trail, Lycoming and Loyalsock Creeks and others, general views of Williamsport, including Dickinson Seminary, the 1936 flood, and others. *Monroe*: views of waterfalls in the Pocono Mountains, Delaware Water Gap; Jacob Stroud Home; tomb of J. Summerfield Staples; and others. *Montgomery*: churches, including Bryn Athyn Cathedral; historic and public buildings including Pottsgrove Mansion, Graeme Park, King of Prussia Inn and others; industry, including the Mack Truck Company, Doehler Die Company; schools including Bryn Mawr, Ursinus College, and others; scenic views, and others. *Northampton*: views of Bethlehem, including bridges, historic buildings such as the Simon Rau Company Drug Store, Moravian structures and others; industries such as the Bethlehem Steel Company and the Roller-Smith Company. Views of Easton, including bridges, historic and public buildings and schools; railroad yards and Lehigh Foundries, Inc.; views of Nazareth including the Whitefield House, Lehigh Canal, Chapman's Quarry, the slate industry and recreational and scenic views. *Philadelphia*: bridges including those at Henry Avenue, Walnut Street, University Avenue, Delaware River and Schuylkill River at Market; buildings including the Philadelphia Airport, apartment houses, banks, botanical gardens, KYW and WCAU radio broadcasting facilities; churches, City Hall, clubs, historic and public buildings in Fairmount Park, Germantown and Philadelphia, hospitals, public housing, insurance companies, libraries, curb markets and the Dock Street Market, museums, the 30th Street Post Office, Eastern State Penitentiary, Edgar Allen Poe House, Curtis Publishing Company, Horn & Hardart restaurant, the 30th Street Railroad Station, Reading Terminal, high schools, Girard College, Pennsylvania Academy of the Fine Arts, Temple University, St. Joseph's College, the University of Pennsylvania, John Wanamaker's, Lit Brothers, theatres and the United States Mint; cemeteries; Chinatown;

industries, including the Pennsylvania Sugar Company, J. G. Brill Company, Philadelphia Rapid Transit Company, Lanston Monotype Company, Stetson Hat Company, Philadelphia Storage Battery Company, and LaFrance Industries; Mummers Parades; monuments and statues; the Philadelphia Navy Yard with views of the *Olympia;* blacks, including portraits of Marian Anderson and Henry O. Tanner, black churches and housing conditions, and the Second National Negro Congress, ca. 1935; parks including Fairmount, Cobbs Creek, League Island, Pennypack and Shibe Park; street views of Broad, Camac, Clinton, Delaware, Elfreth's Alley, Franklin Court, Franklin Parkway, Logan Circle, Market Street, Rittenhouse Square, Washington Square and others; subways; waterfront activities; city skyline views, the Philadelphia Zoo and miscellaneous items. *Schuylkill:* buildings in Lorraine, Orwigsburg, Pottsville, Tamaqua, and other towns; coal mining at Cameron Collieries and the 1939 disaster at Shenandoah; scenic views, copies of engravings of the Molly Maguires from *Harper's Weekly,* and others. *Washington:* agriculture, bridges, churches, the LeMoyne Crematory, Washington and Jefferson College, Jefferson Log College, the monument to Colonel George Morgan, and others. *Westmoreland:* bridges; housing conditions and life at Hannastown, Mount Pleasant, and Norvelt; the Westmoreland Fair, scenic views of fishing and the Lincoln Highway.

Miscellaneous views of the following counties are included: Bedford, Blair, Butler, Centre, Clarion, Clearfield, Columbia, Cumberland, Fayette, Forest, Fulton, Greene, Indiana, Jefferson, Juniata, Lawrence, Lebanon, McKean, Mercer, Montour, Northumberland, Pike, Potter, Snyder, Sullivan, Susquehanna, Union, Tioga, Venango, Warren, Wayne, Wyoming and York.

Job #44 *The Highland Park Zoo* was never published. Files contain forty-five 8x10 prints of animals and their keepers at this Pittsburgh zoo.

Job #63 *The Negro in Philadelphia* was never published. Files contain fifty-two 8x10 prints showing black housing, churches, etc., the 1938 "First Colored Food Show" at the Octavius Catto Lodge; and a copy of a photograph of Catto, ca. 1880.

Job #134 *Pennsylvania Germans* was never published. Files contain fourteen 5x7 prints of buildings at the Aurora Colony in Marion County, Oregon and woven coverlets made by Pennsylvania members of the Harmony Society, ca. 1840.

Job #172 *Conservation* was never published. Files contain eleven 8x10 prints of scenic views relating to conservation in Pennsylvania. Included are views of the Safe Harbor Dam.

Job #207 *The Education Building* (1939). Files contain fifty-eight mostly 8x10 prints of the state Education Building, Harrisburg. Interior and exterior views show artwork, murals, etc., State Library stack areas, and Forum Auditorium.

Pennsylvania Historical Records Survey

Administrative File, 1938-1942, .5 cu. ft.
The files include thirty-three 8x10 prints by Frederick W. Ritter and others showing Federal Writers Project employees at work at the Philadelphia unit.

Museum Extension Project, Photographs, ca. 1938-1939, 34 items.
The images are 5x7 prints showing staff making, assembling and shipping plaster-of-paris scale models of historic Pennsylvania structures, including Independence Hall, Carnegie Museum, the Eagle Hotel at Waterford, the Nixon Tavern at Fairchance, and others. Included are views of staff measuring the exterior of Independence Hall in preparation for the model.

RG-15
RECORDS OF THE DEPARTMENT OF JUSTICE

The Department of Justice represents the Commonwealth in litigation and provides legal advice to the Governor and all state agencies. The head of the department is the Attorney General. The agency oversees the Board of Pardons and the Bureau of Corrections.

Office of the Attorney General

Ephrata Cloister File, 1929-1956, 1.5 cu. ft.
Includes three 8x10 prints of the Brothers and Sisters Houses at Ephrata Cloister. These are second generation reproductions of original prints ca. 1900 made during the negotiations for the purchase of the property by the Commonwealth.

Bureau of Corrections

Press Office History File, ca. 1950-1970, 4 cu. ft.
This is a series of miscellaneous original documents collected by the office pertaining to the history of state prisons. Approximately one cu. ft. is 5x7 and 8x10 prints by staff photographers, ca. 1950-1970, of activities at Eastern State Penitentiary, Western State Penitentiary, Dallas, Graterford,

Huntingdon, Mercer, Muncy, Rockview and White Hill prisons. Also included are several mug shots of prisoners at Eastern and Western State Penitentiaries, ca. 1890-1940. This series is currently unprocessed.

Western State Penitentiary Prison Administration and Construction Records, 1818-1946, 6.5 cu. ft.

Includes one cu. ft. of photographs, 1861-1928, relating to facilities at Pittsburgh and Rockview. Items for the penitentiary at Pittsburgh include an album, ca. 1922, "Photographic Record—Officials, Officers, Matrons, Employees," containing formal portraits with names of the prison staff; forty-two prints of varying size relating to the Ohio River flood of 1913 and the "Riverside Riot" of 1921; 107 2 1/2 x 4 formal portraits of guards with names and dates of service; one folder of miscellaneous prints including cabinet cards and other portraits of wardens, chaplains and other officials by local photographers, one group portrait of the State Pardons Board, ca. 1950, and a ca. 1861 carte-de-visite of the prison building by G. S. Hough of Pittsburgh.

Items for the penitentiary at Rockview include 5x7 and 8x10 contact prints showing construction of the main building, the temporary prison, formal portraits of guards and officials; and an album of views of the prison farm showing prisoners at work raising crops and tending animals.

RG-16
RECORDS OF THE DEPARTMENT OF LABOR AND INDUSTRY

The Department was created in 1913 to enforce the Commonwealth's laws relating to the welfare and safety of industrial employees. It also administers programs relating to workmen's compensation, unemployment insurance, labor relations and conditions, fair employment practices and employment security.

Bureau of Employment Security

Public Relations Office Motion Picture Films, ca. 1938-1943, 10 reels

These 16mm films were obtained by the Bureau primarily from federal government agencies and used to educate the public. Most were made during World War II and deal with the role of women in the war effort and the use of railroads by the military. Some are in color and vary from 400-600 feet. Subjects include:

"All Out for Victory," "Glamour Girls of 1943," and "Women on the

Warpath," produced by the U.S. War Manpower Commission; "Community at War," "Railroaders Always," and "Women Power" produced by the U.S. Army Pictorial Service (Signal Corps); "Lifeline of the National Railroads," produced by Carl Dudley Productions; and "Your Job Insurance," ca. 1936, produced by the U.S. Social Security Board, explaining procedures for obtaining workman's compensation in Pennsylvania (includes footage of President Roosevelt, Governor Earle, and others).

RG-19
RECORDS OF THE DEPARTMENT OF MILITARY AFFAIRS

The Department is responsible for administering the Pennsylvania National Guard, the State Armory Board, and various programs pertaining to veterans' assistance. The department head is the Adjutant General, and the agency was known as the Adjutant General's Office prior to 1923.

Office of the Adjutant General—World War I Service

American Expeditionary Forces Photographs, .25 cu. ft.

This is a series of 360 contact prints of varying size, usually 5x7, by the Signal Corps of the U.S. Army. All items show activities of the 28th Division in France, May 1918-March 1919. Most are numbered, labeled and dated. Accompanying the series is a chronological index repeating the above information. The photographs appear to have been removed from an album.

Subjects cover: soldiers and officers on guard, in trenches, in field hospitals (many individuals are identified by name); ruins of French towns and fields; "no man's land," captured German, Italian and Russian prisoners; 28th Division soldiers' graves; Red Cross nurses; Y.M.C.A. huts; freed Allied prisoners after the Armistice; and a series of prints made from captured German negatives showing enemy camp life and other activities.

Pennsylvania War History Commission General File, 1915-1920, 1928, 30 cu. ft.

The War History Commission collected documents and ephemera pertaining to Pennsylvanians serving in the Army. The General File is made up of these documents, arranged numerically by divisional unit. Photographs are occasionally interfiled to help illustrate a unit's activities. Also infrequently found are typed lists of photographs pertaining to a particular unit taken by the Signal Corps. The lists are arranged by negative number and contain a brief description of the subject. Also present are "Rosters to Accompany Photos," taken by Ewing, Inc. of Little Rock, Arkansas. The rosters are an index to panoramic portraits of companies, often giving the individual soldier's name and hometown. The original photographs, however, are not present.

Pennsylvania War History Commission, Photographs of the 28th Division, 1919, 216 items

The photographs cover 28th Division activities shortly after the Armistice. One group of images is a series of 148 panoramic prints by Ewing, Inc. of Baton Rouge, La., showing formal portraits of various companies of the 103rd, 107th, 108th, 109th, 110th, 111th and 112th battalions. Other views include ruins of the Argonne, Vaux, Chateau-Thierry and A.E.F. cemeteries. Also included are sixty-eight views, largely 8x10, of the Division's victory parade in Philadelphia, May 25, 1919. Most prints were collected from local

RG-19 Department of Military Affairs--Pennsylvania War History Commission: "Men of the 28th leaving Snyder Avenue Wharf," Philadelphia, May 1919 for a victory parade.

newspapers including the Philadelphia *Inquirer*, *Ledger*, and *Record*. Views show marching troops, Civil War veterans and others in the crowd, personalities at the reviewing stand at Independence Hall such as Governor William Sproul, General Daniel Muir, Philadelphia Mayor Thomas B. Smith, and others.

RG-20
RECORDS OF THE DEPARTMENT OF GENERAL SERVICES

The Department of Property and Supplies, created in 1923, was chief purchasing and distributing agent for the Commonwealth. It assumed duties previously assigned to the Board of Public Grounds and Buildings, Department of Public Printing and Binding, and several memorial, park and monument commissions. This entailed acquiring and managing real estate space and facilities, state vehicles, and demolition and disposal of surplus property. In 1975, Property and Supplies merged with the General State Authority to become the Department of General Services.

Office of the Secretary of Property and Supplies

General Correspondence, 1939-1960, 8 cu. ft.

Included in the files of Secretary Chester M. Woolworth, 1946-1949, are four 8x10 prints of an artist's conception of the proposed Soldiers and Sailors Memorial Bridge, Harrisburg.

Office of the Deputy Secretary of Property and Supplies

General Correspondence, 1909-1931, 6.5 cu. ft.

Among the files of Deputy Secretary Walter G. Scott is a "Historical File," 1909-1931, of the Department's work. Interfiled with memoranda and correspondence are photographs of varying size of the following: the construction of the South Office Building, 1921 (107 items) and cleaning and repair of the Barnard Statuary on the Capitol, 1928 (12 items) at Harrisburg; the Curtin-Parke Civil War Monuments at Vicksburg, Miss., 1928-1930 (3 items); unveiling the Robert Morris Monument, 1923-1926, Philadelphia (1 item); the construction of the pedestal of the General Meade Monument at Gettysburg, 1923 (5 items).

Board of Commissioners of Public Grounds and Buildings

Capitol and Capitol Park Extension Photographs, 1896-1928, 1950, 5 folders

These are the remains of an album containing forty-six prints of varying size of the Capitol and Capitol Park area, Harrisburg. The views date from October 1, 1896 to January 5, 1918, and show the "old" Capitol, construction of the dome of the new Capitol, structures to be razed to make way for Capitol Park, and the planting of a tree in the Park by Governor Brumbaugh for Arbor Day, 1917.

Also present are twenty-two 8x10 prints by the J. Horace McFarland Company, December 11, 1919, of the northern State Street Bridge area prior to razing; eight photographic copies of an artist's conception of the proposed Soldiers and Sailors Memorial Bridge, 1928; seven photographs by J.W. Roshon of artist's conceptions and a model of the proposed Capitol Park by architect Arnold W. Brunner; six views of Harrisburg from the Capitol dome and five miscellaneous views of Capitol Park during the 1920s; and one oversize aerial view of Capitol Park, 1950, by Pennsylvania Aerial Surveys, Inc.

Bureau of Construction

Works Progress Administration Construction Projects, 1927-1941, 4.5 cu. ft.

Includes approximately 400 8x10 prints of the construction of the following, many by local photographers: Harrisburg Capitol Complex (Education, Liquor Control Board, North Office, Revenue Buildings; Department of Highways Testing Laboratory; Soldiers and Sailors Memorial Bridge); state hospitals at Blossburg, Fairview, Harrisburg, Warren and Wernersville; Mansfield State Teachers College; Scotland Soldiers Orphans School; and the State Industrial School for Women at Muncy (see also RG-9).

Bureau of Real Estate and Insurance

Building Demolition Files, 1951-1966, 1.5 cu. ft.

Includes thirty-eight 8x10 prints by Department of Highways photographers of the Harrisburg residential area demolished to make way for a Capitol Park Extension Project. Photographs show the area roughly bounded by North, Forster, Third and Sixth Streets, razed to make way for Transportation, Museum and Archives, and Health and Welfare Buildings.

RG-22
RECORDS OF THE DEPARTMENT OF EDUCATION

The origins of the Department can be traced to the Free School Act of 1834, relating to the administration of public schools. The position of Superintendent of Public Instruction was created in 1874. The agency became the Department of Public Instruction in 1923 when the State Library and Museum, the State Board of Censors, and other agencies were placed under its aegis.

Bureau of School Administration

Division of Physical Plant and Construction, Photographs, ca. 1930, 23 items

One folder of prints of varying size, of exterior and interior views of schools throughout the Commonwealth, most unidentified. Identified schools include: Reading High School, Reading; Ramsay High School, Mt. Pleasant; Connelly Trade School, Pittsburgh; and Lower Heidelberg Consolidated School, no location given.

State Board of (Motion Picture) Censors

Records, 1915-1956, 5 cu. ft.

This Board was created to monitor films of questionable moral value before being distributed to theatres. Records include Applications for Examinations, 1915-1951; General Correspondence, 1924-1926; Legal Briefs, 1915-1940; Minutes, 1939-1956; Reports, 1925-1951; Rules, Procedures and Forms, 1915-1952. Though the Board collected copies of the films it monitored, none of these has survived.

State Library

Rare Books Room, Photograph Albums, 1878-1879, 2 vols.

Two leather bound albums, "The Government's Officers and Legislators of Pennsylvania," one for 1878 and one for 1879, were created by photographer C. S. Roshon of Harrisburg. Each album contains approximately 250 cabinet card portraits of state legislators and heads of various agencies, many autographed by the sitter. The district and county are also given. Not all legislators are present.

Lantern Slide Section, ca. 1900-1950, approximately 100,000 items.

The Lantern Slide Section began under the State Museum, originally part of the State Library. The Library eventually absorbed the Museum Slide Section and created the Lantern Slide Section. These glass slides were loaned and circulated like books. The Museum and Library had its own facility for the creation of new slides, or purchased them from firms such as the Keystone View Company; William H. Rau; Williams, Brown & Earle and many others. Many items are hand drawn, hand colored or tinted.

Subjects cover the broad spectrum of education, including Pennsylvania and world history, religion, politics, industry, biology, geography, architecture, art, music, science and nature. Most are arranged in sets to be part of a lecture. Though at one time arranged by subject, the original order has been lost and the slides are currently unprocessed. Lecture manuals (7 cu. ft.) accompany these sides. Like the slides, the manuals were either produced by the Library staff or provided by the photographic firm that sold the slides.

Division of Slides, ca. 1950-1980, approximately 50,000 items

These slides superceded the lantern slides above with a 2x2 format, and cover many of the same topics. Most were purchased from commercial view companies and have accompanying lecture manuals (15 cu. ft.). Most items are in color. This file is unprocessed.

RG-23
RECORDS OF THE DEPARTMENT OF PUBLIC WELFARE

The Department can be traced to the Board of Public Charities created in 1869 and the Board's Committee on Lunacy. In 1921 these agencies were abolished and the Department of Public Welfare created. As the primary agency concerned with the social welfare and financial needs of the Commonwealth's citizens, it administers a wide range of services including state hospitals, medical and public assistance, aid to the mentally and physically disabled, and many others.

Office of the Aging

Governor's White House Conference on Aging Records, 1959-1962, 3 cu. ft.

Includes 100 8x10 prints of a workshop on aging held September 13-14,

1960, in Harrisburg. Participants include Governor David Lawrence, Genevieve Blatt, and Ruth Grigg Horting of the White House Conference. Most persons, however, are unidentified. Views show participants delivering speeches or seated at a banquet. Some prints are duplicates. The original negatives are present.

Office of Mental Health

Harrisburg State Hospital Records, 89 cu. ft.

Includes 1.5 cu. ft. of collected photographs, engravings, drawings and postcards, ca. 1885-1967, of varying size of the hospital facilities, staff at work, patients receiving treatment, etc. Many of the items are second-generation copies made about 1970 for an exhibit on the hospital's history. Also present is the Charles Johnson Collection, 1900-1927, 58 items. Images show hospital staff, patients, and interior and exterior views of buildings, most by J.W. Roshon or LaRue Lemer. Of note is a salted paper print by Langenheim Brothers of the hospital's Board of Directors, May 20, 1851.

Dixmont State Hospital Records, 63 cu. ft.

Includes thirty-three prints, ca. 1912-1940, mostly 8x10, of Dixmont facilities, staff at work, patients receiving treatment, etc., by various local photographers. Notable items include two views of Dixmont's Red Cross Nurses participating in a parade with Boy Scouts, ca. 1917.

Retreat State Hospital Records, 8 cu. ft.

Includes 3.5 cu. ft. of prints and color slides by staff photographers of activities at Retreat, 1950-1975. Views include staff and patients participating in carnivals, Christmas, civil defense and disaster drills, construction projects, Mental Health Week, patient therapy, volunteer recognition and miscellaneous unidentified events.

Bureau of Public Education

16mm Motion Picture Films, 1948-1976, 300 reels

These films, part of a lending library maintained by the agency, were either produced for or by the Bureau or purchased from commercial firms. Most are in color, vary in length from five minutes to over an hour and deal with various aspects of mental health and well-being. Many are intended for a general audience to increase public awareness about the plight of the socially disadvantaged or mentally and physically handicapped. Others are training films for social workers for teaching the mentally handicapped, conducting psychiatric interviews, dealing with personality conflicts, etc.

Notable items include "After Agnes: The Quiet Crisis," dealing with the Department of Public Welfare's response to the victims of Hurricane Agnes in 1972.

RG-25
RECORDS OF SPECIAL COMMISSIONS

Usually created by the governor, these commissions were temporary as they performed a specific function, then disbanded. They were usually independent of any department, serving primarily as investigative or planning bodies, or as the means by which to erect public monuments and to commemorate events. Their functions were usually explained by their titles.

Commission to Supervise the Transfer of Flags from the Library and Museum Building to the Cases in the Rotunda of the Capitol Building of Certain Flags of Pennsylvania Commands, 1914
These records include twenty-three photographs of varying size of the parade June 14, 1914, of Civil War veterans carrying their battle colors to the Capitol, Harrisburg.

Fiftieth Anniversary of the Battle of Gettysburg Commission, 1909-1914
These records include approximately three hundred photographs of varying size taken at Gettysburg, July 1-4, 1913. They were collected by the Commission from various sources including the American Press Association, International News Service, W.H. Tipton, Mumper Studios, and others. The prints were used in the publication of *Fiftieth Anniversary of the Battle of Gettysburg: Report of the Pennsylvania Commission*, Harrisburg: State Printer, 1913, and have crop marks, captions and other identifiers attached to them. Views include veterans reminiscing at pertinent battlefield sites; reenacting Pickett's Charge; using field hospitals, mess tents, sleeping quarters and other temporary facilities set up for the occasion; Boy Scouts, State Police, Red Cross and other groups enlisted to help; visiting dignitaries such as President Woodrow Wilson delivering the July 4 address; ex-President William H. Taft; Vice President Thomas Marshall; Secretary of War William Garrison; Governor William Stuart; State Police Commissioner John C. Groome, and many other federal and state officials. Many portraits are signed.

Pennsylvania Constitution Commemoration Commission, 1937-1938

These records include 372 primarily 8x10 photographs (some duplicates) relating to activities celebrating the 150th anniversary of the U.S. Constitution. The prints were collected by the Commission from newspapers all over the state, especially Philadelphia and Pittsburgh. Views include: placing bronze tablets at the graves of Constitution signers, September 29, 1937, with Governor George Earle; activities December 12, 1937, celebrating Pennsylvania's ratification; Philadelphia activities, including a city parade, a festival at Franklin Field and a Crispus Attucks Pageant in June, 1938; Pittsburgh activities with Mayor Cornelius D. Scully; regional finalists and winners of a statewide high school essay contest; portraits of members of the Constitution Commission; and a scrapbook, "Pennsylvania Constitution Commemoration Committee—Pittsburgh Southwest Region, 1938," showing activities therein.

Pennsylvania Three-Hundredth Anniversary Committee (Swedish Tercentenary), 1937-1938

Records include sixty-eight photographs, usually 8x10, of activities relating to Governor and Mrs. George Earle's visit to King Gustaf V of Sweden, 1937. Most are formal portraits of the above and members of the committee, including Emma Guffey Miller, Senator Joseph Guffey, Repre-

RG-25 Special Commissions—Fiftieth Anniversary of the Battle of Gettysburg Commission: "Pickett's Charge of July 3, 1913" by members of Pickett's Division Association, Gettysburg Reunion.

sentative Roy E. Furman, and others; members of the Finnish and Swedish delegations; Crown Prince Gustaf; miscellaneous views include the Governor receiving a portrait of Johann Printz and views of Printz's burial place in Sweden. Also present is one folder of correspondence by the committee relating to the collection of the above photographs from a variety of sources including Blank & Stoller, Bachrach Studios, Photo-Crafters, Trinity Court Studios, and various Stockholm photographers.

Capitol Investigation Commission, 1897-1911

Records include nine 8x10 photographs taken in May 1908 by an unidentified photographer of the interior of the State Capitol, Harrisburg, in light of corruption charges during its construction. Items show Woodruff files, shoeshine stands, miscellaneous offices, etc.

Commission to Locate the Site of the Frontier Forts of Pennsylvania, 1894-1896

Records include original galleys, drawings, maps, photoprints, etc., used for the publication of *Report of the Commission to Locate the Site of the Frontier Forts of Pennsylvania*, Harrisburg: State Printer, 1896. Photographs are nine items of varying size including two 1894 views of Ralston and Brown Fort by W.V. Walter; the remains of the magazine at Fort Augusta, by Roshon Studios; five views of Forts Jenkins, McClure, Rice and Freeland, by "M. Kulp," ca. 1895 and an undated view of Hendrick's Blockhouse by the American View Company.

Commission on Modern State Government, 1967-1969

Records include seventeen 8x10 prints taken at a 1969 conference by Department of Highways photographers of Governor Raymond Shafer posing with members of the Commission. Most are identified by name on the reverse.

Commission for the Investigation and Control of Chestnut Tree Blight, 1911-1914

Records include 774 photographs taken between April 1912 and November 1913 relating to the study of chestnut tree blight. The prints, taken by photographers hired especially by the Commission, are 5x7 mounted on heavy board containing negative number, subject, location and date. Views show affected trees all over the state, closeups and microphotographs of the blight, and attempts at treatment and control.

A typewritten listing of the above prints is filed with the Commission minutes. There is also a listing of lantern slides maintained by the Commission, now apparently lost.

RG-30
RECORDS OF THE PENNSYLVANIA STATE POLICE

The Department of State Police was created in 1905 to help preserve law and order throughout the Commonwealth. In 1937 the Highway Patrol was transferred from the Department of Revenue and joined with the Department to become the Pennsylvania Motor Police. The name of the agency was again changed in 1943 to become the Pennsylvania State Police.

Office of the Commissioner of State Police

Pennsylvania Motor Police Photographs, 1937-1938 and undated, 4 folders

This series contains 161 publicity prints by staff photographers of Motor Police activities. Of these, 143 are 8x10 prints of trainees at Myerstown and Hershey Training Schools; Governor George Earle and Police Commissioner P.W. Foote inspecting troops; the Motor Police airplane at Harrisburg Airport; troopers participating in the National School Safety Parade, Washington, D.C.; winners of a 1938 police pistol match; and on duty at a Gettysburg Civil War Veterans Reunion. Eighteen items are 20x24 undated exhibit prints of unidentified automobile accidents.

Records of Special Duty at Gubernatorial Inaugurations

Inauguration of John Fine, 1.5 cu. ft.

Contains seventy-seven 8x10 photographs of Governor John Fine's inaugural parade, ceremonies and ball, 1951, by staff photographers. Many views prominently show the state troopers on duty.

Bureau of Personnel

Diary of Trooper Wallace Keely, 1905-1949, 1 volume

Keely was an officer with Troop C, Crumrue Township, Berks County, and later Pottsville. The diary is actually a scrapbook of annotated photographs and newsclippings highlighting Keely's career. Views show Troop C buildings, places where Keely made arrests and mug shots of persons he arrested, and Keely in uniform and as an undercover officer performing Special Duty for the Governor's Office and the Fish Commission. Also included are three prints of varying size showing Keely on his mounts "Crumrue" and "Commodore," and the headquarters of Troop C in Berks County, 1905.

Records of Special Duty and Investigations, 1930-1950

Motion Picture Films, .2 cu. ft.
Includes two 400 ft. reels of 16mm silent color motion picture film of the dedication of the International Peace Light Memorial by President Franklin Roosevelt at Gettysburg Battlefield, 1938.

RG-31
RECORDS OF THE DEPARTMENT OF COMMERCE

The Department was created in 1939 to promote the development of business, industry and commerce in the state. It superseded the State Publicity Commission and for a time included the State Planning Board. In the late 1960s and early 1970s it administered the Bicentennial Commission for the celebration of the nation's 200th anniversary in Pennsylvania. The Department serves industry and community development by coordinating state and federal commerce programs and by making available pertinent technical and statistical information.

Office of the Secretary of Commerce

General Correspondence, 1954-1965, 12 cu. ft.
Interfiled among these records are 8x10 publicity stills by staff photographers showing departmental activities. Many are from original negatives filed with the Bureau of Vacation and Travel Development photographs (see below). Among the correspondence of Secretary Andrew J. Sordoni are sixty-two prints of Pennsylvania Week, October 10-17, 1954. Pennsylvania Week was an annual event staged by the department to promote the Commonwealth's goods, industry, and people. Views show Sordoni, Governor John Fine, and other officials delivering speeches, shaking hands, etc. Also included are portraits of regional Pennsylvania Week coordinators, and the 1954 Distinguished Daughters of Pennsylvania, including actress Grace Kelly.

Among the correspondence of Secretary William R. Davlin are twenty-seven publicity prints of the 1960 Industrial Development Clinic at Harrisburg, sponsored by the Department. Views show conference participants, most unidentified.

Bicentennial Commission

General Correspondence, 1968-1977, 34 cu. ft.

Included is one folder of negatives and prints of varying size, mostly 8x10, of the Commission's preparations for 1976. Shown are the Pennsylvania float at President Nixon's Inaugural Parade, 1969; Governor Raymond Shafer promoting bicentennial license plates and other items; a meeting of the State Bicentennial Commission, 1971; and Governor Milton Shapp at an unidentified Bicentennial exhibit.

Special Records File, 1974-1977, 2.5 cu. ft.

Includes photographic prints, negatives, color 2x2 slides, and motion picture film of the Bicentennial Wagon Train in Pennsylvania and other states. This file is unprocessed.

State Planning Board

Maps and Aerial Photography Survey, 1937-1947, 36 cu. ft.

Between 1937-1942 the U. S. Department of Agriculture's Adjustment Administration Cartographic Section conducted a vertical aerial survey of the state. Contractors hired included the Aero Service Corporation, Philadelphia; Abrams Aerial Surveys, Lansing, Michigan; Wallace Aerial Surveys, Spokane, Washington; Wolf Studios, Des Moines, Iowa, and others. The survey includes all counties except Philadelphia.

Arranged by county, the survey is made up of 8x10 contact prints (27 cu. ft.) which bear code numbers and are grouped by units within each county. The scales is 1:20,000 ft. Each unit has an accompanying 19x24 composite photograph made from the prints (9 cu. ft.). There is a three volume index to these composites.

Bureau of Vacation and Travel Development

Black and White Photograph File, 1938-1954, 17.5 cu. ft.

Created by the State Publicity Commission, the file was "inherited" by the Bureau when the Department of Commerce was established in 1939. Most of the photographs were taken by staff photographers Elmer L. Burkett and Edwin F. Hansen, or obtained from news and other information sources.

The file consists of over 2,900 prints (4.5 cu. ft.), usually 8x10 and arranged by subject, and matching 4x5, 5x7 and 8x10 negatives (4 cu. ft.) arranged by number. The prints are mounted on cardboard bearing information on subject, negative number, and when, who and where taken. Negative envelopes often contain the same data. Many items are missing.

There is a card file subject index (1 cu. ft.) to the prints, and a separate file containing extra copy prints and the original negative envelopes (8 cu. ft.).

The photographs were used by the Department to promote Pennsylvania industry, agriculture, scenic wonders, etc. Subjects cover buildings, city and town views, county views, highway scenes, industry, monuments and markers, recreation, and miscellaneous.

Buildings include historic structures such as Daniel Boone Homestead, James Buchanan's Birthplace and "Wheatland," Bushy Run Park, Carlisle Barracks, Ephrata Cloister, Fort Augusta, Fort Indiantown Gap, Fort Necessity, Friendship Hill, Robert Fulton Birthplace, Governor's Mansion, Grand View Ship Hotel, King of Prussia Inn, Landis Valley Museum, Joseph Priestley House, Studebaker Wagon Works, Conrad Weiser Homestead; various historic Presbyterian, Lutheran, and Roman Catholic churches and Mennonite and Quaker meetinghouses; the State Capitol in Harrisburg; courthouse buildings for Bedford, Blair, Butler, Cambria, Cameron, Carbon, Centre, Chester, Clinton, Columbia, Cumberland, Dauphin, Delaware, Erie, Fayette, Forest, Franklin, Huntingdon, Juniata, Lancaster, Lebanon, Lehigh, Luzerne, McKean, Mercer, Mifflin, Montour, Northampton, Schuylkill, Sullivan, Union, Venango, Warren and York Counties; and a miscellany of unique or unusual structures.

City and town views including Altoona, Bedford, Bethlehem, Eagles Mere, Emporium, Erie, Gettysburg (including Battlefield), Harrisburg, Hershey, Hummelstown, Johnstown, Kittanning, Liverpool, Mauch Chunk, McConnellsburg, Millersburg, Philadelphia, Phoenixville, Pittsburgh and Valley Forge (including historic area).

County views include Adams, Bedford, Berks, Blair, Bradford, Bucks, Cameron, Carbon, Centre, Chester, Clarion, Clearfield, Clinton, Columbia, Cumberland, Dauphin, Elk, Erie, Fulton, Huntingdon, Juniata, Lackawanna, Lancaster, Lehigh, Luzerne, Lycoming, McKean, Mifflin, Monroe, Montgomery, Northampton, Perry, Pike, Potter, Somerset, Sullivan, Susquehanna, Tioga, Union, Warren, Westmoreland and Wyoming.

Highway scenes along U.S. Routes 6, 22, 30, 40, 220, 322, 611, the Pennsylvania Turnpike and many smaller state routes.

Industry views include anthracite and bituminous coal mining; coal dredging in the Susquehanna; coke ovens; cement factories in Lebanon and Lehigh Counties; the Lewisburg Chair and Furniture Company; glass and bottle making in Clarion and Washington Counties; iron furnace ruins in Cumberland, Clarion and York Counties; Cornwall and Hopewell Village Historic Sites; lime kiln ruins near Portland; Armstrong linoleum works in Lancaster; flour mills, including Cattaloosa Mill, Ludwig Derr's Mill, White Horse Mill, Laughlin Mill, McConnell's Mill, Neely's Mill, Bare Mill, Stouffer Mill, Wagner Mill, and Wierman's Mill; oil fields in Delaware

(Marcus Hook), Venango and Washington Counties, and the Drake Well replica and monument near Titusville; paper mills in Blair and Elk Counties; pottery factories in Berks and Clearfield Counties; electric power plants at Safe Harbor and in Cameron County; sand and gravel mining in Bedford, Bucks and Cambria Counties; a sawmill near Lewistown; various steel factories throughout the state; a textile factory in Cambria County and miscellaneous industries such as tanneries.

Monuments and markers are shown at the graves of General Edward Braddock, John Harris, Molly Pitcher, Wyoming and Penn's Creek Massacre victims and unknown Revolutionary War soldiers in Lehigh and Pike Counties; commemorating Whistler's Mother, Mary Jemison, Mary Shaw Leader, William H. McGuffey, Robert Peary, "the Madonna of the Trail," Arthur St. Clair, Shikellamy, Tom Quick, John Hanson Steelman, the Bucktail Regiment, and the Civilian Conservation Corps Camp in Cameron; road, site or trail markers for William Penn's Landing Place, the Walking Purchase, the Standing Stone at Huntingdon, the Sullivan Trail, the National Road, Forbes Road, "Pine Ford" over the Susquehanna, and Route 30; military sites including Forts Bigham, Halifax, Ligonier, Littleton, Kreamer, and Robinson; Camp Curtin, the 28th Division Shrine, the Battles of Jumonville, Hanover and Gettysburg and Washington's Crossing; miscellaneous items include James Buchanan's Birthplace, a land grant marker at Cherry Tree, the Atlantic/Mississippi Watershed marker in Potter County; the site of French Azilum; and others.

Recreation includes bicycling; boating, swimming, fishing, canoeing, and other water sports; horseback riding; and hiking the Horse Shoe and Appalachian Trails. Activities are shown in the following state parks: Blue Knob, Bucktail, Caledonia, Cherry Spring, Colerain, Cook Forest, Samuel Elliott, French Creek, Leonard Harrison, Halfway, Kettle Creek, Kooser, Laurel Hill, Ole Bull, Parker Dam, Poe Paddy, Presque Isle, Promised Land, Ravensburg, Trough Creek, Washington Crossing and Worlds End. Also included are Girl and Boy Scout camps; yacht racing, tennis, golf and other sports at various places; ice skating, skiing and tobogganing, especially in the Pocono Mountains and at Laurel Mountain; scenes of the Devon Horse Show, Chester County; and at Mount Gretna Lake and Harveys Lake.

Miscellaneous subjects cover agriculture, showing prosperous farms and orchards; agricultural beauty queens; the Amish; bridges, including some covered; civil defense; Department of Commerce exhibits at trade shows, especially the State Farm Show; fairs at Allentown, Port Royal, and York; hunting for bear, deer, pheasant, turkey and other small game; state and national emblems, including Hemlock trees, Mountain Laurel, Ruffed Grouse and Bald Eagle; the dedication of the John Morton Homestead, ca. 1950; transportation with canal boats, Conestoga wagons, steam and electric locomotives, and views of the Johnstown Inclined Plane, the Gravity Railroad at Hawley; waterfalls at Ohiopyle, throughout the Poconos, and elsewhere; portraits of state government officials including Governors Bell, Fine and Duff, the House of Representatives, electoral college, the Pennsylvania Aeronautics Commission, President Harry S Truman, and various state senators and representatives.

RG-31 Department of Commerce--Black and White Photograph File: "Mushrooms ready for the market. Seven months intervene between taking spores that result in the final crop," ca. 1938.

Kodachrome Transparencies, 1938-1954, 6 cu. ft.

This file contains over 1,400 4x5, 5x7 and 8x10 Kodachrome transparencies covering many of the same topics listed above. The transparencies are arranged numerically, with an index card file arranged by subject. Some items are missing.

RG-41
RECORDS OF THE NAVIGATION COMMISSION FOR THE DELAWARE RIVER AND ITS NAVIGABLE TRIBUTARIES

The Commission was originally established as part of the Department of Forests and Waters. Its responsibilities are to appoint wardens for the Port of Philadelphia, administer the Pennsylvania Maritime Academy, direct traffic, moor seagoing vessels, and carry out related duties.

Records of the Port of Philadelphia

Photographs, 1917-1936, 1952, 1 folder

These images were probably collected by staff for reference and publicity purposes. Most are 8x10 prints produced by the Aero Service Corporation of Philadelphia, 1923-1930, and the Philadelphia City Department of Wharves, Docks and Ferries, 1917-1936. The Aero Service items are ninety-five aerial views of the Delaware and Schuylkill Rivers at the Port of Philadelphia. Notable among these is the construction of the Delaware River Bridge. Items by the City Department of Wharves, Docks and Ferries are eighty-six views of the harbor and activities therein, such as loading and unloading at Municipal Piers; the Baldwin Locomotive Company's Eddystone Plant; the William Cramp and Sons Boatyards; Port Richmond and other areas. Also present is a 1952 portrait collage of the Pilots' Association for the Bay and River Delaware.

Pennsylvania Maritime Academy

Photographs, 1916-1941, 2 folders

The Pennsylvania State Nautical Schoolships *Annapolis* and *Seneca* were used as training vessels for the United States Merchant Marine, 1921-1941, and berthed at Philadelphia. One folder contains remains of an album of about 100 prints of varying size probably taken by *Annapolis* crew members, 1922-1928. Views show daily life aboard ship, various foreign cruises, graduation exercises, etc. Most are labelled and dated. The second folder contains ninety miscellaneous views, 1916-1941, usually 8x10 prints, pertaining to life aboard the *Annapolis* or *Seneca* in Philadelphia harbor. These include views by the Aero Service Corporation, Philadelphia City Department of Wharves, Docks and Ferries, Ledger Photo Service and the Philadelphia *Inquirer*.

RG-45
RECORDS OF THE DEPARTMENT OF MINES AND MINERAL INDUSTRIES

The Department of Mines was created in 1903 to succeed the Bureau of Mines of the Department of Internal Affairs. It became the Department of Mines and Mineral Industries in 1956, and had responsibility for enforcing mining laws, inspecting mines and colleries, promoting uses and markets for coal, and other related duties. The department was abolished in 1971 and its responsibilities transferred to the Department of Environmental Resources.

Office of the Secretary of Mines and Mineral Industries

General Correspondence, 1903-1965, 65 cu. ft.
Interfiled with these records are 8x10 photographs relating to controlling mine fires, especially in Lackawanna and Allegheny Counties and other areas; sealing mine openings, reclaiming strip mines; the 1953 Minooka Mine Fire; and a visit by United Mine Workers President John L. Lewis to an unidentified mine. Most were taken by the Bureau of Mines, U.S. Department of the Interior; the rest are unidentified.

Mine Disaster File, 1939-1964, 3 cu. ft.
Interfiled with these records are 8x10 photographs relating to the 1959 Knox Mine Disaster at Pittston (1 folder) and the 1957 Robena Mine Disaster at Marianna (1 folder). Most were taken by the Bureau of Mines, U.S. Department of the Interior; the rest are unidentified.

RG-52
RECORDS OF THE DEPARTMENT OF TRANSPORTATION

PennDOT was created in 1970 as a merger of the Department of Highways, the Pennsylvania Aeronautics Commission, the Bureau of Motor Vehicles and related agencies. It is the supervising authority of all state highways, airports and other matters dealing with transportation.

Commonwealth Media Services

Main File, 1970-1976, 12.5 cu. ft.
This is a continuation of the Main File of the Department of Highways (see RG-12) and numbers over 10,000 black and white and color negatives of varying size with matching contact prints or enlargements. The file, arranged by number, is accompanied by a logbook with numerical entries containing subject, date, photographer, etc. Topics cover activities of the department, publicity shots, news events and include: Secretaries of Transportation Jacob Kassab and James Wilson with Governors Raymond Shafer and Milton Shapp at ceremonies for opening new highways, swearing in highway officials, signing legislation, etc.; views of flood damaged areas from Hurricane Agnes, 1972, and Hurricane Eloise, 1975; scenic views of highways, historic sites, rest areas, bridges and covered bridges; aerial views of highways; airports, especially Capital City Airport and Harrisburg International Airport; automobile, train and airplane accidents; staff retirement parties; and other festivities.

Films and Videocassettes, 1965-1985, 56 items
Includes black and white and color films of varying length produced by CMS for PennDot and other state agencies. Subjects cover a wide range relating to transportation and safety, depending upon the intended audience, from public service announcements to publicity and staff instruction. Topics include drunken driving, car safety belts, highway job recruitment, snow removal, roadside herbicide spraying, motorcycle safety, safe speeds, highway deterioration, etc. Notable items include Hurricane Agnes Flood, 1972; the 1975 flood; "The Keystone Shortway" (I-80), ca. 1970; the construction of Interstate 95 through Philadelphia, ca. 1975; and document signings, speeches, etc. of Governor Richard Thornburgh, ca. 1980.

MANUSCRIPT GROUPS

MG-152 S. Emerson Bolton Collection: "President delivering his address."
Theodore Roosevelt dedicating the State Capitol Building, Harrisburg,
October 4, 1906. Governor Pennypacker hatless at right. Photograph by
William H. Rau (see p. 69)

MG-23
ARTHUR C. BINING COLLECTION
Ca. 1898-1955, 3.5 cu. ft.

Dr. Arthur Cecil Bining (1893-1957), a native of Wales, was professor of history at the University of Pennsylvania, Philadelphia. He wrote exten-sively on the development of the iron and steel industries in the United States and especially Pennsylvania. His best-known work in this regard was *Pennsylvania Iron Manufacture in the Eighteenth Century* (Pennsylvania Historical and Museum Commission, 1938).

The Collection is materials created or gathered by Bining over the course of his career of research on the iron and steel industry. It is divided into two categories, Research and Graphic Materials. Research Materials (1.75 cu. ft.) include typed or written manuscripts, field notes, letters, etc. Graphic Materials (.75 cu. ft.) include blueprints, engravings, drawings and photographic prints.

Most photographs are exterior views of Pennsylvania iron forges, furnaces and steel mills. Many were taken by Bining on field trips in the 1920s and usually show sites in ruins. Some are older contemporary views by commercial photographers collected by Bining. These often show iron and steel works in blast. Most items are undated, but are usually identified on the reverse by Bining. No original negatives are present.

Views include: the National Tube Works, Clairton Steel Works, and Carnegie Steel Works in Allegheny County; Kittanning Iron and Steel Manufacturing Company in Armstrong County; Everett Furnace in Bedford County; Hay Creek Forge, Dale Furnace, Windsor Furnace, Bird Mansion, Pine Forge Mansion, Sally Ann Furnace and Mansion, Henry Clay Furnace, Charming Forge, Topton Furnace, iron stove plates from Colebrookdale, Robesonia Furnace and Mansion (includes views of the works probably by Bining 1920-1921 and a book of photographs: *One Hundred and Twenty-Five Years of Pig Iron Manufacture at Robesonia Pennsylvania*, 1773-1918) in Berks County; andirons on display at the Mercer Museum in Bucks County; Zinc Furnace in Carbon County; Nittany Furnace, Milesburg Forge, Hecla Furnace and others in Centre County; Worth Steel Company #3 Furnace, Isabella Furnace, Warwick Furnace, Hopewell Furnace, andirons used at Washington's Headquarters, Valley Forge in Chester County; Pine Grove Furnace and stove plates from Boiling Springs Furnace in Cumberland County; Delaware River Steel Company in Delaware County; Dunbar Furnace, Jacob's Creek Furnace and various works of the H. C. Frick Coal and Coke Company in Fayette County; Lehigh Canal and Crane Iron Works in Lackawanna County; Martic Forge, Chickies Furnace, Henry W. Stiegel

Mansion and Robert Coleman Mansion in Lancaster County; Republic Iron and Steel Works in Lawrence County; Cornwall Furnace in Lebanon County; Macungie Furnace in Lehigh County; Youngstown Iron Sheet & Tube Company, Shenango Furnace, and Steward Iron Company in Mercer County; Warrick Iron and Steel Company in Montgomery County; Bethlehem Steel Company, Gideon Furnace 1881 view, by H.B. Eggert and Durham Furnace in Northampton County; Southwark Postal Station Iron Furnace mural and various Franklin stoves in Philadelphia County; Schuylkill Iron Company, High Blast Furnace and Pioneer Furnace in Schuylkill County; American Steel and Wire Company, Eliza Furnace Ore Yards and Lemoyne Crematory in Washington County; Codorus Furnace, and a stove plate made at Mary Ann Furnace in York County; and various sites in Alabama, Connecticut, Georgia, Illinois, Kentucky, Maryland, Massachusetts, New Hampshire, New York, North Carolina, Ohio, Virginia, West Virginia and Nova Scotia. Miscellaneous illustrations include engravings, drawings, etc., of iron plantations and ironmaking techniques in the late eighteenth and early nineteenth centuries and Brown Patent Furnace Hoists.

MG-43
DOCK FAMILY PAPERS
1865-1951, 7.5 cu. ft.

Two generations of the Dock Family of central Pennsylvania were actively involved in art, civic affairs, forestry management, the iron and coal industries, medicine, nursing, and women's rights from the late nineteenth to the mid-twentieth centuries. Notable among these family members are Gilliard (1827-1895), railroad mechanic, machinist and supervisor at various collieries in central Pennsylvania; Gilliard's son George (1860-1951), a renowned physician; his daughter Lavinia (1858-1956), a suffragist and pioneer in the nursing profession, and Mira (1853-1945), member of the Pennsylvania Forestry Commission, 1899-1911, delegate to the International Council on Women, 1899, and founding member of the Harrisburg Civic Club with J. Horace McFarland and others. She was also a lecturer, world traveler, and photographer.

The family's papers were widely distributed to various repositories between 1945 and 1956 by Lavinia Dock and another daughter, Laura. In addition to the State Archives, the following received parts of the collection: the Library of Congress, the U.S. Geological Survey, and the General Federation of Women's Clubs in Washington; the Pennsylvania State University, Department of Forestry, University Park; the Gettysburg College Library, Gettysburg; the Society of Bartram's Gardens and the Botanical Department of the University of Pennsylvania, Philadelphia; the Historical Society of Dauphin County, Harrisburg; the Kittochtinny Historical Society, Chambersburg; and the School of Horticulture, Ambler.

The bulk of the materials at the State Archives are the papers (4 cu. ft.) and photographs (2 cu. ft.) of Mira Lloyd Dock spanning from 1879 to 1945. The journal of Gilliard Dock, 1845-1894, and some miscellaneous papers of George, Lavinia and other Dock family members are also present (1.5 cu. ft.). Most of Dock's papers focus on her career in forestry and civic affairs, but some relate to photography, specifically correspondence with such photographers as William H. Rau and J. Horace McFarland. Two undated notebooks listing slides and prints taken by her are also present, but the originals are apparently lost and unrelated to those in the collection. Also, Gilliard Dock's journal for 1899 mentions Mira photographing scenes in the Broad Top area of Bedford County, where the family often vacationed. In addition to references, pages beginning in September of that year have sixteen of her prints glued to them. These show pastoral spots cherished by the family, and Gilliard on various walking trips. Photographs include glass plate negatives, glass slides and prints. The bulk of these are technical studies of flower and tree specimens in central and eastern Pennsylvania, often identified by their Latin names. Other photographs are artistic studies of people and nature in Pennsylvania and miscellaneous subjects.

Glass plate negatives (215 items) vary in size from 4x5, 5x8, 6x8 to 8x10. Most are undated, but probably were taken between 1889 and 1900. Technical studies include: arbutus, cypress, ferns, habenaria purple, hackberry, Indian pipe, lilies, locust trees, mushrooms, orchids, pansies, phlox, pine, rhododendron, spring beauties, sugar maple, sumac, sunflowers, trillium, white thorn, willows, witch hazel, and unidentified items. Artistic studies include: apple butter making; Gilliard Dock's hunting camp, "Camp Mariah" at Broad Top; forests and gardens in England (copy negatives); various Harrisburg streets and bridges; hikers at High Rocks; a lotus pond in York County; the Susquehanna River at McCall's Ferry; a barn at Mont Alto; and gardens on the State Capitol grounds, Harrisburg.

Glass lantern slides (290 items), were probably taken between 1892 and 1907, with some undated. A few are hand colored. While some are slide versions of the plates listed above, most are commercially produced, probably taken or collected by Dock on her travels. The alphabetically arranged subjects are primarily of forests, parks, playgrounds and individual tree specimens in Pennsylvania, including Adams, Bedford, Bucks, Cameron, Clinton, Cumberland, Erie, McKean, Montgomery, Pike, Potter, Sullivan, Wayne and York Counties. United States and foreign views are also present. Miscellaneous items include apple blossoms, apple butter making, "closed" and "open" forests, logging and lumbering, maple sugaring, tree nurseries, river dumps, playgrounds, forest regeneration and others.

Photographs, 1889-1931 (4 boxes), are prints made by local commercial photographers from negatives made by Dock, and prints and postcards include: Broad Top views, especially Camp Mariah; Rainsburg Gap; chestnut trees, spruce trees and Gilliard Dock on various hiking trips; the Pennsylvania Canal below Dauphin; the Dock Family home in Harrisburg; Harrisburg Cemetery entrance; a lotus pond in York County; views of the Susquehanna at McCall's Ferry taken by Dock and printed by LeRue Lemer; and elm, locust and cedar trees at various locales.

Prints by other photographers include views of trees and historic buildings in eastern Pennsylvania by C. M. Bradford, undated; a New York City penthouse garden and a house in Chester, Pa., by R.R. Brock, undated; ruins of first State Capitol, Harrisburg, 1897, by E.K. Gaugler; Harrisburg playgrounds and sewers; Paxton Creek and Susquehanna River views by J. Horace McFarland, 1900-1910; the Johnson Garden at Germantown by William H. Rau, 1895; and the James Buchanan Birthplace by C.E. Seville, undated.

Miscellaneous subjects, not identified by date or photographer include: bridges; European gardens; Duncans Island in the Susquehanna River; Rockford Plantation, Lancaster County; Mont Alto Forestry School Chapel; various buildings and fountains, Fairmount Park, Philadelphia; Coaley Poultry Farm, Coudersport; miscellaneous views of Easton; Gloustershire, Leamington, Lappenham, and Windsor Castle, England. People include Gilliard Dock, Mira Dock, S.B. Elliott, John Fulton, Robert D. MacMurdy, Governor William Stone and Joseph T. Rothrock; the Mont Alto Forest Academy Basketball Team, 1905-1906; views of San Antonio, Texas; and ceremonies dedicating a plaque at Young Womans Creek Forest Reservation, 1925; and other items.

MG-75
JOSEPH M. HUSTON COLLECTION
Ca. 1898-1918, 10.5 cu. ft.

Joseph M. Huston (1866-1940), member of the Philadelphia Chapter of the American Institute of Architects, won in 1902 a highly publicized

MG-75 Joseph M. Huston Collection: The newly dedicated State Capitol Building at Harrisburg, Winter 1906, by William H. Rau.

competition to design a new state capitol building in Harrisburg. A Philadelphia native, Huston was known locally for designing the Arcade Building, the Witherspoon Building, and others. He and several construction officials were later charged with conspiracy to accept bribes and overcharge the Commonwealth for work on the Capitol. He served in jail for six months and was paroled in 1911. The Collection pertains almost exclusively to Huston's work on the Capitol. Most items are Huston's personal estate and were acquired by the State Archives over the course of several years.

Non-photographic items (7 cu. ft.) include Huston's signed drawings submitted for the Capitol competition (11 folders); other later designs by him for the main building and surrounding park area (7 folders); engravings of the Capitol front and plans for the park (3 folders); three newsclipping albums of varying size presumably compiled by Huston during the building's construction; an undated folio of blueprints for furniture; and miscellaneous items.

Photographs (3.5 cu. ft.) include eighty-one prints by William H. Rau of the Capitol shortly after completion, probably the fall of 1906. Each item, arranged alphabetically, roughly measures 7 1/2 x 9 1/2 and is signed by Rau in pencil or embossed. Subjects include the Capitol exterior, rotunda, governor's and lieutenant governor's offices and reception rooms, offices of the Insurance Commissioner, Auditor General, Deputy Secretary of the Commonwealth, Adjutant General, Attorney General, Treasurer, Appropriations Committee, Supreme Court, Factory Inspector, Superintendent of Public Grounds and Buildings, House and Senate Chambers, caucus rooms, mechanical plant, and first floor and ladies' reception rooms. Additional undated prints by Rau include Huston at his Germantown estate.

Photographs relating to artist George Gray Barnard include twenty-two 22x17 undated studies by Fiorillo of Paris of the Capitol statuary in progress at the sculptor's studio at Moret-Sur-Loing, France; and two images of Barnard outside his studio.

Other items include a photograph album containing approximately 550 prints (3x5 average) by an unknown photographer showing the construction of the Capitol. Most images are dated between July 1903 and November 1905 and follow Huston and companions on visits to the construction site, Vermont granite quarries, on a steamship bound for Europe, and in France and Italy visiting artists and sculptors (including Barnard) at work on various murals and statuary.

Miscellaneous photographs include an undated album of light fixtures, furniture and architectural features planned for the Capitol; six approximately 6x9 copy prints of designs presumably submitted to the Capitol competition by Pittsburgh architects R. Maurice Trimble and Benjamin R.

Stevens; an undated studio view of the statue "Commonwealth" before being placed atop the Capitol dome and other miscellaneous items.

MG-85
J. HORACE McFARLAND COLLECTION
1859-1948, 26 cu. ft.

John Horace McFarland (1859-1948), born in McAlisterville, Juniata County, was a printer by trade and devoted his life to philanthropy, especially the preservation of unique natural areas in the United States. In 1878 he established in Harrisburg his own printing firm, the J. Horace McFarland Company. The company published, among other things, several national magazines devoted to horticulture and gardening, to which McFarland was a frequent contributing author and photographer. With Mira Lloyd Dock and others, he founded the Harrisburg Civic Association which promoted the turn-of-the-century "City Beautiful" movement. He was a founder and president of the American Civic Association, a private organization that advocated preservation of natural areas, including Niagara Falls, N.Y., Hetch Hetchy Valley, Calif., Cumberland Falls, Md., and others, and that helped to establish the National Park Service.

The bulk of the Collection (23.5 cu. ft.) is McFarland's business correspondence, reports, addresses, etc., relating to his work with the A.C.A. and other organizations, and personal correspondence, diaries and other papers. Of interest here is correspondence with photographers Charles Bretzman, Mira Lloyd Dock, the firm of Harris and Ewing, Edwin Hale Lincoln, Frances Benjamin Johnston, Jacob Riis and others. There is also .5 cu. ft. of articles and "how to" lectures on photographing flowers, children and other subjects.

Photographs (1 cu. ft.) include prints collected for the A.C.A. of Niagara Falls, 1906-1934, 180 items; prints by McFarland, probably of his Harrisburg factory, used to illustrate "The Making of Paper" 1905, thirty-five items; Harrisburg area views by local photographers, including the John Harris Mansion, Susquehanna River, Paxtang Park, and others, ca. 1936, twenty-five items; glass lantern slides, some hand colored, arranged for a lecture on the beautification of Harrisburg either by Mira Lloyd Dock or McFarland, ca. 1910, fifty-one items; activities of the "Boyer Joy Giving Car," a trolley operated by the Harrisburg Home Invalid's Union, Old Folks Home and Cheerful Worker's Union, which gave rides to city recreation areas for children, the elderly, the poor or handicapped, ca. 1915, nineteen items; McFarland at a conference at Yellowstone National Park; John Muir and

John Burroughs at Yosemite; and undated scenic views of other national parks, fifteen items; miscellaneous items including formal portraits of McFarland; autochrome plates of unidentified people and places; and a portrait of Alan Seeger, a slain World War I soldier for whom a Centre County natural area was named.

Also included is 1.5 cu. ft. of material relating to Colonel George F. McFarland (1834-?), Horace's father. McFarland was commanding officer of the 151st Pennsylvania Volunteers, a unit suffering heavy losses at Gettysburg. McFarland was later first superintendent of the State's Soldiers Orphans Schools. Illustrative material includes eight Tyson Brothers photographs of the town of Gettysburg and battlefield, 1863; engravings of McFarland, Abner Doubleday, and other commanding officers of the 3rd Division, 1st Corps, 1863; and engravings of various Soldiers Orphans Schools around the state.

MG-130
FRED TSCHUDY COLLECTION
1904-1909, n.d., .6 cu. ft.

The Sons of Veterans Reserves was a national paramilitary organization similar to the Grand Army of the Republic, with members usually sons or relatives of Civil War veterans. Founded in Pittsburgh in 1881, Reserve members wore uniforms, maintained local posts and held annual encampments. Fred Tschudy was commander of the Pennsylvania Brigade, probably between 1904 and 1909, headquartered in Johnstown, Pa. Research has revealed nothing about his personal life beyond this Collection.

The Collection consists of correspondence (.25 cu. ft.) to and from Tschudy regarding S.V.R. business, 1904-1909, and glass plate negatives (forty-four items) of S.V.R. annual encampments, 1907-1909, and undated. The plates, 5x7 and 8x10, are arranged by size and thereunder chronologically. They seem to bear no relation to Fred Tschudy. Some items are identified by time and place, but most are unidentified. The State Archives received the collection in 1958 from Frances Youngblood of Birmingham, Ala.

The photographs include: six plates (8x10) taken at Camp Ezra Ripple, Scranton, Pa., 1907, by John Horgan, Jr., a local photographer. Subjects show flag ceremonies, a sham battle, and various S.V.R. members in front of their tents. Also included are thirty-eight (5x7) plates taken by unknown photographer(s). Subjects include an S.V.R. public worship at Camp Melhuish(?), June 7, 1908; a parade and activities of the 1909 encampment at Camp Joe A. Logan, Milton, Pa.; the S.V.R. Marine Band of Allentown on parade, undated; and an S.V.R. troop on practice maneuvers, undated.

MG-152
S. EMERSON BOLTON COLLECTION
Ca. 1903-1907, 77 items

This collection contains studies probably used by artistic designers for the interior of the present State Capitol in Harrisburg (see MG-75). Most are photographic copies probably for reference purposes during planning stages. Some were never used in the completed building. The Collection was donated in part to the State Archives in 1965 by S. Emerson Bolton, a Philadelphia antiques dealer, and in 1973 by Bolton's family.

The material is primarily photographic studies of works for the Capitol by artists hired on commission. The photos are mounted on heavy cardboard and vary in size from 8x10 to 23x24. Subjects include twelve W.B. Van Ingen watercolors for door entrances. Some are inscribed by the artist to Joseph Huston, the building's architect. Others are seventeen sculptured pediment designs by Attilio Piccirilli, statues of "Hewer" by George Gray Barnard and "Dr. MacMillan" by Alexander J. Calder.

Also included are sixteen original watercolor scale models of interior panels signed by Joseph Huston.

Miscellaneous photographs include four 8x10 prints by William H. Rau of the Capitol dedication ceremonies October 4, 1906. Shown delivering speeches are President Theodore Roosevelt, Governor Samuel Pennypacker and ex-Governor William Stone. Additional views include Huston's office in Philadelphia, chandeliers and bronze doors in the Capitol, and a view of the building from the west bank of the Susquehanna, 1907.

MG-156
EDWARD M. MARTIN PAPERS
1866-1967, 120 cu. ft.

Edward M. Martin (1879-1967), born near Waynesburg, led a distinguished career in military and public service. In 1898 he joined the Pennsylvania National Guard, and saw action during the Philippine Campaign, 1898-1899, the Mexican Border Campaign, 1916, and World War I, 1917-1919. He became a major general and took command of the 28th Division in

1939, and served as a commanding general during World War II. He was also State Auditor General, 1925-1929; State Treasurer, 1929-1933; Adjutant General, 1939-1943; Governor, 1943-1947; and U.S. Senator, 1947-1958.

The bulk of the collection is papers of Martin's governorship, senatorial career, and personal affairs (114 cu. ft.). Photographs relate to his military career, 1898-1943; his public service, especially as governor and U.S. senator and his retirement, 1943-1965 (6 cu. ft.)

Most photographs are in albums, seventeen volumes, collected and compiled by Martin during the course of his life. Most of these bear identification, including subject and date, on the album pages.

Albums include:
An album of activities of the 28th Division, 1918-1919, at Camp Hancock, Ga., and France, taken by the U.S. Army Signal Corps (5 vols.). Also includes the victory parade in Philadelphia, May 1919.

"The Career of Edward Martin," ca. 1916-1960, collected from many sources (7 vols.). The albums are roughly arranged in chronological order. Though they number one through nine, volumes three and nine are missing. *Volume I*: activities of the 10th Regiment, Pennsylvania National Guard, in Puerto Rico, 1898; the Philippine Insurrection, 1898-1899; the Mexican Border Campaign of 1916; at Camp Hancock, 1917-1918; in France, 1918-1919; at Mount Gretna, 1915 and 1921-1923; and PNG camps at Huntingdon and Altoona, ca. 1917; the 3rd Regiment of Infantry at Gettysburg, 1884 (copy); the 28th Division victory parade in Philadelphia, 1919; and the Major Girard Bryce Collection of U.S. Army Signal Corps photographs pertaining to the 28th in France, 1918-1919. *Volume II*: Officers of the 10th Regiment, PNG at Gettysburg, 1904; views of France, 1918, some made with captured German negatives; Martin at Mount Gretna, 1920; at the dedication of the Pennsylvania World War I monument in France, May-June, 1928; posing with President Herbert Hoover, 1932; and portraits of Martin by Fabian Bachrach, and other photographs. *Volume IV*: Martin with the PNG at Mount Gretna, 1920-1928, and Camp Livingston, Va., 1928; inauguration as state treasurer, 1928; with Mrs. Martin at their Washington, Pa. home, 1933; at the construction and dedication of the 28th Division Memorial near Boalsburg, 1938 and 1940; at a Waynesburg Boy Scout Reunion, 1940; at a PNG encampment in Lisbon, N.Y., 1940; at maneuvers of the First Army, 1941; campaigning for governor, 1942; at his inaugural ceremonies and posing for portraits with his cabinet, 1943; Mrs. Martin christening the S.S. *Buena Vista* at Chester, 1943; Martin at Wanamaker's "Ordnance for Victory" show, at the Middletown Air Depot War Bond Flag Ceremony, at the Civilian Defense Corps Review at Indiantown Gap, attending the Thirty-fifth Annual Governors' Conference in Ohio, and attending a ceremony honoring the WAVES, all during 1943; and posing with the cabinet of Governor Arthur James as Chairman of the Council of Defense, ca. 1939. *Volume V*, 1944-1945, shows Martin visiting Middletown Air Depot; speaking to the Erie Businessmen and Industrial Association; reviewing the 95th Division at Fort Indiantown Gap; with Governor John Bricker of Ohio; at the Republican National Convention, Chicago; at graduation exercises for the U.S. Navy Radio School in Bedford Springs; at ceremonies in Oyster Bay, N.Y., on the twenty-fifth anniversary of the death of Theodore Roosevelt; inducting women into the Women's Army Corps; presenting a citation to General Milton G. Baker; and views of the home of James G. Blaine. *Volume VI*, 1945-1946, shows Martin with members of the Mines and Mining Committee inspecting strip-mining operations in Allegheny, Washington and Clarion Counties; dedicating Gotwals Lake at Valley Forge General Hospital; signing legislation for workingmen's compensation, bridge construction and teachers salaries; at the Welcome Home Reception for the 28th Division at Fort Indiantown Gap; with the Civil Aeronautics Patrol; inaugurating Harry Weest as Secretary of Health; addressing a meeting of his cabinet; receiving an honorary degree from Lafayette College; at a reception honoring George C. Marshall; with Generals Carl A. Spaatz and Omar Bradley at a Pottstown Homecoming Celebration; *Volume VII*: 1944, 1946-1947 and 1960 show Martin touring a Washington County bituminous mine; inspecting Byberry and Norristown State Hospitals; at the State American Legion Convention; campaigning for U.S. senator; delivering resignation speech as governor; with interim Governor John C. Bell; at ceremonies returning the 28th Division flags to the State Museum; at the inauguration of Governor James Duff; presenting the Edward Martin trophy; and at ceremonies honoring the birthplaces of Philander C. Knox and James G. Blaine. *Volume VIII*, 1947-1955, shows Martin at the deactivation of the Pennsylvania State Guard; posing with Governor John Fine, Thomas Dewey, James Duff, Dwight Eisenhower, and others; and a series of portrait studies of Senator Martin for the Philadelphia *Inquirer*.

Other albums include the second and third annual encampments of the Pennsylvania National Guard at Indiantown Gap, 1944-1945 (2 vols.); an album of the first annual encampment of the Pennsylvania State Police at Indiantown Gap, 1945 (1 vol.); the Thirty-sixth Annual Governors' Conference in Harrisburg, 1944, showing the governors also visiting Gettysburg Battlefield, Carlisle Barracks, Hershey and Philadelphia (1 vol.); "Major General Edward Martin of the Commonwealth of Pennsylvania and Members of His Cabinet, 1943-1947," containing formal portraits, many signed by the cabinet members (1 vol.); and an album presented to State Treasurer Martin dated April 28, 1933, by the staff of the Treasury Department, containing portraits of all the agency's employees (1 vol.).

Miscellaneous loose prints include stereoviews of the 10th Regiment, PNG, during the 1916 Mexican Border Campaign; aerial views of PNG maneuvers at Manassas, Va., 1939; general views of the PNG at Indiantown Gap, 1940-1941; Martin with his horse "Chief"; at a victory parade for Generals Omar Bradley and Carl A. Spaatz, 1945; dedicating Memorial Lake at Indiantown Gap, 1946; stereoviews of the PNG in Waynesburg, ca. 1910; at ceremonies inaugurating Ralph C. Hutchinson as president of Lafayette College, 1945; the inauguration of Governor James Duff; Governor and Mrs. Martin at their home in Washington, Pa.; studies of Martin for *Life* magazine by Paul Shutzer, 1955; the renovation of the David Bradford House in Washington, Pa., 1965; portraits of Martin's ancestors in Ireland; a signed portrait of John Glenn, 1964; and items pertaining to Grover Cleveland and Dwight Eisenhower from the Washington (D.C.) *Times Herald*.

MG-171
SAMUEL W. PENNYPACKER PAPERS
1703-1916, 48 cu. ft.

Samuel Whitaker Pennypacker (1843-1916) was born and raised at the family homestead, "Pennypacker Mills," in Montgomery County. He practiced law in Philadelphia, became a judge and subsequently was elected governor, 1903-1907. He had a strong interest in history, writing and lecturing widely, and was also president of the Historical Society of Pennsylvania, 1900-1916. Pennypacker's descendants donated his papers to the State Archives in 1969 and 1971.

The bulk of the Papers is executive and personal correspondence and other materials relating to his governorship (47 cu. ft.). Photographs are prints of varying size relating to his career or historical interests, ca. 1897-1913 (1 cu. ft.). Most are identified and dated on the reverse, probably in Pennypacker's hand. Photographers' imprints or logos often also appear.

Photographs relating to Pennypacker's political career show him inaugurated as governor, 1903, by L.G. Harpel and others; at the dedication of the State Capitol, October 4, 1906, with President Theodore Roosevelt by C.S. Roshon; in the parade at Roosevelt's second inauguration in Washington, D.C., 1905, by William H. Rau; participating in a session of the State Senate, ca. 1890; at the dedication of monuments to Pennsylvania regiments at Andersonville, Antietam, Chattanooga, and Vicksburg; dedicating the Hawkins Monument, Pittsburgh; at the Soldiers and Sailors Home, Erie, 1903-1905; at the 1913 Gettysburg Reunion with former President William H. Taft by D.B. Schuey; speaking at Indian Rock on the Wissahickon; a view of the "old" State Capitol by J. Horace McFarland; and landscapes of eastern Pennsylvania by H.W. Fegley.

Items relating to Pennsylvania history include views of historical sites in eastern Pennsylvania, especially by William H. Richardson (forty-five prints). Richardson, at one time president of the Montgomery County Historical Society and the Pennsylvania German Society, was also an amateur photographer. Most views are 4x5 prints mounted on cards signed and dated by Richardson, and show sites in and around Montgomery County. Subjects include Valley Forge; Pennypacker Mills; sites relating to General Howe's campaign of 1777 in Pennsylvania and Delaware; Mennonites and Mennonite meetinghouses at Franconia, Harleyville, Indian Creek, Methatchen and Upper and Lower Skippack; the Salford Schwenkfelder Meeting; the Kriebel House on Skippack Creek; and the Snow Hill Seventh-Day Baptist Cloister. There is also one folder of correspondence between Richardson and Pennypacker, 1895-1910. Additional documents and photographs by Richardson are among the collections of the Montgomery County Historical Society.

Miscellaneous items collected by Pennypacker are by various photographers, most unidentified. Topics cover buildings, including views of Valley Forge buildings by Frank H. Taylor and others; scenes near Goshen Meeting House from the "Brinton Photographic Collection of Revolutionary and other Historical Sites in Pennsylvania Maryland and Delaware," by Douglas E. Brinton; views of the General Anthony Wayne statue at Newburgh, N.Y., the birthplaces of Matthew S. Quay, John Hartranft, Robert Fulton and the Daub Family; Carpenter Mansion, "Cedarcroft" and Chew Mansion in Germantown; the Fountain Inn, Phoenixville, and Red Lion Inn, Torresdale; the "Emlen" House, Abraham Schwenk House, Peter Wentz House, Longwood Meeting House, Birmingham Meeting House, and other homes and religious buildings; graveyards and tombs include the Bertolet Mennonite Graveyard, Thomas Holme Family Graveyard, Anderson Family Graveyard, Prince Gallitzen's grave at Loretto and John Waterman's grave at Valley Forge. Portraits include a carte-de-visite of President Andrew Johnson; David Thomas, Principal Engineer of the Erie Canal; Civil War soldiers T. Buchanan Read and Corporal John L. Smith; and Coffin Colket by Frederick Gutekunst, and others. Miscellaneous items show two views by A. F. Bonine of flag raising ceremonies at G.A.R. Post #19, Lancaster, ca. 1910; the U.S.S. *Pennsylvania* by Gutekunst, photographic copies of a George Washington letter, 1791; maps of parts of Berks and Philadelphia Counties; and monuments and statues at Gettysburg by W.H. Tipton, Mumper and Company, and others.

MG-196
HORACE M. ENGLE COLLECTION
Ca. 1865-1980, 25 cu. ft.

Horace Matthew Engle (1861-1949) was born and raised near Marietta. He was, at various times, a fruitgrower, schoolteacher, prohibitionist and photographer. His personal effects and other ephemera were discovered in 1971 by Edward Leos of Lemont. Engle's story is described in Leos's *Other Summers: The Photographs of Horace Engle*, University Park: Pennsylvania State University Press, 1980. Leos subsequently donated the materials to the State Archives. Engle at first specialized in candid photography, using a Gray-Stirn Concealed Vest Camera, also known as a "detective camera." This could be worn under a jacket or coat, with the lens opening through a buttonhole. The camera took round glass plates, 5 1/2" in diameter, each holding six negative images. Engle later used Kodak Model 2 and 3A cameras.

The bulk of the Collection consists of Engle's personal and business correspondence, technical notes, newsclippings and other papers; and index cards, research notes, copy prints and negatives from Engle's photographs by Edward Leos (21.5 cu. ft.). The remainder are Engle's photographic negatives and prints (3.5 cu. ft.).

Subjects on the Gray-Stirn plates, 1888-1889 (31 items) include: the Engle Family Nurseries near Marietta; town views of Lancaster, Gettysburg, and the Columbia Centennial celebration of 1888; a prohibition rally in Indianapolis, Indiana; an 1889 flood on the Susquehanna near Marietta; C.K. Siefert, itinerant photographer, posing with his wagon; and others, usually portraits of relatives and friends. There is an album of contact prints of these by Engle, with notations in his hand. Not all negatives are represented in the album.

Views taken by the Kodak 2 and 3A cameras include over 1,000 negatives, ca. 1889-1931, some with matching contact prints. The Model 2 negatives are round, 3 1/2" in diameter, and the Model 3A negatives are approximately 3x5. Subjects include: relatives in the Engle, Ellis, Grove, and Musser Families; self-portraits of Engle; floral displays, wildflowers, etc.; the Marietta Centennial Celebration; street views in Roanoke and Shawsville, Va., Cochran, Ga., Charlestown, W. Va., Ontario, Canada, and Elmira, N.Y.; Pennsylvania towns including Brandywine Manor, Brinton, Bainbridge, Chester Springs, Conoy, Marietta, Maytown, Schocks Mills, Troutville, Washington Boro, West Chester and Womelsdorf; notable items include the construction of Holtwood Dam; the State Capitol, Harrisburg; the Indian

Steps Museum near Wrightsville; the Serpentine Quarry near Delta; and others.

Also included is an album of cabinet card portraits, ca. 1883, with most subjects unidentified, by B. Frank Saylor of Lancaster and other photographers; and cartes-de-visite, ca. 1860, of Engle's relatives by photographers C.W. Williams and William Bailey of Columbia.

MG-199
RAILROAD MUSEUM OF PENNSYLVANIA COLLECTIONS
Ca. 1830-1974, 600 cu. ft.

This is a group of acquisitions arranged by donor relating to railroads, especially in Pennsylvania. The materials were collected over many years by the staff of the Railroad Museum of Pennsylvania, Strasburg.

Some collections are stored in the State Archives in Harrisburg, and others at the Museum's library at Strasburg.

MG-199 Railroad Museum of Pennsylvania Collection-Munson Paddock: Mauch Chunk, ca. 1880 by "Jas. Zelner, Artist."

Collections at the State Archives:

Luther P. Cummings Collection, including photographs of trolleys, trams, and traction lines in Pennsylvania, ca. 1900-present, 3.0 cu. ft. All items were either taken or collected by Cummings. Arranged alphabetically by name of company and includes some out of state.

Walter A. W. Fister Collection relating to his career as a superintendent with the Reading Railroad, 1921-1963, 1 cu. ft. Includes photographs taken or collected by him of Reading locomotives, rolling stock, workers, floods, wrecks and other disasters.

Howard G. Hill Collection of locomotive photographs, ca. 1860-present, 4.5 cu. ft. The photographs, taken or collected by Hill, are arranged alphabetically by name of railroad and thereunder by locomotive number. Each is mounted on cards containing technical information as to size, type, builder, etc.

Walter A. Lucas Collection of stereographs relating to railroads and scenic views in America, ca. 1875-1927, over 1,300 items. Includes views by such photographers as Purviance, E. & H.T. Anthony, William H. Rau, Keystone View Company, B.W. Killburn, William Henry Jackson and many others. Railroads include the Baltimore and Ohio, Delaware and Lackawanna, Denver and Rio Grande, Erie, Lehigh Valley, Maine Central, Michigan Central, New York Central, Pennsylvania, and many others. Notable items include a Keystone View Company series on the B&O Centenary Exhibition and Pageant, September 24, 1927.

Elwin Mumford Collection of photographs and postcards taken and collected by him of Reading Railroad and Delaware, Lackawanna & Western locomotives, rolling stock and support facilities in the eastern Pennsylvania and New York area, 1890-1974, 1 cu. ft. Some items are color.

Robert E. Phillips Collection of research materials and photographs taken and collected by him pertaining to the history of the Reading Railroad, ca. 1890-1965, 2 cu. ft.

Collections at the Railroad Museum of Pennsylvania

These include the combined collections of rail buffs Clinton T. Andrews, F. Stewart Graham, George M. Hart, Walter A. Lucas, Munson Paddock, Thomas T. Tabor, Thomas T. Tabor III, and James H. Westbay, the Baldwin Locomotive Works, and the Union Switch and Signal Co. These total over 40,000 negatives and prints taken or collected by the above and pertain to railroads in Pennsylvania, the United States, and the world. Arranged alphabetically by name of railroad.

MG-212
WILLIAM E. STEWART COLLECTION
Ca. 1860-1946, 1.5 cu. ft.

William Stewart (b. 1904), a retired clothing salesman from Pittsburgh, is a lifelong collector of American paper memorabilia. The emphasis of the collection (1.1 cu. ft.) is on published items, such as booklets, brochures, business receipts, trade cards, calendars, premium catalogues, envelopes, ink blotters, invitations, political election handouts, theatre and dinner programs, World War II ration coupons, and other types of documents relating to people and businesses in western Pennsylvania, ca. 1860-1930. The State Archives gradually obtained the collection from Stewart over the course of several years.

Photographs (.4 cu. ft.) are arranged by type and include cartes-de-visite, cabinet cards, greeting postcards, photographic postcards and miscellaneous photographs, ca. 1860-1930. Most of these are not identified by subject, though the photographer and location, usually somewhere in western Pennsylvania, are sometimes given on the reverse. Some of the photographers are: Hendricks and Co., J.R. Pearson, Stewart and Co. of Allegheny City; J.G. Vallade, Altoona; Laughner's of Braddock; J.W. Ward of Connellsville; I. Grotzinger of Saltsburg; Aufrecht's of Pittsburgh; E.A. Lingo of Uniontown; and Lon M. Porter and Rothwell, of Washington Pa.

Unidentified photographs found in the collection deal with the following subjects: automobiles; community bands; holiday celebrations; college football players; farm houses; machinery and animals; fishermen; floods; hunters; ice harvesting; logging camps; parades, especially Fourth of July, Old Home Week and Women's Christian Temperance Union; formal portraits of people; residences; World War I soldiers; stores; train wrecks; and miscellaneous subjects.

Identified subjects are: Ulysses S. Grant, Tom Mix, Lillian Russell, Evelyn Nesbit Thaw, the U.S.S. *Pennsylvania* (armored cruiser), Victoria Woodhull, and the "Manhattan" postcard series on Robert Fulton and Henry Hudson.

Miscellaneous postcard subjects include general greetings, novelty items, American historical events, and holiday cards for Christmas, Easter, Fourth of July and others.

MG-213
POSTCARD COLLECTION
Ca. 1895-PRESENT, 6.5 cu. ft.

This collection contains approximately 24,000 picture postcards and business trade cards relating to Pennsylvania persons, places and events. Most items date from 1900 to 1925 when postcards in the United States were produced cheaply and sold by the millions. At a time when few newspapers published photographs, and the telephone and hand-held box camera were not quite universal, the picture postcard was an inexpensive and swift means of communication. Today these cards provide a glimpse of the physical, social and cultural changes that Pennsylvania communities have experienced.

Types of cards range from silver gelatin prints on postcard stock by local photographers to commercially produced halftone prints, chromolithograph cards, white border cards, "linen" cards, accordion folders and glossy photochrome cards. Most items measure 3 1/2 x 5 1/2, with some oversize cards. The State Archives obtained the postcards from a variety of sources over the course of many years.

The collection contains three series: the County File (6 cu. ft.), the Subject File (.25 cu. ft.), and the Business and Advertising File (.25 cu. ft.). The County File is arranged alphabetically by county and thereunder by municipality. All sixty-seven counties are present. A large municipality is often further divided into such subject categories as amusement parks, bridges, buildings, community events, industries, novelty cards, community and state parks, panoramic and scenic views, street views and miscellaneous. A very small municipality is filed under miscellaneous county towns. The Subject File contains broader categories not easily classified by county, and includes highways, industries, railroads, and United States and foreign subjects. The Business and Advertising File consists of trade and business cards from Pennsylvania businesses.

Municipalities in the County File include:
Adams County - Biglerville, Gettysburg (town and battlefield), Mount Pleasant, and miscellaneous towns.

Allegheny County - Aspinwall, Bellevue, Ben Avon, Braddock, Carnegie, Clairton, Claremont, Coraopolis, Duquesne, East Pittsburgh, Edgewood, Elizabeth, Glassport, Homestead, McKeesport, McKees Rocks, Millvale, Munhall, Natrona, Oakmont, Pitcairn, Pittsburgh (includes Allegheny City, Oakland, and other local neighborhoods and suburbs), Sewickley, Sharpsburg, Swissvale, Tarentum, Turtle Creek, Verona, Wilkinsburg,

Wilmerding, and miscellaneous towns.

Armstrong County - Apollo, Ford City, Freeport, Kittanning, Leechburg, Parkers Landing, and miscellaneous towns.

Beaver County - Aliquippa, Ambridge, Beaver, Beaver Falls, Economy Village and Harmony Society, Monaca, New Brighton, Rochester, and miscellaneous towns.

Bedford County - Bedford, Bedford Springs, Everett, Grand View Point and Ship Hotel, the Lincoln Highway (U.S. Route 30), Saxton, Schellsburg, White Sulphur Springs, and miscellaneous towns.

Berks County - Kutztown, Reading, Roadside America, Wernersville, Womelsdorf, and miscellaneous towns.

Blair County - Altoona, Bellwood, Hollidaysburg, Horseshoe Curve, Roaring Spring, Tipton (includes National Guard Camp Lindsey), Tyrone, and miscellaneous towns.

Bradford County - Athens, Canton, French Azilum, Sayre, Towanda, Troy, Ulster, and miscellaneous towns.

Bucks County - Bristol, Doylestown, New Hope, Newton, Perkasie, Washington Crossing State Park, and miscellaneous towns.

Butler County - Butler, Chicora, Evans City, Harmony, Mars, Saxonburg, Slippery Rock, Zelienople, and miscellaneous towns.

Cambria County - Barnesboro, Carrolltown, Cresson (includes State Sanitarium), Ebensburg, Hastings, Johnstown (includes 1889 flood), Loretto, Patton, Portage, South Fork, and miscellaneous towns.

Cameron County - Driftwood, Emporium, and miscellaneous towns.

Carbon County - Glen Onoko, Jim Thorpe (Mauch Chunk), Lehighton, and miscellaneous towns.

Centre County - Bellefonte, Penns Cave, Philipsburg, State College (includes Pennsylvania State College), Woodward Cave, and miscellaneous towns.

Chester County - Brandywine Creek and Battlefield, Coatesville, Downingtown, Kennett Square, Oxford, Phoenixville, Spring City, Valley Forge, West Chester, and miscellaneous towns.

Clarion County - Bradys Bend, Clarion, Cook Forest State Park, East Brady, Foxburg, New Bethlehem, and miscellaneous towns.

Clearfield County - Clearfield, Coalport, Curwensville, DuBois, Falls Creek, Osceola Mills, and miscellaneous towns.

Clinton County - Lock Haven, Mill Hall, Renovo, and miscellaneous towns.

Columbia County - Berwick, Bloomsburg, Catawissa, and miscellaneous towns.

Crawford County - Conneautville, Hydetown, Linesville, Meadville, Pymatuning Lake, Saegertown, Shadeland, Spartansburg, Springboro, Titusville, Townville, and miscellaneous towns.

Cumberland County - Boiling Springs, Carlisle (includes Indian School and Carlisle Barracks), Mechanicsburg, Mount Holly Springs, New Cumberland, Shippensburg, and miscellaneous towns.

Dauphin County - Harrisburg (includes Capitol Complex), Hershey, Hummelstown, Middletown, Millersburg, Steelton, and miscellaneous towns.

Delaware County - Chester, Lansdowne, Media, Middletown, Prospect Park, Radnor, Ridley Park, Swarthmore College, Wayne, and miscellaneous towns.

Elk County - Johnsonburg, Ridgeway, St. Marys, Wilcox, and miscellaneous towns.

Erie County - Corry, Edinboro, Erie, Girard, North East, Presque Isle State Park, Union City, Waterford, and miscellaneous towns.

Fayette County - Belle Vernon, Brownsville, Connellsville, Fort Necessity, Friendship Hill, Masontown, Ohiopyle, Perryopolis, Point Marion, the Summit Hotel, Uniontown, and miscellaneous towns.

Forest County - Cook Forest State Park and miscellaneous towns.

Franklin County - Caledonia State Park, Chambersburg, Greencastle, Mercersburg, Waynesboro, and miscellaneous towns.

Fulton County - McConnellsburg and miscellaneous towns.

Greene County - Carmichaels, Waynesburg, and miscellaneous towns.

Huntingdon County - Birmingham, Franklinville, Huntingdon (includes Pennsylvania Industrial Reformatory), Mt. Union, and miscellaneous towns.

Indiana County - Blairsville, Cherry Tree, Glen Campbell, Heilwood, Homer City, Indiana (includes National Guard Camp), Marion Center, Saltsburg, and miscellaneous towns.

Jefferson County - Big Run, Brookville, Punxsatawney, Reynoldsville, and miscellaneous towns.

Juniata County - East Waterford, Lewistown, Mifflintown, Thompsontown, and miscellaneous towns.

Lackawanna County - Carbondale, Rocky Glen, Scranton, and miscellaneous towns.

Lancaster County - Columbia, Elizabethtown, Ephrata, Lancaster, Pennsylvania Farm Museum, Lititz, Marietta, Millersville, and miscellaneous towns.

Lawrence County - Ellwood City, Enon, McConnells Mill, New Castle, New Wilmington, Rock Point Park, and miscellaneous towns.

Lebanon County - Indiantown Gap, Lebanon, Mount Gretna (includes resort and Camp Roosevelt), Myerstown, and miscellaneous towns.

Lehigh County - Allentown, Slatington, and miscellaneous towns.

Luzerne County - Harveys Lake, Hazleton, Nanticoke, Pittston, White Haven, Wilkes-Barre, and miscellaneous towns.

Lycoming County - Jersey Shore, Montgomery, Montoursville, Muncy, Williamsport, and miscellaneous towns.

McKean County - Bradford, Eldred, Kane, Kinzua Bridge, Mount Jewett, Port Allegany, Rock City, Smethport, and miscellaneous towns.

Mercer County - Greenville, Grove City, Mercer, Sharon, Stoneboro, and miscellaneous towns.

Mifflin County - Lewistown, Newton-Hamilton, and miscellaneous towns.

Monroe County - Buck Hill Falls, Delaware Water Cap, East Stroudsburg, Mount Pocono, Pocono Manor, Stroudsburg, and miscellaneous towns.

Montgomery County - Bryn Mawr, Collegeville, Glenside, Norristown, Pottstown, Willow Grove Park, and miscellaneous towns.

Montour County - Danville (includes Exchange), and miscellaneous towns.

Northampton County - Bangor, Bethlehem, Easton, and miscellaneous towns.

Northumberland County - Fort Augusta, Milton, Mount Carmel, Northumberland, Shamokin, Sunbury, and miscellaneous towns.

Perry County - Duncannon, Newport, and miscellaneous towns.

Philadelphia County - City of Philadelphia and suburbs, Fairmount Park, Germantown, League Island Navy Yard, and miscellaneous towns.

Pike County - Bushkill, Dingmans Ferry, Greentown, Lackawanna, Milford, Shohola, and miscellaneous towns.

Schuylkill County - Ashland, Mahanoy City, Pottsville, Shenandoah, Tamaqua, and miscellaneous towns.

Snyder County - Beaver Springs, Middleburg, Selinsgrove, and miscellaneous towns.

Somerset County - Addison, Berlin, Boswell, Confluence, Elk Lick, Markleton, Meyersdale, New Baltimore, Somerfield, Somerset, Stoystown, Windber, and miscellaneous towns.

Sullivan County - Eagles Mere and miscellaneous towns.

Susquehanna County - Great Bend, Hallstead, Heart Lake, Hop Bottom (Foster), Jackson, Lanesboro, Montrose, New Milford, Starrucca Viaduct, Susquehanna, and miscellaneous towns.

Tioga County - Blossburg, Elkland, Gaines, Mansfield, Morris, Pine Creek Gorge, Tioga, Wellsboro, Westfield, and miscellaneous towns.

Union County - Lewisburg and miscellaneous towns.

Venango County - Drake Well Park, Emlenton, Franklin, Monarch Park, Oil City, Pleasantville, Polk, and miscellaneous towns.

Warren County - Chandlers Valley, Clarendon, Columbus, Kinzua Dam and Bridge, Sheffield, Sugar Grove, Warren, Youngsville, and miscellaneous towns.

Washington County - Arden Trolley Museum, Bentleyville, California, Canonsburg, Centerville, Charleroi, Claysville, Donora, McDonald, Monongahela, Washington, and miscellaneous towns.

Wayne County - Beach Lake, Hawley, Honesdale, Lake Ariel, Newfoundland, Waymart, and miscellaneous towns.

Westmoreland County - Bolivar, Derry, Greensburg, Idlewild Park, Jeannette, Latrobe, Ligonier, Manor, Monesson, Mount Pleasant, New Kingston, Ridgeview Park, Scottdale, Trafford City, Vandergrift, West Newton, Woodlawn, and miscellaneous towns.

Wyoming County - Factoryville, Meshoppen, Nicholson, Tunkhannock, and miscellaneous towns.

York County - Hanover, York, and miscellaneous towns.

The Subject File includes: Highways: Buffalo-Pittsburgh Highway (U.S. Route 219), the Lackawanna Trail (U.S. Routes 11 and 611), the Lincoln Highway (U.S. Route 30), the National Road (U.S. Route 40), the Pennsylvania Turnpike, and the Roosevelt Highway (U.S. Route 6); Industries: coal, oil, and railroads; the John Kennedy Lacock Postcard Series on the Braddock Road and the Cumberland Road, and the H.T. MacNeil Series of historic Pennsylvania buildings; and U.S. and foreign countries.

MG-214
WARREN J. HARDER COLLECTION
Ca. 1910-1968, 10 cu. ft.

Warren John Harder (1905-1968), lifelong resident of Harrisburg, was a news correspondent, commercial photographer and amateur local historian. As an active member of the Historical Society of Dauphin County, he often wrote historical pieces for various newspapers and in 1949 prepared, using his photographs, the "Do You Remember When?" series for the Harrisburg *Evening News*. He owned a lantern slide projector and as late as 1962 gave illustrated historical talks and nostalgia shows with glass slides from his collection. Especially interested in nineteenth-century technology and inventions, Harder wrote extensively on the coming of the telephone and electricity to central Pennsylvania. In 1960 he published the biography of a competitor of Alexander Graham Bell, *Daniel Drawbaugh, the Edison of the Cumberland Valley* (University of Pennsylvania Press).

The Collection is divided into two categories, Research and Photographic Materials. The Research Materials (2 cu. ft.) contain rough drafts, correspondence, notes, photographs and other items relating to the preparation of *Daniel Drawbaugh*. Also included are drafts of speeches and articles such as "Down Memory Lane," "The Electric Speaking Telephone," "The Telephone Comes to Harrisburg," and "Between the Lines of the Drawbaugh Story." The Photographic Materials (8 cu. ft.) are primarily second generation negatives, prints and glass slides divided into the following categories: Historical File, Civil War File, General File, Portrait File, Lantern Slide File and Harrisburg Area Subject File.

The Historical, Civil War, General, and Portrait Files (2 cu. ft.), contain 4x5 and 35mm copy negatives (some with contact prints) of news articles, engravings and lithographs of persons, places and events in World, American and Pennsylvania history. The Historical File contains items relating to nineteenth century technology and inventions, such as automobiles, bicycles, bridges, burglar alarms, Thomas Edison's inventions, electricity, fire escapes, fire engines, flying machines, guns, phonographs, photography, printing, railroads, sewing machines, ships, stoves, telegraphs, telephones, and writing equipment. The Civil War File contains portraits of such prominent figures as John Wilkes Booth, John Brown, Jefferson Davis, U.S. Grant, Robert E. Lee and Abraham Lincoln. Other military and political officials, and views of battle areas such as Appomattox, Chambersburg,

MG-216 Carlisle Indian School Collection: Album, "Indian Industrial School, Carlisle, PA." Woodworking Shop by Frances Benjamin Johnston. (See p. 85.)

Fort Moultrie, and Gettysburg are included. It also covers slavery, war prisons, and Lincoln's administration and assassination. The General File contains such broad topics as "ancient times" to the American Revolution, the Molly Maguires, Indians, and Senator Joseph McCarthy. The Portrait File includes U.S. presidents from George Washington to Andrew Johnson; seventeenth, eighteenth and nineteenth century Pennsylvania governors; and well-known historical figures such as Daniel Boone, Cleopatra, Christopher Columbus, John C. Calhoun, P.T. Barnum, Robert Fulton, William Penn and others.

The Lantern Slide File (1.5 cu. ft.) contains black and white and tinted glass slides copied or purchased by Harder. Items are grouped by lecture topic. Topics include the Colonial era; Harrisburg area scenes (including bridges, canals, railroads, and wheel clubs); the Spanish-American and First World Wars; Southern scenes; sing-along slides and theatre signs.

The Harrisburg Area Subject File (4.5 cu. ft.) primarily contains 8x10 prints copied by Harder from original photographs in the collections of the Historical Society of Dauphin County and other sources. Others are first generation photographs taken by Harder, usually to demonstrate change through time in a particular subject. Each print has an index number and historical information affixed to the reverse. There is a 3x5 card index to this file. Subjects include Harrisburg, Camp Hill and Lemoyne area buildings, bridges, canals, community activities and events, floods, industries, the State Capitol buildings, street scenes, and uptown and downtown redevelopment.

The Collection was obtained by the State Archives in 1969 from the executors of the Harder Estate. Harder's lantern slide projector is in the Industry and Technology collections of The State Museum of Pennsylvania, Harrisburg.

MG-216
CARLISLE INDIAN SCHOOL COLLECTION
1878-1969, .5 cu. ft.

The Bureau of Indian Affairs, U.S. Department of the Interior, operated a school for American Indian children at Carlisle Barracks, Carlisle, Pa., 1878-1918. The purpose of the school was to acculturate these children into contemporary American life by providing classroom education and formal training at various trades. Jim Thorpe, 1912 Olympic medal winner, was a graduate of the school. The Collection was acquired by the State Archives over the course of many years from several different sources.

The Collection contains documents (.2 cu. ft.) and photographs (.3 cu. ft.) pertaining to the school and its students. Photographs include an undated album (1 vol.) by photographer Frances Benjamin Johnston showing students in class, on athletic teams, and training at various crafts such as woodworking, printing, etc.; and an album, 1887-1903, by Carlisle photographer John N. Choate containing class portraits. Also present are loose items such as cabinet card before-and-after portraits of students in tribal costume and in mainstream American clothing; and school portraits, 1878-ca. 1880.

MG-217
HARRISBURG *HOME STAR* COLLECTION
1948-1971, 5 cu. ft.

The *Home Star*, also known at various times as the Harrisburg *Guide* and Harrisburg *Home News*, was a weekly community newspaper published between 1948 and 1971. Edited by Paul Walker, a local journalist, the *Home Star* published information and advertisements pertaining to shopping, political campaigns, community events and achievements, and visits by local, state and nationally known politicians and celebrities of the 1950s and 1960s.

The Collection was the working photograph file of the *Home Star* staff. The photographs, arranged alphabetically by subject, are usually 8x10 formal portraits or publicity stills. Most items have crop lines on the front and a tag on the back containing instructions to the printer for preparing a lithographic negative. In many cases, the litho negative that was produced is present. Informational material on a subject such as campaign flyers, news releases and other data is also often included. Most photographs are undated, though many contain the deadline date needed for publication.

The *Home Star* staff probably took some of the photographs, but many were obtained from local and national news services and Harrisburg area commercial photographers, such as Brown's Studios, Samuel W. Kuhnert, Sterling Studios, Allied Pix Service, Inc., and others. The *Home Star* ceased publication in 1971 and the collection was donated subsequently by Walker to the Archives.

Subjects include: Spiro Agnew, the Allenberry Playhouse, Walter Alessandroni, the American Red Cross, the Art Association of Harrisburg, Lucille Ball, Count Basie, Genevieve Blatt, George Bloom, Victor Borge, the Broad Street Market, Raymond J. Broderick, Glen Campbell, Central Pennsylvania Business School, Bennett Cerf, the Dauphin County Medical

Society, Dwight Eisenhower, Arthur Fiedler, Gerald Ford, George Gekas, the Harlem Globetrotters, Maurice K. Goddard, M. Lee Goldsmith, Mr. and Mrs. Barry Goldwater, Goodwill Industries, Mr. and Mrs. Virgil "Gus" Grissom, Harrisburg Chamber of Commerce, Harrisburg area schools and hospitals, Harrisburg Community Theatre, R. Dixon Herman, Woody Herman, Hubert Humphrey, Chet Huntley, George Jessel, the Kingston Trio, Ernest P. Kline, John C. Kunkel, the Lettermen, Liberace, the Lone Ranger, Henry Mancini, Eugene McCarthy, Thomas Minehart, Rev. James Morecraft, the Mount Gretna Playhouse, the Muscular Dystrophy Association, Michael Musmanno, Richard Nixon, John O. Pastore, Joe Paterno, Thomas W. Pomeroy, Jr., Ronald Reagan, Stephen Reed, James Reston, Nelson Rockefeller, George Romney, Franklin D. Roosevelt, the Salvation Army, Herman T. Schneebeli, Richard Schweiker, Hugh Scott, Mr. & Mrs. William Scranton, Raymond Shafer, Milton Shapp, A.H. Stackpole, Leonard Staisey, Harold Stassen, Sylvester K. Stevens, Harold Swenson, David Susskind, George Szell, John K. Tabor, the Duquesne University Tamburitzans, M. Harvey Taylor, Craig Truax, George N. Wade, George C. Wallace, Barbara Walters, Rose Mary Wood, James E. Van Zandt, the Veterans of Foreign Wars, the Young Men's Christian Association, the Young Republicans of Dauphin County, and Leroy S. Zimmerman.

MG-218
PHOTOGRAPH COLLECTIONS
Ca. 1850-PRESENT, 20 cu. ft.

This is a group of smaller acquisitions collected over the years by the State Archives, arranged by donor or photographer and covering industry, transportation, bridges, buildings, floods, politics, the military, people, and miscellaneous subjects.

James A. Beaver Photograph Album containing thirty-one formal cabinet card portraits of members of Beaver's gubernatorial administration 1887-1891, especially the staff of the Adjutant General's Department. Also included is a portrait of historian William Henry Egle.

Josephine Foster Bright Album of the State of Pennsylvania's exhibit at the 1939 New York World's Fair, one volume. In addition to interior and exterior views of the exhibit, celebrities such as Mayor Fiorello LaGuardia, actor Dick Powell, and state officials are present.

David Bussick Collection of 4x5 glass negatives by an unidentified photographer of scenes in Harrisburg, Gettysburg, Philadelphia and possibly Mount Gretna, ca. 1900, seventy-seven items.

Colonel Robert M. Carroll Collection of his Pennsylvania National Guard activities, 1913-1937, fourteen items. Shows ground-breaking ceremonies at the Harrisburg Military Post, and panoramic prints of the Governor's Troop at Mount Gretna, and other regiments at various encampments.

Chandler of Philadelphia (photographers) Portrait Album of the "Commissioners on Constitutional Amendment and Revision," 1920, including Gifford Pinchot, William Sproul and others, one volume.

Cowperthwaite Family Albums of portraits of members and descendants from Ireland and Pennsylvania, ca. 1855-1901, two volumes. Most subjects are unidentified.

William Cramer Collection of H.C. Frick Co. photographs, taken by H.B. Springer, ca. 1910-1915. The prints are second generation copies of life in southwestern Pennsylvania bituminous mining towns, 235 items.

Barbara Davis Civil War Cartes-de-Visite Album of various Union generals, unidentified soldiers and family members, probably from eastern Pennsylvania, one volume. Includes "Admiral Dot" of P.T. Barnum's Circus.

Delaware and Hudson Canal Company Photographs, ca. 1850-1940 (copy prints), forty-nine items. Views include portraits of company officials, the "Stourbridge Lion," the Gravity Railroad at Hawley, scenes along the canal and railroad, and others.

Mrs. Jacob Dubs Collection of views of ruins of the State Capitol after the February 2, 1897 fire, eleven items.

Colonel Durkee Cabinet Cards and Cartes-de-Visite of members of various Erie area families, ca. 1860-1880, thirty-nine items. Surnames include Silverthorn, Hathaway, Gould, Abbey, Harris and others.

Rebecca Edge Photographs of the ruins of the State Capitol after the fire of February 2, 1897, eleven items.

Mrs. Thomas Edge Cabinet Card Portrait Album of State Department of Agriculture officials, with Governors Hartranft, Hoyt, Pattison, Beaver, Hastings, and Stone, ca. 1870-1905, one volume.

Louis L. Emmert Photographs of Ephrata Cloister taken by him in October 1905, forty items. The 6x8 prints show interior and exterior views of the buildings, grounds, graveyard, Cocalico Creek, the Revolutionary War monuments, etc.

Joseph Feagley Album of activities during "Pennsylvania Week," 1950, one volume. Feagley was State Chairman. The 8x10 prints show business meetings, promotional campaigns and Pennsylvania celebrities such as Alexis Smith, "Ham" Fisher, and others.

Cecil Fulton, Jr., Collection of Purviance's "Photographic Views Along the Penn Central Railroad," including Horseshoe Curve and scenes near Altoona, Johnstown, Tyrone, Pittsburgh, and other places, ca. 1870, fourteen items.

Governor Hotel (Harrisburg) Collection of photographic copies of the governors' portrait paintings in the State Capitol, from William Penn to Milton Shapp, fifty-nine items. The copies hung in the lobby of the hotel until it closed in 1976.

D. L. Imbrie Cartes-de-Visite Albums of delegates to the 1872 and 1873 Pennsylvania Constitutional Conventions, including Matthew Quay, Simon Cameron, Andrew Curtin, and many others, two volumes.

Joseph Kingston Collection of 8x10 photographic prints of the 1972 Hurricane Agnes Flood in Pennsylvania taken by newspaper photographers of Reading, York, State College, Pittsburgh, Hazleton and Milton, 250 items.

Pauline Lawson Scrapbook of views and newsclippings of the 1889 Johnstown Flood, one volume.

Lawrence E. Lechleitner Photograph Album containing ninety-nine 8 x 10 views of the construction of the Pennsylvania Railroad Roundhouse and an addition to the Passenger Station at Harrisburg, 1937-1938.

Paul Lenker Collection of glass plate negatives by a unidentified photographer showing bridge construction activities, probably by the Phoenix Bridge Company of Phoenixville and Philadelphia, ca. 1880, sixty-one items.

Darwin Lesher Collection relating to the history and operation of the Millersburg Ferry, Millersburg, ca. 1971, sixty items.

William Allen March Collection relating to his career before and after World War I, twenty-two items. Includes signed photographs of John J. Pershing and Herbert Hoover.

Edward Martin Collection relating to his career during both World Wars, eight items.

Duncan McCallum Collection relating to his association with Gifford Pinchot as governor, six items. Includes an autographed portrait of Pinchot.

Mrs. William Moody Collection of views of the Madras District, India. ca. 1870-1904, approximately sixty items. The views relate to the activities of Dr. Anna Kugler of Montgomery County and Dr. Edward Chester and his wife Susan Kistler Chester of Perry County. They were missionaries of the United Lutheran Church, Philadelphia, which established a school and hospital in Guntur, India.

A. Morse and Company of Philadelphia Photographs, 1880, eight items. Shown are the Morse Family in front of their photography studio at 61st Street and Haverford Avenue, their traveling darkroom, and such subjects as coke ovens and the Bluestone Quarry at Smithton, the Lutheran Church at Radnor, an Edgwood Company Railroad locomotive, and a Philadelphia street car.

A. Morse and Company Photograph Album containing forty-six views of the countryside in and around Philadelphia, ca. 1880. Views include U.S.

Centennial Buildings, General Anthony Wayne Inn and Wayne's grave marker, an unidentified military battlefield and the Morse photography wagon.

Mary Mowry Collection of coal dredging operations on the Susquehanna River near Harrisburg, ca. 1960, twenty-five items.

Charles Nash Photographs of Pennsylvania Railroad activities in Enola, Hollidaysburg, Rockville and other central Pennsylvania locales, 1903-1907, 169 items. Includes views of the March 1904 Susquehanna River ice jam.

National Park Service Collection of monuments to various states' regiments at Gettysburg, ca. 1960, thirty items.

J. Thompson Neely Lantern Slides of the Panama Canal construction, 1914, 115 items. Neely, a native of Bucks County, was an engineer living in Cancun, Canal Zone, and probably took or collected the images. Some are hand colored.

Frank Neidly Collection of cabinet card portraits of vaudeville and legitimate entertainers who played the Reading Opera House, Reading, in 1879, sixteen items. Shown in costume are Frances Bishop, Ullie Ankstrom, Fritz J. Schmeiser, Annie Summerville, "Beatrice," Anna Berger, Laura Shrimer-Mapleson and others.

Samuel W. Ochs Collection of 8x10 glass negatives of panoramic and street scenes of Oxford, Chester County, ca. 1868-ca. 1940, forty-one items.

Mark Richards Civil War Cartes-de-Visite pertaining to Walter S. Williams of the 11th Pennsylvania Volunteers and his friends, including the regimental dog "Sal," twenty-seven items.

Daniel Roland Collection of builders' photos of locomotives and rolling stock at the Pennsylvania Railroad's Altoona Car Shops, ca. 1900, thirty-seven items.

Henry Sartor Photographs of views of rural north central Pennsylvania, ca. 1880, nineteen items. Sartor, a photographer for the Union View Company of Rochester, N.Y., is shown with his traveling darkroom. Also included are his views of the 1880 Milton fire, and unidentified families in front of their homes.

Mrs. E.G. Schermerhorn Civil War Cartes-de-Visite collected and inscribed to her father, Captain Frederick Tiedemann of the 75th Pennsylvania Volunteers, sixty-eight items. These are officers and enlisted men of the 40th, 73rd and 75th Pennsylvania Volunteers and the 58th New York State Volunteers serving under General Franz Sigel. Included are Generals Sigel, Ambrose Burnside, John C. Fremont, U.S. Grant, Joseph Hayes, Philip Kearney, John A. Logan, George G. Meade, Philip Sheridan, William T. Sherman, George Thomas, and Admirals D.G. Farragut and David Porter.

MG-218 Photograph Collection - Rowland Stebbins Cartes-de-Visite: "Lieu. Bruce Rice, Co. I, 1st Rifles, P.R.V.C. Killed at Strasburg." Rice was a member of the Bucktail Regiment.

Civil War era politicians and personalities include John Brown, Parson Brownlow, William Lloyd Garrison, Horace Greeley, Abraham Lincoln, Edwin M. Stanton, Charles Sumner and John Greenleaf Whittier.

G. L. Shanon Album of Pennsylvania covered bridges, ca. 1898-1963, one volume. Some color items.

Paul Smith Postcard Photographs of Port Royal, Pa. and vicinity, ca. 1925, fifty items. Includes buildings, street views, Juniata River views, Port Royal Fairgrounds and others.

Mrs. P.A. Snay Civil War Cartes-de-Visite primarily of soldiers of the 5th Pennsylvania Reserves, ninety items.

Rowland Stebbins Civil War Cartes-de-Visite pertaining to Samuel H. Quail of the 9th Pennsylvania Reserves and soldiers of other regiments, thirty-seven items.

Isaac Newton Swope Family Album of portraits and descendants of this Mapleton Depot, Huntingdon County family, ca. 1880-1960, one volume. Family surnames present include White, Boring, Hess and Smithson.

Stereograph Collection, ca. 1870-1915, including views of the Penn Central Railroad by the Purviance View Company, E. and H.T. Anthony, and others; the Lehigh Valley Railroad by M.A. Kleckner, George F. Gates, and others; Gettysburg Battlefield by W.H. Tipton, E. and H.T. Anthony, B.W. Kilburn and others; the 1876 Centennial Exhibition in Philadelphia by the Centennial Photographic Company; Shippensburg views by H. Frank Beidel; Harrisburg and vicinity by LeRue Lemer, C.W. Woodward, and others; Uniontown views by Farwell; Pennsylvania coal, coke and steel industry views by the Keystone View Company; Pittsburgh, Allegheny County and Dixmont Hospital by Thomas Wood, the Pittsburgh Photographic View Portrait and Copying Company and others; a Keystone View Company series on World War I (incomplete); and miscellaneous views of Lafayette College, Easton, President and Mrs. William McKinley, out-of-state and foreign views, blacks, American Indians, and the life of Christ.

Ernest Terral Collection of railroad workmen erecting electrical transformers in Cambria, Blair and Venango Counties, ca. 1912-1913, forty-one items.

Dr. Frederick Tilberg Collection of views taken by him of the 1936 flood in the Harrisburg area, forty items.

George Walton Collection of 5x7 glass negatives of the buildings at Ephrata Cloister taken about 1908 by his father, Joseph Walton, seven items.

Thomas Whyel Collection of activities at the Consolidated Coke Company, Connellsville, Fayette County, ca. 1920, two items.

William Penn Memorial Museum Collection of Pennsylvania iron furnaces and forges, lime kilns, railroads, canals, gristmills, bridges and covered bridges, churches, schools and county courthouses either taken or collected by staff, ca. 1960, over 1,000 items.

Maxwell Whiteman Collection of Associated Press, United Press International, and other wire service photographs of George Leader's gubernatorial campaign and early administration, 1954-1956; and mine accidents in Pennsylvania and other states, 1937-1949, 376 items.

Miscellaneous items include oil region views, ca. 1875, some by L.P. Greenlund of Warren; Abraham Lincoln's funeral train at Harrisburg in April 1865, by D.C. Burnite; canal boat construction at Highspire for the Schuylkill Navigation Company, ca. 1860, by C.S. Roshon; historical bridges at Harrisburg and elsewhere, ca. 1900; "The Game of Philadelphia Buildings," by Mary S. Holmes, copyright 1899, containing game cards with

MG-218 Photograph Collections - Stereographs: Keystone View Company #75-20049 "Miners going into the Slope, Hazleton, PA, ca. 1915."

pictures of the city's landmarks; an unidentified flood, probably 1889, near Harrisburg by LeRue Lemer; a Matthew Brady Studios carte-de-visite album of Abraham Lincoln, his family, Andrew Curtin and Union military officers, ca. 1862; composite portrait photographs of the members of the State House of Representatives for the years 1868, 1877-1878, 1879-1880, 1883-1884, 1891-1892, 1911-1912, 1913-1914, by C.S. Roshon and LeRue Lemer; Musser Studios views of the gubernatorial inaugurations and portraits of Governors Sproul, Fisher, Pinchot, Earle, James and Duff; Governor Stone with the Pennsylvania National Guard at Gettysburg, 1902, and Governor Pennypacker and the Pennsylvania National Guard at President Roosevelt's Inauguration, 1905, and at President McKinley's Inauguration, 1901; a Civil War carte-de-visite album "Our Generals," showing Grant, Meade and others; views of the ruins of Chambersburg, 1864, by C.L. Lochman; the Union prisoner-of-war camp at Andersonville, Ga., ca. 1864, and later scenes of the park and monuments; dedication ceremonies of monuments to various Pennsylvania regiments at Chickamauga and Chattanooga and others at Gettysburg, Petersburg and Shiloh; soldiers and veterans of the Ringgold Light Artillery of Reading; cabinet card portraits of unidentified members of Grand Army of the Republic Post 58, Harrisburg, by W.C. Fox; G.A.R. encampments at Gettysburg; Warren's statue and the 11th Pennsylvania monument at Gettysburg by W.H. Tipton, ca. 1880; National Guard encampments at Gettysburg with General J.S. Gobin, at Mount Gretna with General John Pershing, Camp Meade (Philadelphia), the Argonne Forest of France, and Camp Benson (Wilkes-Barre) during the

1877 Railroad Riots; United States Army company portraits at New Cumberland Army Depot, 1919; the U.S.S. Armored Cruiser *Pennsylvania*; the families of Governors Edwin S. Stuart, Francis Shunk and Andrew Curtin; several cartes-de-visite and cabinet card albums of unidentified people by photographers of Harrisburg, Hummelstown, Lebanon, Reading, etc.; and views of the Harrisburg area, an unidentified seacoast resort, and family portraits by an unknown female photographer, ca. 1889; views of the reburial of James Wilson at Christ Church, Philadelphia, November 22, 1906, by William H. Rau; and many others.

MG-219
COMMERCIAL MUSEUM PHOTOGRAPHS
Ca. 1897-1954, 13 cu. ft.

The Commercial Museum, dedicated by President William McKinley in 1897, exhibited artifacts pertaining to international commerce, industry, and trade. Located at 34th and Vintage Streets, Philadelphia, the Museum shifted thematic directions in the 1950s, modified many of its exhibits, and is today the Museum of the Philadelphia Civic Center. The photographs were culled and given by the Commercial Museum to the State Archives in 1961.

The photographs are the curators' reference files of over 6,000 prints of varying size, usually 8x10. They were taken, collected, copied or purchased from a variety of sources by the Museum staff. Used to illustrate commerce, trade, business and industry in the United States and the world, most images were gathered from Pennsylvania and the Philadelphia area. Included are original prints obtained from William H. Rau, Joseph T. Rothrock, Dallin Aerial Views, various U.S. Government agencies or the Museum's own photographers. Some are stills made from the Museum's motion picture and lantern slide collections. No original negatives are present. Each print is stamped on the reverse with the Commercial Museum's identifying mark. Often the subject, date or negative number is on the front margins or reverse, though dates more frequently reflect when the print was obtained rather than when taken. Some envelopes filed with the prints also provide donor information.

The images are arranged in three categories: The Pennsylvania File, the Philadelphia Area File, and the Subject File. Often the same subject is found under different categories. Though prints often bear the Museum's negative numbers, the original filing system is now lost. The State Archives has inaugurated its own numbering system. On the reverse of each print, the number is usually in the upper right hand corner.

The Pennsylvania File

The file contains miscellaneous scenes of the state arranged alphabetically by the following counties and regions (not all are represented).

Allegheny: The Pittsburgh Point, Carnegie Steel Company and the 1911 Centennial Celebration of Steamship Navigation on Inland Waters.

Beaver: bathing beaches at Beaver Falls and Monaca and an encampment at Bradys Run by the 100th Regiment, Pennsylvania National Guard.

Berks: Weinrich Sanitarium at Wernersville.

Blair: a copy of a ca. 1840 engraving of Hollidaysburg.

Bucks: Bowman's Hill, Pennsbury Manor, the Union Mills Paper Manufacturing Company, the Delaware Canal at Kintnersville, and various Delaware River Bridges.

Cambria: a copy of a ca. 1840 engraving of Johnstown.

Carbon: Lansford and Mauch Chunk.

Centre: Pennsylvania State College.

Chester: French Creek Falls, Moore Hall, Knox Residence, West Chester and Valley Forge.

Clinton: Lock Haven.

Anthracite Coal Region: Mauch Chunk, Pottsville, Wilkes-Barre and other unidentified towns.

Columbia: Friends Meeting House at Catawissa.

Cumberland: Dickinson College and the Indian School at Carlisle.

Dauphin: the State Capitol at Harrisburg, 1906-1907, by William H. Rau.

Delaware: harbors at Chester and Marcus Hook, Delchester Farms in Edgemont, buildings at Swarthmore College, the W.H. Sayer residence and various county scenes.

Delaware River Region: the Delaware Water Gap, harbor activities at Philadelphia and Camden, New Jersey, the Hog Island Yards and the Delaware River Bridge, 1929.

Erie: the public docks at Erie, 1914.

Forest: virgin white pines.

Lancaster: Ephrata Cloister.

Lebanon: the July 1916 State Mobilization Camp at Mount Gretna.

Lehigh: the Finley Chain Suspension Bridge.

Lycoming: Williamsport, 1922 and erosion control at various farms.

Mifflin: Lewistown, Jacks Mountain, Peace Mountain, and ruins of the Pennsylvania Canal by Joseph T. Rothrock and William H. Rau.

Montour: the State Hospital for the Insane at Danville.

Montgomery: Bryn Mawr College, St. James Church at Evansburg, King of Prussia Inn and quarry, Old York Road at Ogontz, and the Percival Roberts Residence.

Northampton: Lehigh University buildings, remains of the Sullivan Road near Wind Gap, bridges over the Delaware and Lehigh Rivers and aerial views of Bangor, Easton, Nazareth, Portland and Wind Gap by the Aero Service Corporation and Dallin Aerial Views.

Northumberland: Fiddler Colliery and J.H. and C.K. Silk Mill at Shamokin.

Pike: Winona and Buck Hill Falls, by Joseph T. Rothrock, and Delaware River views at Matamoras and Lackawaxen.

Potter: Cross Fork and Galeton, 1914.

Schuylkill: Mahanoy Valley and Mahanoy Plane.

Sullivan: Eagles Mere, Little Glen, Ticklish Rock, and various forest views.

Susquehanna: the Starrucca Viaduct.

Wayne: Lake Wallenpaupack and Pocono Mountains, 1927.

Wyoming: a street view, possibly in Tunkhannock.

York: power plant and dam at McCall's Ferry and river views at Wrightsville.

The Philadelphia Area File

The file is arranged by name of subject, usually buildings, streets, parks or other landmarks in the vicinity and includes: Fairmount Park and buildings therein, libraries, museums, railroad stations, bridges, markets, historic homes, department stores, factories, churches, and parks. Views of buildings include the Baldwin Locomotive Works, Bank of North America, Bellevue-Stratford Hotel, the Bourse, Broad Street Station (including the 1923 fire), Carpenters' Hall, Cliveden, Christ Church, City Hall (including construction), Congress Hall, Convention Hall, U.S. Custom House, Disston Saw Works, Fairmount Waterworks, Fern Rock Woolen Mills, Frankford Arsenal, Franklin Institute, Free Library of Philadelphia, various Friends meeting houses, Girard Bank, Independence Hall, Masonic Temple, Metropolitan Opera House, Mercantile Club, Pennsylvania Hospital, Museum of Art, Old Swedes' Church, Post Office, Reading Terminal, Ring's Spinning Mills, Betsy Ross House, Pennsylvania Salt Manufacturing Company, Schlicter Jute Cordage Company, Strawbridge and Clothier Department Store, Trinity Church, Union League, UGI Building, U.S. Mint, University of Pennsylvania, Widener Memorial Library, White Lead Works, YWCA and many others. Street scenes include Arch, Broad, Center Square, Chestnut, Delaware, Dock, Filbert, Fourth, Franklin Parkway, Front, Girard, Juniper, Market, Second, South, Spring Garden, Spruce, and Walnut Streets. Events include the Mummers' Parades of 1916 and 1921, Rittenhouse Square Flower Show, 1917, Founders Week Parade, 1908, by William H.

Rau, Commercial America Trade Conference, 1954 and the United States Sesquicentennial, 1926. Miscellaneous items include firefighting, waterfront activities at Port Richmond and Girard Point, the Philadelphia Yacht Club, City Troop on parade, city subway construction and many others.

The Subject File

The file is arranged alphabetically with the majority relating to agriculture, industry and transportation:

Agriculture views show planting, cultivation, harvesting by field workers or machinery, processing and marketing. The majority of images were taken by Commercial Museum photographers at New Jersey truck farms and deal with the following fruits and vegetables: apples, asparagus, lima and string beans, blackberries, cantalopes, cauliflower, cherries, corn, cranberries, cucumbers, grapes, lettuce, onions, peaches, pears, peas, peppers, rhubarb, strawberries, sweet potatoes and watermelons. Views in other states include the apple industry in New Hampshire, New York, Virginia and West Virginia; bean picking in Maryland; blackberry picking in Virginia; cabbage fields in Utah; horse, sheep, pig, goat, beef and dairy cattle herding in Pennsylvania, New Jersey, New York, Maryland and other places; cherry picking in New York; chicory harvesting and drying at E.B. Muller Company, New York and Michigan; cocoa bean drying and processing at Hershey Chocolate Company, Hershey, 1925; chocolate milling at Stephen F. Whitman & Sons, Philadelphia, 1924; corn planting, cultivating, harvesting and processing in Crawford County, Pennsylvania, Ohio and other places; flax retting and hackling by hand in Frankford, Pa., 1917, and by machine at the Barbour Flax Spinning Company, New Jersey; flour milling at Milbourne Hills, Philadelphia, and in New York and Indiana; hemp growing in Hanover, Pa., 1907; hay cutting, raking and staking at an unidentified locale; meat grading, processing, and packing at the Armour Company, Chicago, Ill., and other places; milk, ice cream and butter production at Abbotts Dairies, Philadelphia, 1926-1941; mushroom growing and canning, Kennett Square, 1941; onion growing in Ohio; oyster boat fleets and unloading, shucking and canning oysters in Baltimore, Md., New Haven, Conn., and southern New Jersey; peanut processing, North Carolina, 1941; potato cultivating and processing at various locales, poultry farming in Bucks and Chester Counties and other places; growing rye in North Carolina, 1913; growing sorghum in Virginia, 1941; soybean cultivation and oil processing in Illinois; cane sugar processing at Franklin Sugar Refinery, Philadelphia, 1922, and in Yonkers, N.Y., 1919; maple sugar gathering, New England; tea warehouses, New York; tobacco cultivation, harvesting, stripping, drying, and moistening, Lancaster County; wheat planting, harvesting and processing at the Shredded Wheat Biscuit Company, New York. Miscellaneous items pertaining to agriculture include 1941 views of various small family farms in Pennsylvania taken by the Pennsylvania State College, College of Agriculture; plowing and reaping by animal and machine at various places in the United States; and specimens of native commercial American trees in Pennsylvania, New Jersey and New York.

Industry views cover the development of products from mining or harvesting to refining, assembly, storage, shipping and marketing. Images show airplane manufacturing at the Naval Aircraft Factory, League Island, Philadelphia, 1918, and the Curtiss Aeroplane Company, New York, 1916-1918; bauxite mining and aluminum refining, and casting and finished products by the Aluminum Company of America; asbestos mining and refining at the Keesby and Mattison Company, the Asbestos Shingle Slate and Sheathing Company, Ambler, and the Johns-Manville Company, Waukegan, Illinois; automobile production at the Autocar Company, Ardmore, 1923, and other places; bread baking at Kolb's Bakery, Philadelphia; baseball manufacturing at an unidentified factory; brick manufacturing at Chambers Brothers Company, Philadelphia, and Harbison-Walker Company, Pittsburgh; clay mining, preparation, and firing and brick shipping yards, New York; refining carborundum at The Carborundum Company, Niagara Falls, N.Y.; carpet manufacturing at Hardwick and Magee Company, 1925, and the Kensington Company, Philadelphia; cement girders at Universal Atlas Cement Company, Chicago; charcoal manufacturing, Ohio; cloth cutting at Snellenburg's Clothing Company, Philadelphia; fossils in coal shale, Pittston; anthracite coal mining, processing, and shipping by the Lehigh Valley Coal Company, Hudson Coal Company and others in Coaldale, Hazleton, Kingston, Mahanoy City, Natalie, Scranton, Shenandoah, Summit Hill, Wilkes-Barre, and in Indiana and Ontario; bituminous coal mining processing, shipping and by-products courtesy of the Bituminous Coal Institute, Washington, D.C. showing the Pittsburgh Coal Company and others in Carmichaels, Johnstown, Pittsburgh, and West Virginia and other states; coke production at Connellsville, Johnstown, Lebanon, Robesonia, and Pittsburgh, and other states; copper mining and copper and brass production at the Raritan Copper Works, Perth Amboy, N.J., 1924; cultivating cork oak trees, and stripping and packing corkbark in Spain and Portugal; manufacturing cork products at the Armstrong Cork Company, Pittsburgh, 1922; cotton milling machines on display at the Industrial Art School, Philadelphia, 1918, and in production at various places; crab fishing and processing, probably near Baltimore; retail drugstore displays in Philadelphia, Leechburg, and Washington; harvesting American wormseed for druggists in Maryland; manufacturing dental equipment at the Electro Dental Manufacturing Company, Philadelphia,

MG-219 Commercial Museum Collection #1898: "Ice Cream Making, Abbott's Dairies, Philadelphia. Pouring the different flavors into the tanks. From Abbott's Negative, Sept. 1927" (see p. 96).

1923; color dye manufacturing and testing at DuPont Dye Works, New Jersey, 1925; electric blast furnaces, Bethlehem Steel Company, Bethlehem; uses of electric power in production lines at the Westinghouse Air Brake Company, Wilmerding, the Westinghouse Electric and Machine Company, East Pittsburgh, and in generators at Conowingo Dam, Maryland, 1929; trapping and skinning muskrats, N.J., and processing animal fur, Philadelphia; refining and storing coal gas at United Gas Industries, Philadelphia, 1906-1914; making lantern mantles, location unknown; manufacturing glass and glass products at Gillinder and Sons Company, Philadelphia, 1906, the Pittsburgh Plate Glass Company, 1926, and other states; leather working and glove manufacturing at the Glove Craft Company, Troy, N.Y., and other places; kitchen and household hardware displays at unidentified department stores; silk hosiery manufacturing at the German-American Hosiery Company, Brown-Aberle Company, Wallace Wilson Hosiery Company, Gotham, Inc., Philadelphia, 1922; producing straw and felt hats at Stetson Hat Company, Philadelphia, 1910-1931; iron refining at Pencoyd Iron Works, Pencoyd, 1906; rolling steel from open hearth blast furnaces at Follansbee Brothers Company, Edgar Thomson Steel Works, Carnegie Steel Company and Homestead Steel Company, in the Pittsburgh area, 1908, and at the National Tube Company, McKeesport, the Cambria Steel Company, Johnstown, 1907-1910, Bethlehem Steel Company, Coatesville, 1931, the Spang Chalfont Steel Company, Aetna, the Midvale Steel Company, Philadelphia, and in Alabama, Texas, New York, Wisconsin and Ohio; iron furnace ruins in Delaware, Berks and York Counties; iron mining at Cornwall Ore Mines, Cornwall, 1936, and New York; iron ore shipping and handling in Pittsburgh, Johnstown, New York and Ohio, especially by Great Lakes steamships; ivory products, including dice, chess pieces, and other articles by an unidentified manufacturer; kaolin mining at Hockessin and Brandywine Summit, Pa., and North Carolina; machine made lace at Lehigh Manufacturing Company, Philadelphia; leather skin tanning, hide dressing and preparation at the Suipass Leather Company and Foerderer's Factory, Philadelphia, and Girard Leather Company, Ohio, 1936; a licorice root warehouse in New Jersey; oil cloth and linoleum manufacturing at Thomas Potter and Sons, Philadelphia; linseed oil milling at Grove Oil Manufacturing Company, Philadelphia; locomotive assembly at Baldwin Locomotive Works, Philadelphia, and locomotive shipping, New York; lumbering and virgin hardwood stands at various places in northern Pennsylvania, Ohio and New York; lumber shipping at the Philadelphia docks; log rafts, various places; forest fire devastation in northern Pennsylvania; handling logs in the Adirondack Mountains, New York, 1914; the Pennsylvania Railroad's tree nurseries in Morrisville, N.J.; macaroni production at an unidentified factory; machinery production at various locales, including making lathes, plating, welding, compressing and milling machines, Farrar boilers, electric hoists, and others; views of production at the Standard Cast Iron Pipe and Foundry Company, Bristol, 1916; and vault assembly at the York Safe and Lock Company, York; mining marble at the Beaver Dam Marble Company, Baltimore, Md.; casks of palm oil shipped from Africa at Philadelphia wharves, 1924; paper from the Dill & Collins Paper Factory, Dennison Manufacturing Company, Diamond State Fiber Company, Philadelphia; use of paper in rug manufacture by William Sholes & Co. and in piano roll production by the Rose Valley Company, Philadelphia; making wallpaper at the William Campbell Wall Paper Company, Hackensack, N.J.; paper manufacturing at plants in North Carolina, New York, Massachussetts and West Virginia; petroleum drilling in northwestern Pennsylvania, 1861-1906; transporting oil, petroleum drilling and views of Drake Well, Franklin, Oil City, Titusville, and other places by John Mather, 1861-1906, and other photographers; derricks, crude oil storage and transport in Ohio, New Jersey, New York and Texas; the Atlantic Refining Company's Philadelphia Yards, 1926-1929; ceramic pot forming, glazing, firing and decorating at Mercer Pottery Co., Trenton, N.J., 1926; clay mining, New Jersey; terra cotta production, Los Angeles, Calif.; printing press operations at the Curtis

MG-219 Commercial Museum Collection #3195: "Running Molten Steel from 50 ton ladle into Ingot Moulds, Homestead Steel Works. Obtained from Chautauqua Photo. Co., Pittsburgh, 4/17/08" (see p. 98).

Publishing Company, Philadelphia; manufacturing push pins at the Moore Push-Pin Company, Philadelphia; radio entertainment and broadcasting at KYW and WDAB Studios, Philadelphia, and WGY, Schenectady, N.Y.; advertising stills of Westinghouse radios, uses of Radio Corporation of America equipment on trains and ships, and exhibit booths at an unidentified radio communications trade show, probably at the Commercial Museum; radium and tungsten mines, Colorado; and various experimental plates showing radioactivity of pitchblende; rayon production and employee life at the American Viscose Company, and the DuPont Chemical Company, 1926, Marcus Hook, and the Delaware Rayon Company, 1931, New Castle, Delaware, Tennessee and Ohio; producing rope at the Schlicter Jute Cordage Company, Philadelphia, and the Wall Rope Works, Beverly, N.J., 1918; refining rubber, and tire production at the Firestone, Goodyear and Goodrich company plants, Cleveland and Akron, Ohio; making tennis shoes and rubber cement at United States Rubber Company, N.Y., and other places; salt mining and refining by the International Salt Company at various locations; manufacturing saws at Disston Saw Works, Philadelphia; cutting lumber at sawmills in Pennsylvania and Ohio; shipbuilding and launching ceremonies of the *Quistconck*, 1917, and *Malolo*, 1926, and others by designer Archibald Carrick at Hog Island Yards, Philadelphia; shipyards in Maine and Massachussetts; silk fabric production at the Sauquoit Silk Manufacturing Company, Philadelphia, 1918; silver refining at an unidentified locale; the use of steam and steam shovels produced by Marion Steam Shovel Company, Marion, Ohio; assembling elevated street railway cars at J.G. Brill Company, Philadelphia, 1920-1927; quarrying stone at Slatington and Lansdowne, 1931, and Lumberton, N.J.; cutting stone at Johns Maxwells Sons Yards, Philadelphia; soapmaking at Yewdall and Jones, Philadelphia, 1906; views of the Emory Testing Machine for strength and durability and a conflagration chamber for testing building members at Underwriters' Laboratories, Chicago; utilizing ticker tape machines at the Western Union Company, New York; telephone equipment at Pennsylvania W & P Company, Baltimore; the automatic dial system at the Bell Telephone Company, Scranton, and switchboard room, Philadelphia, 1931; manufacturing tin plate at N. & G. Taylor Co. Philadelphia, 1926, Follansbee Brothers and the American Sheet and Tin Plate Company, Pittsburgh; manufacturing cigars, Reading and out-of-state; making violins, Baltimore, Md.; collecting and recycling of waste and garbage including paper, rags and tin, Philadelphia; manufacturing steel wire in Pittsburgh and Youngstown, Ohio; manufacturing wire cloth and screen at Audubon Wire Cloth Co., N.J., 1927; combing and spinning wool by machine at S.B. & B.W. Fleisher, Inc., Hardwick & Magee Company, and Yewdall and Jones, 1906, Philadelphia; wool scouring, washing, dying, and packing at the Pendleton Wool Scouring & Packing Company, Oregon and other states.

Transportation: The aircraft industry showing models, artists' conceptions and views on the ground and in the air of dirigibles, airplanes, helicopters and autogiros including the *Los Angeles* and *Shenandoah*; cross country air mail flights by National Air Transport, 1927; views of the Pan Am Clipper, Curtiss Aeromarine, the Ford TriMotor with the Byrd Antarctic Expedition, Vought-Sikorsky helicopters and Pitcairn autogiros, TWA Stratoline B-17, Fairchild, Lockheed, Curtiss, Erco, Boeing, Martin and other military, commercial and pleasure aircraft. The automobile, truck and related industries showing assembly and publicity shots of Chrysler army tanks, 1941, Plymouth sedans for 1940 and 1941, the Diamond T Truck Company with cowboy Gene Autry, Stewart Motor Company's manufacture of trucks for United Parcel Service, REO "Speed Wagon" Trucks, advertising Studebaker cars with circus man Clyde Beatty, Autocar Company Trucks and Messinger Farm Equipment, electric trucks made by Commercial Truck Company, 1922, and many others. River, canal and ocean transportation, including barges, boats, canal boats, ferries, sailboats, steamships, tugboats with views of American Bridge Company vessels, 1919; whaling ships in various Massachussetts harbors; models and paintings of historic clipper ships; the ocean liners, S.S. *Mauretania*, in New York

Harbor, 1909, *Lusitania, Olympic, Great Eastern* and others, early steamboats by Robert Fulton and John Fitch; warships, gunboats and armoured cruisers, a "Neptune Party" crossing the equator and others; Railroad transportation, including the Allegheny Portage Railroad; models and builders' photos of steam and electric locomotives at the Baldwin Locomotive Works; the *John Bull* of the Camden and Amboy Railroad; Baltimore and Ohio Railroad locomotives; the Cumberland Valley Railroad locomotive *Pioneer*; abandoned rights-of-way of the Columbia Railroad in eastern Pennsylvania; New York Central Railroad locomotives; Pennsylvania Railroad locomotives; Philadelphia & Columbia Railroad train and subway station views in Philadelphia; Reading Railroad; Southern Pacific; West Jersey Railroad and others; Conestoga wagons and stagecoaches. Canals, including scenes along the Delaware & Hudson; the Pennsylvania Canal, including the Delaware, Susquehanna and Juniata Divisions; the Schuylkill Canal; Union Canal; Delaware and Chesapeake Canal; Delaware, Chesapeake and Ohio Canal through West Virginia and Maryland; the Morris and Essex Canal, New Jersey; the Erie Canal, Troy, N.Y., 1915; the New York State Barge Canal, and the Intercoastal Waterway in Delaware. Scenic river views at various locales of the Delaware and Susquehanna in New York, Pennsylvania, Delaware, New Jersey and Maryland; the Monongahela near Pittsburgh; the Ohio in Pennsylvania, West Virginia and Kentucky; the Schuylkill in Pennsylvania; the Mississippi in Iowa and Louisiana; the Raritan, Hudson and Trenton in New Jersey; the Harlem and East plus the harbor in New York City, and others.

Natural History: Extinct dinosaur and mammal fossils on exhibit at Carnegie Museum, Pittsburgh, 1927; views of a total solar eclipse from various locales, August 31, 1932; closeups of the sun, moon, planets and astronomical phenomena; miscellaneous photographs and engravings of birds; deer and duck hunting; the fishing industry; technical studies of exotic and native flowers blossoming in and around the Philadelphia area, 1918-1920; live and mounted insect specimens, especially bees and beehives, silkworms and silkworm cultures.

Miscellaneous categories include photographic copies of portraits of Thomas Jefferson, Benjamin Franklin, American Indians; aerial views of Trenton and Phillipsburg, N.J. and Wilmington, Del.; colonial flags, historical clocks and watches on exhibit at various Pennsylvania museums; activities of various Boy Scout troops in the Philadelphia area, 1911-1930, including those aboard the training ship *Emily*, Red Cross work, drying peach pits, scouts on parade, selling bonds for the Second and Third Liberty Loans during World War I, camping, and blind scout activities.

102

MG-240
WILLIAM W. STOEY PHOTOGRAPHS
1895-1925, 11 cu. ft.

William Wesley Stoey, 1846-1925, born near Carlisle, spent most of his life in Harrisburg. He served in the Civil War in Company A, 7th Pennsylvania Reserves, was captured in 1864 at the Battle of the Wilderness, and was sent to Andersonville Prison. Afterward, Stoey earned his living as a taxidermist at a shop at 1126 North Front Street, Harrisburg. His avocations included photography, which led to occasional employment, and natural history, which involved him in the Natural Sciences Association of Harrisburg. Stoey and his friends, who included Mira Dock, J. Horace McFarland and others, often went on natural history excursions with their cameras in south central Pennsylvania.

The photographs are 2,282 glass plate negatives taken by Stoey between November 5, 1895, and August 31, 1925, a few months before his death. Some plates were taken by his daughter Ida L. Stoey. Stoey often experimented with the camera, making exposures by flashlight, and working at night with special lenses or techniques. He also copied the photographs of others, such as C.S. Roshon, LeRue Lemer, William H. Rau and others. Most plates are 4x5, with some 5x7 and odd sizes such as stereo and half plate. The plates are arranged numerically and each bears a number scratched on the edge by Stoey. No original prints are present. PHMC contact prints of each plate were created in 1984-1985 for reference purposes.

Accompanying the plates is Stoey's index (1 vol.). Entries are numerical and usually include the date, subject, often the time of day, size and type of plate, and light conditions. There is also a PHMC subject card index to the plates. Though there are 2,414 entries, only 2,282 individual plates are present. The index contains a diary kept by Stoey between December 27, 1893, and April 28, 1895, "Things We Do, Hear and Say." Entries mostly record his natural history walks in the Harrisburg vicinity. There are also notes on a No. 4 Falcon bicycle, and a cyclometer record for 1895.

The diary and plates were donated by Stoey himself a few months before his death to the State Museum of Pennsylvania and transferred to the Archives sometime afterward. Some of Stoey's taxidermy is in the Natural History Section of the State Museum.

Though the bulk of the images is of Harrisburg, rural areas in south central Pennsylvania, especially in Dauphin, Cumberland, Lancaster and Perry Counties are present. There are five subject categories: natural history, people, town views, transportation and miscellaneous.

Natural history includes images of farm and domesticated animals, plus

MG-240 William W. Stoey Collection #601: "Straub & Bowers, river road,
June 24, 1898" (north of Harrisburg).

examples of Stoey's taxidermy; wildflowers; flower gardens; floral arrangements (usually funerary); plants and trees; scenic views of the Susquehanna and Juniata Rivers, especially at Chickies Rocks, Clarks Ferry, Dauphin Cliffs and Narrows, Fite's Eddy, Fort Hunter, Jack's Narrows, McCall's Ferry, Safe Harbor and Shenks Ferry; scenic views of bridges, creeks, hotels and private homes, hunting, runs, roads, waterfalls, springs, valleys and others, especially Beaver Creek, Cameron Creek, Clarks Creek, Conodoguinet Creek, Conestoga Creek, Conowago Creek, Conowingo Creek, Cumberland Creek, Doubling Gap, Eslingers Creek, Fishing Creek, Hummelstown Cave, Indian Steps, Manns Run, Mud Run, Paxton Creek, Poorhouse Run, Rock Run, Sterretts Gap, Stoney Creek, Tuquan Creek,

Tumbling Run, Trout Run, Wetzel's Swamp, Wislers Run, Yellow Breeches Creek, and others; natural phenomena such as clouds, the Harrisburg Ice Storms of 1904 and 1920, and the solar eclipse of June 28, 1908.

People are usually both formal and casual portraits of adults and children in their homes or yards, with a few postmortem images. The sitters were often Stoey's family, friends or neighbors. Family surnames include Aukamp, Backenstoss, Barkley, Becker, Berrier, Boak, Bowers, Butler, Carr, Chubb, Demming, Dintaman, Doren, Ellinger, Fager, Fetter, Fisher, Hassenplug, Graff, Hartz, Hemperley, Keeney, King, Landis, Lingle, Miller, Morgan, Peiffer, Rather, Rinehart, Schlagle, Sees, Sellers, Sensaman, Sensenig, Shook, Smith, Sourbier, Spangler, Stephens, Stevenson, Sullenberger, Taylor, Venable, Weaver, Weber, Williams, Yingst, Yoder, Zimmerman and others, including a series of prisoner mug shots taken for Dauphin County Prison and a copy of a daguerreotype of Governor Joseph Ritner.

Town views are primarily of Harrisburg, but the following are represented: Boiling Springs, Bridgeport (Lemoyne), Craighead, Dauphin, Gettysburg (battlefield), Middlesex, Port Deposit, Md., Rockville (including bridge), Safe Harbor, Salunga, Sibletown, Speeceville, West Fairview, Wormleysburg and York Haven. Harrisburg views include: boat wharves; bridges, especially Camelback, Mulberry and Walnut; businesses and industry, many identified by the family names listed above, such as beauty salons, blacksmith shops, carpet, upholstery and furniture stores, cigar factories, coal dredging, dairy, ice and coal wagons, dams, distilleries, greenhouses, grocery stores, hotels, hydroelectric plant, ice cream parlors, iron furnaces, mills, nailworks, sawmills, stone quarries, Harrisburg Waterworks, wharves, and others; buildings include interior and exterior views of homes of many of the people listed above, the old and new Capitols, with the ruins of the fire of 1897, and the Grand Opera House fire of 1907; Harrisburg Cemetery monuments and tombstones, plus gravediggers and landscapers at work; recreation and celebration, including Christmas and Halloween, bicycling, excursion boating, card playing, fishing, hockey, skating, swimming, activities at the Harrisburg River Carnival, September 2, 1907, and Old Home Week, 1905; and street views, including of Cameron, Crystal, Cumberland, Front, Broad, Second, Market, Reily, State, Seventeenth, and Third.

Transportation includes boatyards on the Susquehanna, the Fort Hunter Ferry; the Pennsylvania Canal and canal boats and locks at Clarks Ferry, Dauphin, Harrisburg, Lochiel, Middletown, Rockville and Speeceville; railroads at Bridgeport (Lemoyne) including the President McKinley funeral train, Enola and Rockville.

Miscellaneous includes farm machinery manufactured by the Jackson Company, and the Reliance Chick Brooder and Incubator; a Spangler Car

Fender; paintings by B.I. Lingle; and copies of photographs of points of interest all over the world, such as the pyramids of Egypt, the Grand Canyon and others.

MG-240 William W. Stoey Collection #1518: "Pennsylvania State Capitol from Second and Barbara Avenue, March 2, 1907."

MG-247
THE LOGAN FAMILY COLLECTION
Ca. 1680-1945, 4 cu. ft.

Algernon Sydney Logan (1849-1925) was a descendant of James Logan, provincial secretary to William Penn. The Logan Family owned several estates in the Philadelphia area. Algernon spent time managing family affairs and engaging in various pursuits including writing and photography. He periodically displayed prints at the Philadelphia Photography Club and other organizations.

The bulk of the Collection (2.5 cu. ft.) is portrait photographs of Logan, his wife, Mary Wynne Wister, and their families, ca. 1845-1930. Also included are photographs taken by Algernon S. Logan, and some probably collected by his son, Robert Restalrig Logan. Non-photographic materials (1.5 cu. ft.) include copies of manuscripts pertaining to James Logan, the poetry and novels of Algernon S. Logan, and genealogical data relating to the family. The Logans donated this and other artifacts relating to the family to the State Archives over the course of several years.

Subjects cover: Logan and Wister Family Portraits, including photographic copies of paintings of John Logan and Isaac Norris; three albums of cabinet cards, cartes-de-visite, and miscellaneous prints of the John Dickinson Logan Family, the Charles Jones Wister Family, Owen Wister, and the Wister home, "Grumblethorpe," near Philadelphia. Many of these are by Philadelphia area photographers, including Frederick Gutekunst, David Hinkle, The Monarch Company, M.P. Simons, C.H. Spielers, and many others. Notable items include cased photographs, mostly daguerreotypes, of unidentified family members, ca. 1845-1925. Some of these are by Isaac Rehn, Charles Evans and John Plumbe, Jr.

Photographs by Algernon Sydney Logan, ca. 1871-1925, include self-portraits; views of Logan Family homes in the Philadelphia area; a view of Rittenhouse Square, Philadelphia; farms near Jones Neck, Delaware; bathers and beach scenes at Spring Lake Beach, New Jersey; and "Sand Dunes," an entry in the Reading Lantern Photographic Exhibition of 1903. Also present is *Biographical Sketch of Algernon Sydney Logan,* by Robert Restalrig Logan (Philadelphia National Publishing Company), 1934, containing references to his photographic pursuits.

Miscellaneous items include 133 stereographs of an unidentified branch of the Logan Family on vacation in California, 1921.

MG-250
HARRISBURG COMMUNITY THEATRE COLLECTION
1927-PRESENT, 12 cu. ft.

Founded in 1925, the Harrisburg Community Theatre still stages productions at a theatre on Sixth Street, Harrisburg. The collection was donated to the State Archives in 1975 by the HCT Guild and is periodically updated. The bulk of the collection is 9.5 cu. ft. of accounts, correspondence, reports, minutes of the Board of Governors, newsclippings, posters, programs, scrapbooks, etc., 1927-present.

The photographs are 2.5 cu. ft. of mostly 8x10 stills of productions, 1930-1976. The stills are arranged chronologically and include: *Abe Lincoln in Illinois; Annie Get Your Gun; Arsenic and Old Lace; Bell, Book and Candle; Bells*

Are Ringing; Blythe Spirit; Bye Bye Birdie; Cabaret; Camelot; Cat On a Hot Tin Roof; Charley's Aunt; The Crucible; Death of a Salesman; Dial M for Murder; Fiddler on the Roof; Funny Girl; A Funny Thing Happened on the Way to the Forum; Good News; Guys and Dolls; Gypsy; Harvey; How to Succeed in Business Without Really Trying; I Remember Mama; Inherit the Wind; The King and I; Kiss Me Kate; L'il Abner; The Little Foxes; The Lower Depths; Man of La Mancha; The Man Who Came to Dinner; The Mikado; The Mousetrap; The Music Man; My Fair Lady; The Odd Couple; Oklahoma; Oliver; Our Town; The Petrified Forest; The Philadelphia Story; Play It Again Sam; Pride and Prejudice; The Prime of Miss Jean Brodie; A Raisin in the Sun; The Royal Family; See How They Run; Showboat; The Sound of Music; South Pacific; A Streetcar Named Desire; Teahouse of the August Moon; West Side Story; You Can't Take It With You; and many others.

Also included are stills of various children's productions; portraits of directors; backstage views; rehearsal and performance photos; ground breaking ceremonies for the HCT building, 1950; and unidentified productions.

MG-254
AUDIO-VISUAL COLLECTION
1926-Present, 4.5 cu. ft.

These are miscellaneous acquisitions of motion picture films, videotapes and sound recordings. Items include:

Pennsylvania State Police produced for the Department of Public Instruction for use in the U.S. Sesquicentennial Exposition of 1926. The story explains the establishment and duties of the State Police and the true-life story of Trooper Francis Haley, killed in the line of duty. Silent, with titles. One reel 16mm, black-and-white, 1,000 feet. Copy of the original 35mm film.

Sherm Lutz films taken by him of his activities as a trainer for the Civilian Pilot Training Program at Boalsburg Air Field, ca. 1935-1941. Scenes show trainees checking planes, practicing take-offs and landings, etc. Also included are scenes at the State College Air Depot, ca. 1945-1955, most notably showing the landing of the first DC-3. Seven reels, 16mm, silent, color, 1,800 ft.

Village Life at Laurelton State Village, ca. 1945-1950, taken by medical director Dr. Catherine Edgett. Scenes show the facility and patients receiving treatment. Two reels, 16mm silent, color, 800 ft.

Pennsylvania Week produced by the Department of Commerce, probably October, 1949. This was a commercial to promote the state's annual campaign for commerce and industry. Includes a speech by Governor James

Duff. Copy of the original 35mm film. One reel, 16mm, sound, black-and-white, 250 feet.

Ike at Gettysburg, probably taken by Harrisburg *Patriot-News* photographer Guy Pugliese, June 1952. Scenes show a reception given by the presidential candidate and Mrs. Dwight Eisenhower at their Gettysburg Farm. Personalities include U.S. Senator James Duff, Governor John Fine, and State Senator M. Harvey Taylor. One reel, 16mm, color, silent, 625 ft.

Left Bank, Right Bank, produced by the Pennsylvania State University, 1976, concerning the voyage of the Bicentennial Raft on the Susquehanna. Accompanied by the booklet "The Bicentennial Raft and the Rafting Era in Pennsylvania," by O. Linn Frank. One reel, 16mm, sound, color, 1,000 feet.

On the Road to '76 with Charles Kuralt. Produced by CBS News for the 1976 Bicentennial celebration in Pennsylvania. One reel, 16mm, sound, color, 250 feet.

The National Governors' Conference, July 4-6, 1976, held at Hershey, produced by WITF Television. Two inch videotape, ten reels (original version) and three-quarter inch videotape, nine reels (augmented version).

Liberty the Second, produced by CTV Television, Meadville, concerning the 1985 salvaging of *Liberty the Second,* a speedboat sunk in Conneaut Lake in 1922. VHS videotape, one-half inch, fifteen minutes.

MG-263
GEORGE A. RICHARDSON COLLECTION
1869-1974, 12 cu. ft.

George Atwell Richardson (1886-1976) of Bethlehem, Pa., was in his lifetime a surveyor, aeronautical engineer, metallurgist, lecturer, historical writer, photographer, motion picture film producer and traveller. The bulk of the Collection (11.7 cu. ft.) contains documents and photographs pertaining to his vocational and avocational interests. The remainder (.3 cu. ft.) is primarily annual diaries, 1869-1881, of his father George Carr Richardson.

Born in Milwaukee, Wisc. and raised in Evanston, Ill., Richardson attended the University of Pennsylvania, 1909-1912, earning a bachelor's degree in mechanical engineering. While there he became interested in the technical aspects of aviation, and organized and participated in some of the first intercollegiate hot-air balloon and glider meets held in the East. In 1910 he founded and became president of the Intercollegiate Aeronautical Association of America. From 1904-1908 and during the summers of 1909-1911 and 1912 Richardson worked on and supervised surveying and mapping crews for the engineering department of the Chicago, Milwaukee and St. Paul Railroad in Illinois. From 1913-1916 he performed various engineering jobs for the Midvale Steel Company, Chicago, later becoming advertising manager, a position he held until 1923. At this time he produced and directed promotional and instructional motion pictures for the firm. He then moved to Pennsylvania and managed the Bethlehem Steel Corporation's Technical Publicity Department from 1923-1933. From 1933-1938 he collaborated with his brother Edward on numerous patents pertaining to diesel engines, aviation, and metallurgy. He also became an historical writer and lecturer, creating a series of slide programs for community use on aviation, the Appalachian Trail, and other topics. From 1939 to the 1950s he was sales manager of Metallurgical Laboratories, Inc. of Philadelphia. After retiring and until his death at age 90, he was active with local historical societies and community groups. Richardson is listed in *Who's Who in America* for 1925 and *Who's Who in Engineering* for 1954.

An avid traveller and hiker, Richardson made numerous "trampings," as he called them, throughout the United States and Canada. He was an ardent supporter for the establishment and maintenance of the Appalachian Trail, especially in Pennsylvania, and was for many years a troop leader in the Boy Scouts of America. He was also an enthusiastic photographer and made his first glass plates at the age of thirteen in 1899. He photographed and made most of the slides used in his lectures. Richardson most likely saw photography as a useful recording and communications tool, for most of his images are of a technical, rather than artistic, nature.

The Collection was donated to the Historical and Museum Commission by the Richardson Family in 1976. Artifacts relating to it are housed at the State Museum of Pennsylvania. Approximately 300 safety film negatives taken by Richardson of canal sites in eastern Pennsylvania during the 1930s are located at the Hugh Moore Park and Canal Museum, Easton, Pa. Additional documents and photographs created by Richardson during his careers at Midvale Steel and Metlab are located at Eleutherian Mills, Wilmington, Del.

Documents (6.5 cu. ft.) in the Collection often complement the photographs and include personal business accounts, 1911-1921; correspondence, 1904-1968; yearly diaries, 1910-1911, 1913-1924; family and genealogical data; technical literature on photography and aeronautics, 1908-1927; souvenir programs from Chicago area theatres, 1896-1906; issues of the following aviation magazines: *Aero*, 1910-1912; *Aero and Hydro*, 1912-1914; *Aeronautics*, 1909-1912, 1915; *Aero Club of America Bulletin*, 1910-1912; *Aircraft*, 1911; *Aviation and Aeronautical Engineering*, 1916-1919; *Fly*, 1908-1912, and *The Intercollegiate*, 1910-1912; research material and rough drafts for lectures on the history of aviation, frontier forts of Pennsylvania and the

East Coast, the Sullivan Trail and the Appalachian Trail, ca. 1912-1965; poetry; and historical articles on a variety of topics, 1903-1970.

Photographs (5.2 cu. ft.), 1899-1961, include glass plate and film negatives, glass and film slides and some contact prints. The Collection is arranged numerically by type of negative. Each negative is numbered and identified in Richardson's handwriting, and with the envelope often indicating the type of camera used, lens aperture and time setting, the date, time of day, and weather conditions, together with miscellaneous notations about the subject. The prints often carry on the reverse the negative number and information concerning subjects, but these are unarranged and uncatalogued. The slides are usually copies made from the prints and are arranged in lecture formats.

Glass plate negatives and their subjects include:
3 1/4 x 4 1/4 (102 items) of Richardson and his family at their home in Illinois, and a trip to visit relatives in Maine, 1899-1900.

4x5 (460 items) of Richardson and his family, 1912-1918; with surveying crews in the Illinois railyards of the Chicago, Milwaukee and St. Paul Railroad (includes views of immigrant Italian workers), and copies of engineering drawings and records used by the railroad, 1912; Richardson and his fellow students in various activities at the University of Pennsylvania, including technical studies for use in student theses, 1912-1913; copies of engravings, newsclippings and photographs relating to the early history of flight, ca. 1912; a "tramping" to the Philadelphia Zoo and Barnegat Point, N.J., 1914; the Midvale Steel Company, 1915; Richardson as a Boy Scout leader with his troop in Pennsylvania, 1917; with his brother Edward in Home Defense uniforms, 1917-1919; and a trip to Valley Forge, 1918. Accompanying these plates are two albums of about 200 contact prints made from selected negatives.

5x7 (30 items) of architectural and engineering drawings of the Godfrey and Bensonville yards of the C.M. & St.P.R.R., 1911-1912.

Film negatives
Negatives are arranged in twelve Kodak Negative Albums of varying size (approximately 100 negatives per album) and include:

Album #1 - tramping to Canada and Maine, September, 1908; and to the Badlands and Black Hills of South Dakota, September, 1909.

Album #2 - a University of Pennsylvania circus, Spring, 1909; Port Richmond and Philadelphia riverfront views, June, 1911; Valley Forge, February, 1909; the First Intercollegiate Balloon Race, North Adams to Peabody, Mass., June, 1911; Harvard Glider Meet, Squantum, Mass., October, 1910; Swarthmore Carnival and Glider Contest, May, 1911; gliding at Cornell University, N.Y., Fall, 1910; and a tramping to Harpers Ferry, W.Va., Spring, 1910.

Album #3 - a tramping to the Catskill Mountains, N.Y., July, and Valley Forge and southeastern Pennsylvania, Fall, 1916.

Album #4 - the Union Canal ruins near Bernville, Pa., and miscellaneous family activities, October-November, 1921.

Album #5 - a tramping to the Catskill Mountains, N.Y., with a Boy Scout troop, September, 1921; Aberdeen Proving Grounds, Md., and Union Canal ruins, Pa., October, 1921; the Portage Railroad, Cresson, July 1922; and a western trip through Arkansas, Texas, Mexico and the Grand Canyon, November, 1922.

Album #6 - continuing the above western trip, ending in New Orleans, La., November, 1922; Niagara Falls and the Morris and Essex Canal, N.J., Summer, 1924; a Florida to New York trip on a steamship, March, 1925; and a tramping to Yorktown, Va., and Cahokia Mounds, Ill., Spring, 1927.

Album #7 - a tramping to Richmond and the Rappahannock River, Va., May, 1927; a tramping to Canada and Maine, July, 1927; a mine at Friedensville, Pa., July, 1930; and ceremonies marking the establishment of Delaware Division Canal (Roosevelt) State Park with Governor Gifford Pinchot, New Hope, Pa., October, 1931.

Album #8 - the Richardson family and their cabin at Saddleback Pond, Maine, Summer, 1931, and a 1908 tramping to Maine taken by a friend.

Album #9 - Hereford Furnace and Dale Iron Works, Bally, Pa., July, 1929; an abandoned iron mine near Bethlehem; and a trip from Wind Gap to Lehigh Gap, June, 1930.

Albums #10-12 and an additional 200 loose negatives were taken between September, 1931, and October, 1936, for use in lectures on Pennsylvania frontier forts, the Appalachian Trail, the Sullivan Trail and the Lehigh Canal. Included are panoramas of the Blue Mountains, views along the trails and the sites of Wilson Blockhouse and Mill, Chapman's Quarries, Ralston (Brown's) Fort, Peter Doll's Blockhouse, Teed's Fort, Adam Deshler's Fort, Friedensthal, Fort Dupui, Fort Hyndshaw, Scholl's Mill, Christian's Spring, Gnadenthal, Nazareth Hall, Whitefield House, Rose Inn, Fort Penn, Fort Hamilton, Fort Norris, Fort Lehigh, Bear Rocks, Trucher's Fort, Fort Allen, Gnadenhutten, Wind Gap, Lehigh Gap, Smith's Gap, Little Gap, Johnson's Gap, Fox Gap and Tott's Gap.

Safety film negatives total approximately 500 items of varying sheet and roll film size, 1939-1961, with some later items in color. Subjects include the Richardson family in Pennsylvania and Maine; his marriage ceremony, 1945; the Sullivan Trail; and activities with Metlab.

Glass slides are either black-and-white or color. Subjects include:
3 1/4 x 4, one case (90 items) of University of Pennsylvania publicity advertisements, 1909-1912; one case (109 items) illustrating "Flight," a lecture on the early history of aeronautics, ca. 1910; two cases (138 slides) illustrating "When the Blue Ridge Mountain Was Fortified Frontier"; one case (48 slides) illustrating "The Appalachian Trail"; one case (28 slides) illustrating "The Sullivan Trail," all ca. 1935; two cases (141 slides) illustrating technical lectures for Metlab, ca. 1950, and miscellaneous (69 items) relating to aviation and religion, ca. 1912.

2x2, one case (70 items) pertaining to Metlab, ca. 1950.

Film slides
2x2, color, arranged in lecture format, include "The Sullivan Trail," taken between 1942-1954 (160 items); and historic forts of eastern North America, taken in the 1950s (400 items).

Miscellaneous photographic materials include a 16mm black-and-white silent motion picture film (1 reel, 500 feet) on the construction and maintenance of the Appalachian Trail in Pennsylvania, ca. 1935, and postcards (.3 cu. ft.) collected by Richardson during his travels.

MG-264
I.U. INTERNATIONAL POLITICAL MEMORABILIA COLLECTION
1789-1972, 14.8 cu. ft.

The International Utilities International Management Corporation is a holding company based in Philadelphia. In the years leading up to the United States Bicentennial Celebration of 1976, I. U. purchased historic American political materials from several collectors, notably Harold Griffin of Santa Monica, California. The Collection was used for exhibit purposes as a way of celebrating the Bicentennial. I. U. donated the materials to the Pennsylvania Historical and Museum Commission in July 1976. Artifacts relating to the Collection are among the holdings of the State Museum of Pennsylvania, Harrisburg.

The Collection relates to successful and unsuccessful United States presidential candidates and their vice-presidential running mates. Also included are items on national political issues significant to American history. The bulk (3.3 cu. ft.) includes autographs, ballot tickets, campaign literature, cartoons, envelopes, inaugural programs, letterheads, letters, magazines, newspapers, pamphlets and posters.

Photographs, postcards and engravings comprise 1.5 cu. ft. Most are formally posed images designed to promote the candidate. Often they are shown at various stages of their careers along with their families or with high-ranking government officials. Many are signed, and while some signatures are original, others are mechanically reproduced. Size of items varies, but is usually 8 x 10 or smaller. Types of photographs range from cartes-de-visite and cabinet cards to other types of prints. Political personalities include: John Adams, John Quincy Adams, Spiro T. Agnew, Chester A. Arthur, John M. Ashbrook, Nathaniel P. Banks, Alben W. Barkley, James G. Blaine, General Frank P. Blair, John C. Breckinridge, John W. Bricker, Charles W. Bryan, William Jennings Bryan, James Buchanan, William O. Butler, John C. Calhoun, Lewis Cass, Shirley Chisholm, Henry Clay, Grover Cleveland, DeWitt Clinton, Schuyler Colfax, Calvin Coolidge, Charles Curtis, George M. Dallas, Jefferson Davis, John W. Davis, Charles G. Dawes, William L. Dayton, Thomas E. Dewey, Stephen A. Douglas, Thomas Eagleton, Dwight D. Eisenhower, Edward Everett, Charles W. Fairbanks, Millard Fillmore, Theodore Frelinghuysen, John C. Fremont, James A. Garfield (also includes Charles Guiteau), John N. Garner, Elbridge Gerry, Barry Goldwater, William A. Graham, Ulysses S. Grant, Mike Gravel, Horace Greeley, Hannibal Hamlin, Winfield Scott Hancock, Benjamin Harrison, William Henry Harrison, Warren G. Harding, Vance Hartke, Rutherford B. Hayes, Garret A. Hobart, Herbert Hoover, John Eager Howard, Charles Evans Hughes, Harold E. Hughes, Hubert Humphrey, Andrew Jackson, Thomas Jefferson, Andrew Johnson, Herschel V. Johnson, Lyndon B. Johnson, Estes Kefauver, Edward Kennedy, John F. Kennedy, Robert Kennedy, Rufus King, Frank Knox, Alfred M. Landon, Abraham Lincoln, John V. Lindsey, Henry Cabot Lodge, Jr., John A. Logan, Eugene McCarthy, George McClellan, Peter McClosky, George S. McGovern, William McKinley, Charles L. NcNary, James Madison, Thomas Riley Marshall, Wilbur Mills, William Miller, James Monroe, Levi P. Morton, Edmund Muskie, Richard Nixon, Alton B. Parker, Endicott Peabody, George H. Pendleton, Franklin Pierce, Charles C. Pinckney, James K. Polk, Whitelaw Reid, Joseph T. Robinson, Nelson Rockefeller, Franklin D. Roosevelt, Theodore Roosevelt, Terry Sanford, Winfield Scott, William Scranton, Arthur Sewall, Horatio Seymour, James S. Sherman, Alfred E. Smith, John Sparkman, Edwin M. Stanton, Harold E. Stassen, Alexander H. Stevens, Adlai Stevenson, Sr., William H. Taft, Zachary Taylor, Allen G. Thurman, Strom Thurmond, Samuel J. Tilden, Harry S Truman, John Tyler, Martin Van Buren, George Wallace, Henry A. Wallace, Earl Warren, George Washington, Daniel Webster, William A. Wheeler, Wendell Willkie, Henry Wilson, Woodrow Wilson and Fielding L. Wright. Also included are some composite portraits of presidents, Civil War generals, and Confederate government officials.

MG-272
PENNSYLVANIA MILITARY MUSEUM COLLECTION
1789-PRESENT, 16 cu. ft.

This is a group of collections acquired by the Pennsylvania Historical and Museum Commission's museum at Boalsburg. All relate to military service by Pennsylvanians from the Revolution to the Korean Conflict. Individual collections include commissions, letters, diaries, maps, posters and photographs. Most photographs are prints of varying size relating to the Pennsylvania National Guard and, World Wars I and II. Collections include:

Frank Beary Collection relating to his career as a general in the PNG, 1898-1948, 130 items. Photographs are of activities at Mount Gretna Military Reservation and other camps by L.G. Harpel. Notables appearing with Beary include Governors Edwin Stuart, William Sproul, John Fisher, Gifford Pinchot and Edward Martin; Generals George Richards, Daniel Strickler, John Pershing, Thomas Stewart, J.R.S. Gobin, and many others. Events include camp life at Mount Gretna, reviews and parades, target practice, etc.; an undated dedication of a Spanish-American War Memorial in Lebanon, and a ceremony to deposit battle flags at the State Museum, 1945.

Herbert K. Blouch Collection of his career as a chaplain in the Army Air Corps during World War II, 1944-1945, and with the PNG, 1947-1970, one cu. ft. The photographs, many probably taken by Blouch, show his activities during his tours of duty in Italy, Egypt, Palestine and Trinidad.

Robert E. Brown Collection of his career as a sergeant with the 103rd Cavalry, PNG, 1930-1942, twenty items.

J.T. Burket Collection relating to the 110th Regiment and the 10th Pennsylvania Infantry, PNG, 1903-1924, seven items. Includes the 110th Regiment in France, 1918, and at Mt. Gretna, 1924; and the 10th Pennsylvania Infantry at Camp Stewart, Tex., 1916.

Nathan Cohen Collection relating to his experience as soldier and orchestra leader for the 28th Division musical review "Who Are You?" 1918-1919, five items.

Cyrus Coleman Collection of his career with the 112th Regiment, PNG, 1917-1924, nine items. Photographs are panoramic prints of various companies of the 112th, the A.E.F. cemetery, and various scenic areas in France. Also included is a brochure, "List of Cirkut Photographs Made in France by Ewing, Inc., Commercial Photographers, Baton Rouge, LA"; a list of names on photograph rosters for the 112th; and a portrait of General John Pershing.

Horace A. Decker Photographs, probably taken by him, showing his camp life as a private with the 16th Infantry, PNG, during the Mexican Border Campaign of 1916, 136 items.

George S. Denithorne Collection of his career with various engineering units, PNG, during the Mexican Border Campaign and World War I, 1916-1919, and as Captain of Engineers, Reserves, 1922, thirty-eight items.

Harry Eyer Collection of panoramic prints of Company C, 103rd Engineers, PNG, 1918, three items.

Clara Hay Panoramic Prints of the 10th Regiment and the 110th Infantry, PNG, during the Mexican Border Campaign, 1916, and in France during and after World War I, 1918-1919, six items.

Ivan Hollabaugh Collection primarily relating to his World War I service with the PNG in France and Germany, 1918, 124 items. Includes French and German postcards of local scenes and a photograph of General Charles Muir autographed to Hollenbaugh.

Ellery Hubbard Panoramic Prints of the 28th Division in France during World War I, two items.

John R. Johnsonbaugh Collection pertaining to the Spanish-American War and World War I, 113 items. Includes postcards he collected while serving France and Luxembourg.

Mabel S. Knight Photographs relating to her service as a Red Cross Nurse during World War I in France, four items.

Edward H. Lightner Collection including photographs of the 18th Regiment, PNG, in France, 1917, three items; and a pamphlet, "Notes on Interpretation of Aeroplane Photographs," issued by General Headquarters, 1918.

Fletcher McKnight Collection relating to his World War I service with the PNG, fifty-one items. Includes panoramic prints of Camp Hancock, Ga., and France; a photogrammetric view, probably in Germany; and postcards of Camp Hancock, Fort Dix, N.J., the Salvation Army, and views in France and Germany.

William Allen March Collection relating to his service as a major with the 108th Regiment, PNG, during World War I, seventy-eight items. Includes panoramic prints of Camp Stewart, Tex.; Camp Tobyhanna, Pa.; and LeMans, France. Includes an autographed print of Marshall Ferdinand Foch, 1919.

Luella Davis Oliver Collection relating to her World War I service as an Army Nurse, sixteen items.

William C. Pelton Photographs relating to World War II, including Army Air Corps B-17 and B-24 Bombers over targets in Germany and Japan; the Atom Bomb Test at Bikini Atoll, 1952; Charles DeGaulle's march into Paris, 1944; the 107th Field Artillery at Fort Indiantown Gap, 1941, and others, thirteen items.

H.C. Randolph Photographs pertaining to his World War II career showing activities at Fort Indiantown Gap, 1941; Camp Livingston, La., 1942; and his service in Wales, France, Belgium and Germany, 1944-1945, 218 items.

Harry D. Richards Photographs relating to the PNG, thirty-one items. Richards, a Philadelphia photographer, took views of a PNG parade in Philadelphia, and training at Mount Gretna, ca. 1925.

Warren Schnable Panoramic Photographs relating to his career with the 213th Artillery, PNG, before, during and after World War I, eight items. Views show the 213th at Camp Stewart, Tex., 1916; Ft. Monroe, Va., 1923; Camp Devon, Md., 1919; and at Mount Gretna, 1921-1922.

General Daniel B. Strickler Collection covering his career with the PNG during World War II and the Korean Conflict, sixty-eight items. Includes formal portraits of Strickler and informal views of him meeting with Generals Dwight D. Eisenhower and Mark Clark, Governors James Duff and Edward Martin, Miss America 1950, and others. Views also show Strickler with the PNG in Germany, Korea and at Fort Indiantown Gap.

Francis Weber Collection, including a booklet of ten photographic postcards showing the liberation of Paris in August, 1944.

E.H. Woomer Panoramic Prints primarily showing the 110th Infantry, PNG at Camp Hancock, Ga., 1917-1918 and at Mount Gretna, 1920, seven items. Also included are two portraits of General Edward Martin, 1944.

Carl Zember Collection including three panoramic prints of the PNG at Camp Hancock, Ga., 1917.

Miscellaneous items include panoramic prints of Pennsylvania National Guard activities, 1915-1937, at Mt. Gretna, Indiantown Gap, Camp Stewart, Camp Hancock, and during World War I in France; prints of varying size of the 28th Division liberating Paris in August, 1944; activities of Battery A of the Pennsylvania Volunteer Light Artillery during the Spanish-American War; and others.

MG-273
CHARLES H. BURG PHOTOGRAPHS
1893-1899, n.d., .4 cu. ft.

Charles Burg (1872-?), born in Brickerville, Pa., was a soldier with the 3rd Brigade, Governor's Troop, Pennsylvania National Guard. He served various tours of active duty, notably the Hazleton Coal Strike after the notorious Lattimer Massacre of September 10, 1897, and the Puerto Rican Campaign of the Spanish-American War in August 1898. After his discharge, Burg lived in Camp Hill, Pa., and commanded the Howard Calder Post of the

MG-273 Charles H. Burg Collection: "Strikers on the march Sep. 10th the day of the shooting" (at Lattimer).

Veterans of Foreign Wars in Harrisburg. Little is known of his later life. The photographs and Burg's discharge papers were donated by the estate of his daughter Evelyn M. Hoy in 1977. Burg's hat, medals and other artifacts are among the collections of the State Museum of Pennsylvania, Harrisburg.

The photographs are fifty-four items collected by Burg during his military career and is arranged in three categories, the Hazleton Coal Strike, 1897; the Puerto Rican Campaign, 1898; and miscellaneous. Almost all of the Hazleton Coal Strike photographs were taken by Rise & Gates, a photography firm based in Lebanon. These are 4 3/4 x 3 3/4 mounted prints and identified on the reverse with the firm's logo and subject information.

In the late 1890s, the fledgling United Mine Workers Union engaged in several strikes in the Hazleton area, meeting great opposition from local coal companies. Attempts in 1897 to organize at nearby Lattimer Mines were cruelly rebuffed when a local sheriff and his deputies fired into a crowd of unarmed immigrant Slavic miners on September 10. Twenty men were killed and the Pennsylvania National Guard, including Burg's Governor's Troop under the command of General John Gobin, was called to prevent further violence. The photographs show the Governor's Troop encampment and General Gobin with his staff at Hazleton; coal breakers and strip mining at Hazelton, Lattimer and Beaver Meadows; the streets and homes of Lattimer, some with Italian and Slavic children in the foreground; the strikers marching on the afternoon of September 10 just prior to the fatal shootings; and the site of the massacre after removal of the bodies.

The Puerto Rican Campaign photographs are to a large extent unidentified and were possibly taken by Burg himself. Each print is mounted on heavy cardboard. The Governor's Troop was mustered into U.S. Service and stationed at Port au Ponce in August, 1898. Subjects show camp life at Port au Ponce; natives in their homes and marketplaces; the news headquarters; and scenes on board the troopship.

Miscellaneous items are formal portraits, usually measuring 7x9, of Burg and fellow troopers taken by various local photographers. Subjects show them at encampments at Columbia, 1893, Mount Gretna, 1895 and 1898; on federal service mustering-out day, Harrisburg, November 21, 1898; on patrol duty at Gettysburg, undated; and Burg as commander of the Howard Calder V. F. W. Post, undated. The reverse of some of these prints identifies individual troop members.

MG-274
LEHIGH VALLEY RAILROAD COLLECTION
1849-1963, Approx. 370 cu. ft.

Originally known as the Lehigh, Schuylkill and Susquehanna Railroad, the LVRR competed for the lucrative anthracite coal transport trade in northeastern Pennsylvania. It dominated the industry in eastern Pennsylvania, New York and New Jersey, becoming known as the "route of the Black Diamond." The demise of the coal industry and the rise of auto and air transportation in the 1950s led to its financial ruin and a takeover by the Pennsylvania Railroad in 1960. The Collection was acquired over the course of several years from the main offices of the LVRR.

The bulk of the Collection is approximately 367 cu. ft. of minutes, reports, journals, ledgers, cash books, etc., pertaining to everyday operations. Photographs are 3 cu. ft. (over 500 items) of negatives of varying size, usually 6x8 or 8x10 glass plates taken by staff photographers. Subjects include construction of the Claremont Terminal, Jersey City, N.J., 1917-1923; ruins of the Morris Canal near Washington, N.J.; the 1902 Lehigh River flood near Easton; construction of an unidentified engine and freight house, probably in Buffalo, 1915; and other items.

MG-280
ARTHUR D. BRANSKY PHOTOGRAPHS
1905-1906, .3 cu. ft.

Charles E. Ross (1873-1961), a native of Iowa, ran a photography business with Linnie, his wife, in Stroudsburg during the first quarter of the twentieth century. Later in his career he also became a well-known hunting and fishing guide in the Pocono Mountains.

From the autumn of 1905 to the winter of 1906, newlyweds Charles and Linnie Ross took an extended honeymoon trip through east central Pennsylvania. From Allentown to Williamsport they photographed interesting people and subjects in small towns, hoping to earn money from sale of the prints. Staying in hotels along the way, they captured town panoramas, interior and exterior views of factories, mills, churches, residences, schools, commercial businesses such as saloons, general and specialty stores, barber shops, restaurants, post offices and crafts shops such as blacksmiths, harness shops, and stonecutters. People proudly posed for these photographs next to their residences or places of business, often pausing in their work to smile for the camera. Most views Ross identified only by town. His original 5x7 glass negatives from this trip and others taken during his career, over 1,000 items, are in the possession of Arthur D. Bransky of Breinigsville, Pa. In 1979 and 1980, the State Archives obtained contact prints from 227 of these negatives. The prints are arranged alphabetically by town and deal with the following topics:

Adamsdale: Williams-Marrion Shoe Factory, Adamsdale Park, Adamsdale Church and Cemetery, town panorama, unidentified railroad workers and steam engine.

Alburtis: Geisinger Butcher Wagon, H.K. Snyder Butcher Shop, unidentified carriage maker shop, saloon, blacksmith shop, general store and a farm residence and barn.

Allentown: unidentified saloons, general stores, dry goods stores, clothing stores, restaurant, and school children.

Annville: Helig House Hotel and unidentified children.

Blandon: Blandon House Saloon, Albert D. Gulden's Grist Mill, Grand Central Hotel, Charles and Linnie Ross self-portrait, unidentified hotel barroom, school children, house painters, horses, factory office, funeral wake, log house, and rural road view.

Bower's Station: Post Office/General Store, unidentified saloon, stonecutter's shop, blacksmith shop, and doctor's residence.

Campbelltown: undertaker's residence, T.H. Miller & Son Harnessmaker's Shop, P.E. Wolfersburger Home and unidentified general store.

Centerport: harnessmaker's shop, Charles K. Miller Marble & Granite Works (includes residence and family), J.F. Rentschler Hotel, M.S. Rentschler General Store, and unidentified electrical powerhouse.

Fleetwood: Allentown and Reading Traction Company trolley cars.

Fogelsville: A.H. Ely Boot and Shoe Maker Shop, E.W. Smith Saddle and Harnessmaker's Shop, unidentified blacksmith shop, foundry, store, hotel, post office, and residence.

Hereford Area: unidentified gristmill and farm buildings.

Kutztown: unidentified saloon.

Macungie: unidentified dry goods store and printer's shop.

Monterey: Monterey Hotel, unidentified barber shop, christening of a child, general store, hotel barroom, musicians, sawmill, and a one-room schoolhouse.

Pottsville: unidentified barber shop, cigar store, hotel, saloons, and steam engine.

Reading Area: Lloyd Laundry Company, Rexall Drug Store, unidentified foundry casting room, haberdashery, hotel barroom, grocery store, men's club, plumbing store, saloon, and town panoramas.

Shamokin: C.S. Burkhart Stove Dealer's Shop, Delbaugh's Saloon, Central Hotel barroom, The Grill (restaurant), unidentified barbershops, brewery store, billiard parlor, confectionary and tobacco shops, drugstore, dry goods store, hotel dining room, barroom, lobby and banquet rooms, saloons, and steam tractor and wagon.

MG-280 Arthur Bransky Collection: "Edwin J. Bailey, Blacksmith and Wheelwright, Topton, PA., 1906."

Temple: DeTurk's Farm Machinery Store and residence, Stony Point Granite Works, Temple Hotel, unidentified blacksmith shop, candy store, church, general store, hotels, pianist, and residences.

Topton: Edwin J. Bailey's Barrelmaker, Blacksmith and Wheelwright Shop; Benjamin E. Beiber General Store; Post Office (with G.C. Bortz Bakery Wagon in foreground); Washington House Hotel; and unidentified textile factory workers.

West Leesport: Washington House Hotel, town panoramas, and unidentified church cemetery, residence, and sewing factory workers.

Williamsport (includes Newberry): Enterprise Bread and Cake Bakery, Knights of Columbus meeting, Y. Steiber and Sons General Store, We-Klothe-U-Outfitting Company, and unidentified barbershops, bowling alley, candy store, Christmas tree, church, clothing store, drugstore, fruit store, factory turbine, harness shop, hotel, hotel kitchen, opera house (includes circus act), railroad station, telegraph office, residences and saloon.

MG-281
SAMUEL W. KUHNERT COLLECTION
Ca. 1912-1976, Approx. 30 cu. ft.

Samuel Wilhelm Kuhnert (1890-1978) was born in Steelton and raised on a farm near Halifax. He ran a photography processing business from his home in Camp Hill and later Harrisburg. He had a special interest in aviation and in 1919 began experimenting with aerial photography. For the following two decades he made and sold oblique aerial views of towns and places in central Pennsylvania. Upon his death in 1978, Kuhnert's children donated his photographs, flight suit and aerial cameras to the Pennsylvania Historical and Museum Commission.

The Collection contains over 6,000 photographic prints and negatives (28 cu. ft.), motion picture films (.5 cu. ft.) and miscellaneous business and personal records (1.5 cu. ft.). Photographs are arranged alphabetically by subject and grouped into the following categories: aerial views, aircraft, pilots, and miscellaneous. Most items are 4x5, 5x7 and 8x10 in size and were taken between 1919-1940.

Aerial views are cities and towns or specific buildings or areas within these towns and special events. Included are Adams County orchards, Amity Hall, Andersonburg, Annville, Bedford, Bellefonte, Blain, Bloomsburg, Boiling Springs, Bowmansdale, Bressler, Brookville, Caledonia Mountains,

Camp Hill, Carlisle, Carsonville, Cisna Run, Chambersburg (with Wilson and Penn Hall Colleges), Chesapeake Bay (near Havre de Grace, Md.), Clarks Ferry, Clarks Valley, Cleona, Coatesville, Conodoguinet Creek, Dalmatia, Danville (with state hospital), Dauphin, DeHart Dam, Dillsburg, Duncannon, Elizabethtown, Emmitsburg, Md. (St. Joseph's College), Enhaut, Enola, Enterline, Everett, Fort Hunter, Frederick, Md., Germantown, Gettysburg (airport, battlefield, town and college), Good Hope, Grantville, Hagerstown, Md., Halifax, Hamburg (state hospital), Harrisburg (Capitol Complex, city, and specific buildings), Hanover, Heckton, Hershey, Highspire, Hogestown, Hummelstown, Indian Echo Cave, various Pennsylvania National Guard encampments, Indiantown Gap, Kings Gap (the Cameron Estate), Lambs Gap, Lancaster (with Armstrong Company factory), Landisburg, Lawnton, Lebanon, Lemoyne, Lewisberry, Lewisburg (Bucknell University and federal prison), Linglestown, Liverpool, Loyalsock Valley, Loysville, Manada Gap, Marsh Run, Marysville, Matamoras, Mechanicsburg, Mercersburg, Millersburg, Milton, Mount Gretna (Pennsylvania National Guard encampments), Mount Holly Springs, Mount Pleasant, Mount Union, Mount Zion, New Berlin, Newberrytown, New Bloomfield, Newburg, New Cumberland, New Kingston, Newport, Northumberland, Palmyra, Paxtang, Peachmont Canneries, Penbrook, Perdix, Peters Mountain, Powells Valley, Rockview Prison, Rockville, Rutherford, Safe Harbor Dam (construction), Selinsgrove, Shermansdale, Shippensburg, Shiremanstown, Speeceville, State College, Steelton, Sterretts Gap, Summerdale, Sunbury, Pennsylvania Turnpike, Tyson Orchards, Wagnersville, Wellsville, West Fairview, West Lebanon, Wertzville, White Hill, Williams Grove Park, Williamsport, Willow Mills Park, Wormleysburg and York.

Aircraft include many varieties which passed through the central Pennsylvania area, most notably Bellancas; Boeing B-17s; Curtiss *Jennies*; dirigibles including the Douglas U.S. Navy *Shenandoah* and *Los Angeles*; DC-3s; Ford Trimotors, including those inaugurating the first transcontinental airmail flight, October 1930; Goodyear blimps; Kreider-Reisner *Challengers*; Kuhnert's homemade plane; Lockheed *Vegas*, including Wiley Post's *Winnie Mae*; Pitcairn Autogiros; Travel Airs; WACOs; and brother Walter Kuhnert's hot-air balloon.

Pilots include those who worked at various central Pennsylvania airports, including John Abiuso, Sunbury; Jesse Jones, Lancaster; Fred Nelson, Harrisburg; Pat Brooke, Penn-Harris; and Frank Wilson, Carlisle; pilots and mechanics of Beckley College Aeronautical Division; nationally known flyers and stuntmen including Albert Julian, Wiley Post, Charles Lindbergh, Billie Leonard, and many others.

MG-281 Samuel W. Kuhnert Collection: "Hanover, PA., city, etc. Exposures made on May 18, 1929."

Miscellaneous items include train, airplane and automobile accidents and other disasters photographed by Kuhnert for insurance companies; funerals; 1936 flood in the Harrisburg area; a 1932 snowstorm in Camp Hill; and portraits of Kuhnert's friends and relatives.

Motion picture films include seventeen 16mm reels in black and white and color primarily of Kuhnert's family and friends. Notable items include "A Trip Through the Clouds" showing pilot friends flying their planes, ca. 1935; U.S. Army XB-17s in flight; and the 1936 flood in Harrisburg.

MG-286
THE PENN CENTRAL RAILROAD COLLECTION
Ca. 1828-1969, Approx. 4800 cu. ft.

The Penn Central Transportation Company was created from a 1968 merger between the failing Pennsylvania and New York Central Railroads. Penn Central itself bankrupted in 1970, and today many of its facilities are maintained by Amtrak and Conrail. The collection primarily pertains to one of the nation's leading rail enterprises, the Pennsylvania Railroad Company and its subsidiaries. These records comprise administrative correspondence, minute books, stock ledgers, annual reports, general account volumes, legal materials, freight registers, blueprints and tracings, 1835-1939 (over 4,800 cu. ft.). Other materials include photographs (19 cu. ft.) arranged into three series: the General Office Library Photograph File (7.5 cu. ft.), the Conrail Mechanical Engineering Department Photograph File (6 cu. ft.), and the Penn Central Auction Photographs (5.5 cu. ft.).

The General Office Library Photograph File was donated to the State Archives in 1976. It consists of a historical reference file of Pennsylvania Railroad photographs, ca. 1850-1960, maintained by the company's Office of the Secretary at its headquarters in Philadelphia. The file grew as items were donated over the years by employees and interested persons. Photographs are primarily prints of varying size and glass lantern and film slides. Many of the prints are second generation copies of older photographs. Original items often have the photographer's identification mark on the back. Photographic firms include the Purviance Studios and Keystone Studios and such individuals as William H. Rau of Philadelphia, for a time employed by the PRR as a photographer, E. Walter Histed of Pittsburgh, R.A. Bonine of Altoona, C.W. Derstine of Lewistown, B. Hellmich and M.J. Jahelka of New York City, and many others. Also present are engravings, drawings, cartoons, postcards, newspaper clippings, magazine articles, and brochures. Many individual items, including the photographs, often have historical or explanatory information written on the reverse by the donor. A folder of letters and documents from donors filed at the end of the collection provides identification in some cases.

Arranged alphabetically, topics cover: the Adams Express Company; the Allegheny Portage Railroad; construction of PRR bridges such as Hellgate Bridge, New York City, 1917, South Bridge, Philadelphia, 1922-1923, and others; bus service; city views of Atlantic City, Philadelphia, Pittsburgh, and others; disasters such as the Johnstown Floods of 1889 and 1936, and various train wrecks and fires; historical events such as the 1877 Pittsburgh Railroad riots and moving the Liberty Bell by rail, 1915; exhibitions and expositions; docks, piers and ferries; grain elevators; hotels; steam, diesel and electrified locomotives; passenger service; railroad laborers and officials; photographs and photograph copies of paintings of PRR company presidents, 1847-1963; "piggybacking"; rail cars; railroad track construction; business, freight and ticket offices; support facilities such as shops, switches, towers, control panels and yards; snow and ice removal; PRR stations and terminals in Chicago, Harrisburg, Philadelphia (primarily Broad Street Station), Pittsburgh and smaller towns; locomotives and rolling stock; other forms of transportation such as canals, Conestoga Wagons, stagecoaches, trucks and automobiles; tunnels; and the effects of World Wars I and II on the PRR such as troop transport trains, the employment of women, and a 1918 victory parade by PRR employees in Pittsburgh.

The Conrail Mechanical Engineering Department Photograph File was acquired by the State Archives in 1981 and consists of nearly 2,000 8x10 prints, ca. 1930, primarily builders' views of locomotives and rolling stock. Interior views are sometimes included. The prints are arranged by locomotive and class car number.

The Penn Central Auction Photographs were obtained by the Pennsylvania State Archives in 1972 when Penn Central began divesting its holdings. These are primarily albums commissioned or collected by the PRR. They include:

Broad Street—PRR—West Point, by William H. Rau and C. Barrington, ca. 1890 (1 vol.). Contains twenty-six views of Philadelphia, the Broad Street Station, and scenic views in and around West Point, N.Y.

Johnstown, by R.A. Bonine (1 vol.). Contains sixteen views of the ruins of Johnstown after the Flood of 1889.

June Flood 1889—Views on the Pittsburgh Division—Accompanying General Managers Report (1 vol.). Contains twenty-five views of the ruins of Johnstown and PRR facilities therein using photographs by R.A. Bonine and possibly another photographer. The album was compiled to accompany a report on damage to PRR facilities.

J. Howard Patton Scrapbook of PRR Locomotives, 1909-1912 (1 vol.). Contains 122 nostalgic views of PRR locomotives from the 1840s to the present.

A Collection of Photographs of Locomotives Typical of Each Class on the Pennsylvania Railroad at this Date ...., PRR Motive Power Department, May 1, 1868 (1 vol.). Contains sixty-six builders views of locomotives and equipment produced at the Altoona shops.

Builders Photos of PRR Locomotives (1 vol.). Contains 123 views of locomotives, ca. 1915.

PRR Locomotives Before 1868 (1 vol.). Contains 120 views (primarily copies made ca. 1920) of early locomotives.

PRR Snow and Ice Conditions—Winter of 1944-1945 (1 vol.). Consists of 107 prints compiled by the Company showing snow and ice removal at PRR facilities in New York and Pennsylvania.

Pennsylvania Railroad Suburban Views—Pittsburgh and Baltimore Division (1 vol.). Contains 115 views, ca. 1915, of homes and residential areas near Pittsburgh including Aspinwall, Clairton, Greensburg, Irwin, Parnassus, Valley Camp, West Elizabeth and Wilkinsburg. Areas near Baltimore, Maryland, include Bowie, Brooklandville, Chase, Chattolanee, Lake, Lestra, Lutherville, Severn, Sherwood, Springfield, and Stevenson.

MG-286 Penn Central Railroad Collection: "Viaduct Trestle, Pittsburgh
Division, Johnstown Flood, June 1889," by R.A. Bonine (see p. 126).

Pennsylvania Railroad Suburban Views—Main Line (1 vol.). Contains 124
views, ca. 1915, of homes and residential areas along the PRR Main Line in
and near Philadelphia including Ardmore, Bala Cynwyd, Berwyn, Bryn
Mawr, Chestnut Hill, Croyden, Devon, Downingtown, Germantown, Green
Tree, Haverford, Lafayette, Merion, Narberth, Norristown, Overbrook,
Paoli, Phoenixville, Radnor, Rosemont, St. Davids, Strafford, Torresdale,
Villanova, Wayne and Wynnefield.

*Photographic Views on Line of the Pennsylvania-Schuylkill Valley Railroad
West of Port Clinton, Pa.* (1 vol.). Consists of forty-nine prints taken between
1884-1887 by an unknown photographer for J. N. DuBarry, Capital Superintendent of the P.S.V.R.R. Views show ruins of the Schuylkill Canal; views
of the railroad as it passes through Landingville, Schuylkill Haven, Seven
Stars, Pottsville, Mount Carbon, St. Clair, and the Atkins Pioneer Furnaces
and Diamond Drill Works at Pottsville.

William H. Rau Photograph Album, ca. 1890 (1 vol.). Contains twenty-five views of Philadelphia's Broad Street Station, and an unidentified waterfall.

Log Book of Negatives taken for the PRR including those of William H. Rau, 1887-1924 (1 vol.). Entries show negative size and numbers, subjects and date. Accompanying the log are two pamphlets, "A Catalogue of Photographic Views of the Pennsylvania Railroad," by Rau, largely a published version of the log up to 1900 made available to customers; and "Railroad Photography," 1891-1892, also by Rau, describing how his PRR photographs were made, again accompanied by a list of the above negatives. The two "Pennsylvania Railroad Suburban Views" albums noted above contain prints from negatives listed in the log.

Other photographs obtained through the Penn Central auction include those from the PRR Advertising and Publicity Department, ca. 1920-1950. Subjects cover the railroad's shops, signals, tracks, yards, locomotives, rolling stock, rights of way, industrial sites, cities along PRR lines, aerial views by Tom Hollyman, passenger services, etc. This file is currently unprocessed.

MG-298 Lucille Wilson Collection: "Single Sisters House, Linden Hall Seminary, Lititz. Easter 1881" by R. Witmer.

MG-289
GEORGE M. HART COLLECTION
Ca. 1860-1960, 1.5 cu. ft.

George Hart (b. 1919), a native of Doylestown, has been involved with railroading for most of his life. Since the 1930s he has been photographing and collecting photographs relating to railroads, especially the Reading. He was the first director of the Railroad Museum of Pennsylvania, Strasburg, 1975-1982. The Collection consists of photographs acquired by Hart and donated by him to the Pennsylvania Historical and Museum Commission. Additional materials of his are among the collections of the Railroad Museum.

Subjects include stereographic views on glass of Niagara Falls, N.Y., ca. 1860, by Platt D. Babbitt, twenty-four items; and 8x10 glass negatives of the Philadelphia and Reading Railroad, 1910-1921, by an unidentified photographer, forty-four items. Most views are numbered and dated and show Reading facilities at Mahanoy Plane, St. Clair, Cressona, Trenton Junction and other places.

MG-298
LUCILLE WILSON COLLECTION
1793-1881, .5 cu. ft.

This Collection contains photographs, prints, engravings and drawings relating to the Reverend Eugene Alexander Fruauff, Moravian minister and principal, 1838-1873, of the Linden Hall Seminary for Young Ladies in Lititz. The buildings of Linden Hall were originally the Brothers and Sisters Houses constructed by Moravians who planned and settled Lititz in the mid-eighteenth century. Lucille Wilson of Las Vegas, Nevada, donated the items to the State Archives in September 1978.

The photographs are thirteen prints of varying size, nine of which relate to Linden Hall Seminary. No negatives are present. Six are formal class portraits showing groups of students with teachers taken by "R. Wittwer, Neusalz" or New Salem. The class members are identified on the reverse in German script. All are undated but two, which bear the date of Easter, 1881. An additional two class portraits are identified as taken by "Ebberman's Photographic Gallery, Lancaster." An 1865 view of the main seminary building is by Saylor of Reading. Four other prints are undated (ca. 1880) views of Millersville Normal School, Millersville; "The Old Chapel,"

Bethlehem; the John Mann Farm near Columbia; and Sunnyside College, location unknown.

Non-photographic items include engravings of the Reverend Benjamin Latrobe, 1793; the Reverend Henry Steinhaur, no date; Governor Joseph Ritner, 1837; the church, parsonage and seminaries at Lititz, no date; the Lititz Hotel, 1849; Linden Hall, no date; floor plans of the Pennsylvania House of Representatives, 1852, and Senate Chamber, 1853; floor plans of the General Unity Synod at Herrnhut, Saxony, for 1836, 1848 and 1857. Also present are pen-and-ink drawings of the Boys Academy at Lititz, 1869, by Fruauff, a "Plan of the Turnpike from Lititz to Lancaster," 1853, by "F.F." and a pencil sketch of Eugene Fruauff, 1812. Miscellaneous items include undated engravings of the Hoerner Dairy Farm, Lancaster County, and "Partridge Hall," owned by William Stavely, Bucks County.

MG-323
LEON KARPEL COLLECTION
1920-1955, .75 cu. ft.

This Collection contains 188 halftone photographs of eighteenth-century structures in Pennsylvania, originally published in various magazines such as *American Architect and Architecture, Architectural Forum, Architectural Record*, 1920-1955. The photographs, in various sizes, have been cut from the magazines and mounted on mat board. Most subjects are structures in eastern Pennsylvania, primarily Philadelphia, though buildings in Carlisle, Harrisburg, Reading and other places are present. Subjects include interior and exterior views, schematic drawings and close-ups of unique or interesting features such as doorways, stairways and cornices. The State Archives acquired the collection in August 1979, from Leon Karpel, of Poughkeepsie, N.Y.

The Collection is arranged alphabetically by subject and includes the following structures: the Beltzhoover House, Ephraim Blaine House, Dickinson College, Carlisle Meetinghouse, Tom Moore House in Carlisle; Percy Chandler Estate, Chadds Ford; County Courthouse, Chester; Perkiomen Creek Bridge, Collegeville; St. John's Lutheran Church, Easton; John Freeman House, Freemansburg; Cliveden, Germantown; Maclay Mansion, Harrisburg; Graeme Park, Horsham; Gutman House, Hillis House, Richardson House, Newtown; Pennsbury Manor, Morrisville; John Bartram House, Belmont, Blackwell House, Cedar Grove, The Cliffs, Fairmount Waterworks, Independence Hall, Mount Pleasant, Phillips House, Powell House, St. Peter's Church, Stenton, Stocker House, Whitby Hall, Woodford,

Woodlands, Philadelphia; St. David's Church, Radnor; Trinity Lutheran Church, Mounce-Jones House, Reading; Peace Church, Shiremanstown; Donnel House, Sunbury; Augustus Lutheran Church, Trappe; Washington's Headquarters, Valley Forge; Bull House, Warwick; Hergesheimer Dower House, West Chester; Hope Lodge, Whitemarsh and Valley Inn, York.

Miscellaneous items include unidentified buildings in Allport, Crafton, Danville, and West Chester and schematic drawings of cornices, stairs, and stone laying techniques of various buildings.

MG-325
PINE STREET PRESBYTERIAN CHURCH (HARRISBURG) PHOTOGRAPHS
Ca. 1895-1925 , .3 cu. ft.

This is a collection of 176 color and black and white 3 1/4 x 4 glass lantern slides arranged as a 1920s nostalgia show of Harrisburg City area buildings and landmarks. Topics cover commercial and residential buildings, canals, railroads, parks and monuments, many of which no longer exist. Notable events in the city's history are also included. Many of these slides were copied from prints by nineteenth century photographers, such as C.S. Roshon, LeRue Lemer, William H. Rau, and others.

The Pine Street Presbyterian Church of Harrisburg obtained the slides from Harold R. Jauss and donated the collection to the State Archives in 1961. Each slide is numbered. Accompanying them is a set of 2 x 2 film slides copied from the originals.

Subjects include: John Harris Grave and Mansion; Mayor George A. Hoverter; Market Square buildings such as the Senate Hotel, the Adams Express Company Office and market sheds; other downtown buildings such as the Lochiel Hotel, the Steamboat Hotel, the Post Office Building and the Grand Opera House (includes ruins after fire, February 1, 1907; Capitol (1819), especially interior and exterior views before, during and after fire February 2, 1897; the "interim" Capitol, 1899-1900; laying of cornerstone, construction and dedication of new Capitol, 1898-1906; the Capitol Park Extension; City Waterworks; Camelback, Market Street, and Rockville Bridges; the Cumberland Valley Railroad Station and trains; Bridgeport (Lemoyne) views including President McKinley's funeral train, September 16, 1901; the Lochiel train wreck, May 11, 1905; President Lincoln's funeral train, April 22, 1865; canals and canal locks; Aviation Field, 1920; Old Home Week, October 1-7, 1905; the dedication of the Meade Detweiler Memorial; the visit of King Albert of Belgium; the floods of 1889 and 1920; and others.

MG-327 Ira J. Stouffer Collection #445: "Old Wheel and Bellows,
Springfield Furnace," ca. 1915.

MG-326
BOWERS-RAWSON PHOTOGRAPHS
Ca. 1865-1911, .3 cu. ft.

This collection contains thirty-two photographs of towns primarily in Potter County, especially Austin, Costello, and Germania, ca. 1865-1911. Most of the collection is a series of photographic postcards by an unidentified photographer of the aftermath of the September 30, 1911, flood which destroyed much of Austin and Costello. Other photographs show activities in logging camps near Galeton and Germania, various town panoramas and miscellaneous views.

Photographs vary in size and are usually mounted prints. Most items are identified on the reverse and often include genealogical information on the Rawson Family, whose ancestors appear in some of the views. The photographs were collected over many years by Vivian Rawson Bowers and Mr. and Mrs. Charles G. Rawson of Galeton, who donated the collection to the State Archives in 1980.

Subjects include:
Austin and Costello—Ruins of the Baldwin Home, Bank and Post Office, Bayless Paper and Pulp Company mill and dam, Catholic Church, City Hall, Emporium Lumber Mill and trains, Turner Street, the temporary morgue, and others.

Germania—Logging camp at Raush Place, St. Matthew's Lutheran Church, Germania Fire Company building, and an unidentified parade.

Miscellaneous items include: panoramas of Keating Summit and Watrous, and the community bands of Galeton and Westfield, all of Tioga County; the old Cross Fork Hotel fire, n.d., and others.

MG-327
IRA J. STOUFFER PHOTOGRAPHS
Ca. 1915, .3 cu. ft.

This collection contains 124 photographic postcards of historic sites and structures in Blair, Cambria, Centre, Dauphin, Franklin and Huntingdon Counties taken by Ira J. Stouffer, an Altoona resident. The cards are generally exterior views of abandoned canals, mills, churches, houses, iron furnaces, potteries, and the Portage Railroad, but also include scenic and panoramic views. Each item is numbered and identified, probably in Stouffer's own handwriting. Most are marked with his symbol "S" or stamped with his name and address on the reverse. Some items are duplicates. Little is known about Stouffer beyond these photographs. A business card filed with the postcards describes him as "a Scenic Photographer" with "historic subjects of Pennsylvania a specialty."

The postcards are arranged by county and thereunder by municipality or historic site. Subjects include:

Blair County: Altoona (Baker Mansion, Fort Curtin and Horseshoe Curve); Etna Furnace; Franklin Forge; Chimney Rocks; Springfield Furnace; and a series on the Portage Railroad extending into Cambria County and including planes, levels, bridges, tunnels and the Lemon House.

Centre County: Curtin (Eagle Iron Works and Curtin Mansion).

Dauphin County: Middletown (oldest house, Pennsylvania Canal aqueducts and St. Peter's Kierch).

Franklin County: Path Valley, Tuscarora Tunnel, High Rocks at Pen Mar, and Carrick Furnace.

Huntingdon County: Arch Spring (spring, mill, and church); Cassville (Cass and Greenland Pottery Works, Hyssong Pottery Works, Cassville Seminary and Hotel); Coleraine Forge; Elizabeth Furnace (Martin Bell Mansion and iron furnace); Greysville; Huntingdon (Standing Stone and Pulpit Rocks); Paradise Furnace; Petersburg (canal ruins, lock house, gristmills, pottery works, Sullenberger Log Cabin, and Pennsylvania Railroad Station); Warriors Mark (Porter Mansion ruins); Warrior Ridge (canal lock ruins and hydroelectric plant); Water Street; Union Furnace (Pennsylvania Railroad right of way).

MG-328
WILLIAM C. HARLEMAN PHOTOGRAPHS
Ca. 1910, .3 cu. ft.

This collection contains forty-two black and white copies of color picture postcards. The views are primarily of towns in Carbon and Schuylkill Counties and include Mauch Chunk, Lehighton, Weissport, Glen Onoko, and Tamaqua. Views usually consist of panoramas, individual streets and buildings, parks, factories and others. The original postcards are in the possession of William C. Harleman of Lehighton, who collected them over the course of several years. Harleman permitted the State Archives to copy the cards in June of 1980.

The photographs are 4x5 copy negatives with one 5x7 print for each negative. Each item is numbered and arranged alphabetically according to town. Subjects include: Pulpit Rocks, Onoko Falls and nearby picnic grounds, Glen Onoko; buildings, bridges, the community band, parks, railyards, the Lehighton/Weissport Bridge and others, Lehighton; buildings, panoramic views, the Packerton Railyards, the Switchback Railroad and others, Mauch Chunk. Miscellaneous views include slate pickers at Tamaqua and the Weissport Canal Boat Yards.

MG-329
IVAN L. CARTER COLLECTION
Ca. 1920-1938

Ivan L. Carter (1894-1971), a lifetime resident of Carlisle, was a druggist and amateur photographer occasionally hired to record community events. The State Archives received his negatives in 1980 from Donald Garlin of Palmyra, who obtained them at an estate auction.

The photographs are over 4,000 5x7 and 4x5 glass plate and film negatives dating between 1920 and 1938. Very few original prints are present. Descriptive information on the envelopes in Carter's writing often gives the negative number, date and subject. The majority were taken in and around Carlisle, and especially include Dickinson College and the Medical Field Service School (Carlisle Barracks). Views of Boiling Springs, Chambersburg, Gettysburg, Mechanicsburg, Mifflintown, Mount Holly Springs, Newton-Hamilton, Newville and Shippensburg are also present.

The images reflect typical situations employing a small town photographer. Included are interior and exterior views of buildings such as automobile dealer showrooms, bakeries, barbershops, beauty shops, cafes, a canning factory, a carpet factory, churches, dairy stores, department stores, drugstores, feed stores, fire company houses, gas stations, grocery stores, homes for the elderly, hospitals, hotels, houses, jails, libraries, music stores, a paper mill, restaurants, schools, shoe factories, theatres, and others; news events such as flower and fashion shows, holiday parades, swearing-in ceremonies of newly elected borough and county officials, fires, automobile accidents, and others; meetings, banquets and activities of social and community organizations and clubs, churches and schools including the American Legion, Future Farmers of America, Fraternal Order of Elks, the Civilian Conservation Corps, 4-H, Loyal Order of Moose, Kiwanis, Masons, the Salvation Army, Veterans of Foreign Wars, Young Men's Christian Association and Bible and Sunday School classes, Boy and Girl Scouts, garden clubs, gun clubs, civic clubs, popular orchestras, bands and others; everyday events such as birthdays, funerals, graduations, weddings, wedding anniversaries, elementary and high school plays and athletic events; people such as fishermen, firemen, mailmen, police, local politicians, ordinary residents, Carter's family, friends and others.

Notable items include the "Babes in the Woods" murder case, 1934; a Republican party rally and parade, 1934; the official opening of Hanover Street, 1934; and activities pertaining to Senator Leon Prince in Carlisle; a Wilson College Horse Show, 1934, and Penn Hall College swim teams in Chambersburg; Gettysburg College and Gettysburg High School plays and athletic events in Gettysburg; and the Silver Spring Presbyterian Church 150th Anniversary celebration in Mechanicsburg. Activities relating to Dickinson College are: commencements; proms; dances; theatre; musical bands; men's and women's athletic teams such as archery, baseball, basketball, bowling, equestrian, football, hockey, swimming, track and soccer; social and service clubs, fraternities, sororities; faculty portraits; celebrations such as founder's day, the college's 150th anniversary, 1933; the Dickinson School of Law's 100th Anniversary, 1934; Central Pennsylvania Methodist Conference, 1935, and others. Activities relating to the Medical Field Service School (Carlisle Barracks) are officers' and enlisted men's portraits; sports teams; conferences of chaplains and military surgeons; demonstrations of military equipment; Reserve Officers Training Corps and Officers Reserve Corps parades and reviews; activities in conjunction with local C.C.C. chapters and the 104th Cavalry of the Pennsylvania National Guard; visits by Assistant Secretary of War Harry Woodring, 1933, Secretary of War Dern in 1934, and Governor George Earle and U.S. Senator Joseph Guffey in 1935.

MG-335
VIOLET HARNER WISE PHOTOGRAPHS
Ca. 1945-1964, .1 cu. ft.

Violet Harner Wise (b. 1906) was a Harrisburg employee of the state for various agencies, 1930-1964. She was primarily a technical photographer for the Department of Property and Supplies. As an amateur photographer, she often spent her lunch hours recording interesting scenes and events around the city with a Super Ikonta camera given to her by a soldier returning from World War II Germany. Wise, now retired, lives in Dauphin.

The photographs, all in color, are forty-nine 5x7 prints and 35mm negatives copied from Wise's original 1 5/8 x 2 Anscochrome and Ektachrome slides. The State Archives copied the items in October of 1980. Wise retains the original slides.

The photographs are arranged by subject and include: construction of the Harvey Taylor Bridge, 1950-1951; the dismantling and removal of the Civil War Monument at Second and State Streets, 1958; the widening and repaving of Forster Street, 1950; abandoned buildings awaiting demolition, including Central High School, Reily Homestead, Nissley Mansion, ca. 1960, and miscellaneous items.

MG-347
JEAN F. GERDES PHOTOGRAPH COLLECTION
Ca. 1925-1958, .3 cu. ft.

These 188 photographs are of the life and career of James Henderson Duff, 1883-1969, especially as Governor of Pennsylvania, and United States Senator. Included with Duff are family and staff members, professional entertainers and celebrities, and state and nationally known politicians of the era. Duff, a native of Carnegie, began his career in the 1920s as a lawyer in western Pennsylvania and was a speculator in oil fields. He was State Auditor General, 1943-1946, Governor, 1947-1950, and United States Senator, 1951-1957. In the prosperous post-World War II Pennsylvania economy, "Rough Tough" Duff was known as an agressive, no-nonsense politician.

Collected over the course of Duff's career by his wife Jean T. Duff, the items are usually 8x10 prints. Most were taken by professional Harrisburg or Washington, D.C., photographers and many are from news services such as the Associated Press and United Press International. All are publicity stills or formal portraits. Many items are identified by subject and date on

MG-347 Jean F. Gerdes Photograph Collection: "Senator Duff with President Eisenhower at Public Ceremony." Probably Eisenhower Farm, ca. 1954.

the reverse. The collection was donated to the State Archives in 1981 by Duff's grandniece, Jean F. Gerdes, who appears in some of the photographs. The collection is divided into Duff's activities as governor and senator with some miscellaneous items.

Activities as governor include: inaugural ceremonies and ball, January 21, 1947; campaigning for Harry S Truman, 1948; reviewing the Pennsylvania National Guard at Fort Indiantown Gap, 1949; boarding the "Pennsylvania Week" train, 1948 and 1949, with celebrities Hedda Hopper, Alexis Smith, Robert Montgomery, and James Stewart; leisure activities such as gardening at Indiantown Gap and riding his horse, 1947-1950; lighting the Capitol Christmas Tree, 1950; and others.

Activities as United States senator: campaigning, 1950; taking the oath of office, January 18, 1951, with Vice President Alben Barkley, Senator Edward Martin, and others; at the Republican National Convention with Clare Booth Luce, and campaigning for Dwight Eisenhower, 1952; appearing on "Face the Nation" and "Meet the Press," 1953-1954; with Vice President Richard Nixon and Mrs. Nixon at Independence Hall, ca. 1954; at the National Republican Women's Conferences with Senator Margaret Chase Smith and others, 1954-1955; as a member of various senate subcommittees, 1953-1956; speaking against atomic bomb spies, 1952; visiting Erie, 1955; observing National Marine Corps Day, January 17, 195[?]; performing charity work, 1956; receiving awards and honorary degrees, 1951-1955; attending various functions with Senators John Kennedy, Thomas P. O'Neill, Hugh Scott, Everett Dirksen, Hubert Humphrey, Robert Taft, Barry Goldwater, Henry Cabot Lodge, Representative John McCormick, State Senator M. Harvey Taylor and others; meeting celebrities Sophie Tucker, Walter Cronkite, and others, 1954-1955; traveling on the inaugural trip of the "Pennsy Aerotrain," 1956; and participating in a Senate hearing on corruption in the Teamsters Union, 1958.

Miscellaneous items include formal portraits, ca. 1925-1955, and as state auditor general, 1946.

MG-354
OLD ECONOMY VILLAGE COLLECTION
Ca. 1866-1960, 5.5 cu. ft.

Old Economy Village is a Pennsylvania Historical and Museum Commission site in Ambridge. It preserves the original grounds and buildings of the Harmony Society, a religious community founded by a German mystic, Father George Rapp, in 1805. The Collection is photographic prints and lantern slides amassed over the years by the staff of the historic site and consists of three groups:

B.G. Way Lantern Slides, 1891, seventy-seven items, showing views taken in September of that year of the buildings, gardens, and members of the dwindling Harmonists. Each item has "B.G. Way, Brooklyn, N.Y." on the mount and individual subject identifications. Views show the church, tavern, houses, gardens and grotto, hop pickers, Harmony trustees Jacob Henrici and John Duss, and other Society members. Some items are hand colored.

J.M. Tate Lantern Slides, ca. 1890-1919, showing views taken by Tate of Old Economy buildings, grounds and people, including Jacob Henrici; Harmony in Beaver County; and New Harmony, Indiana. A resident of Sewickley and an amateur photographer, Tate took these over the course of several years, eventually developing them into a slide lecture. He had the text of the lecture printed into a pamphlet in 1925, which is found among the administrative records of the PHMC (see RG-13). Some items are hand colored.

Historical Photograph Collection, ca. 1866-1950, contains over 1,000 photographic prints, postcards, newsclippings, engravings, etc., collected by the staff of Old Economy Village. Each item is numbered and arranged numerically. Subjects include portraits of prominent and unidentified Harmonists, including Jacob Henrici, John Duss, and their families, views of buildings and grounds at Old Economy, Harmony and New Harmony. Notable items show J.S. Coxey's Army as it passed through Economy, 1894; the 1924 Old Economy Centennial; and the Economy Band.

MG-359
104th CAVALRY (PNG) VETERANS ASSOCIATION COLLECTION
Ca. 1914-1975, 2.5 cu. ft.

The 104th Cavalry, Pennsylvania National Guard, was originally organized in 1874 as the Eighth Infantry Regiment. It was also known as the Governor's Troop, an honor guard for ceremonial events surrounding the governor. Mustered into federal service during the Spanish-American War and World Wars I and II, the unit regularly held training at Colebrook and Indiantown Gap Military Reservations. In 1921 it was redesignated as the 104th Cavalry. The 104th Veterans Association, formed in 1966, acquired materials from various members and in turn donated them to the State Archives in 1983.

The collection contains newsclippings, pamphlets, certificates and other documents (.5 cu. ft.), but the bulk is photographic prints (2 cu. ft.).

Individual donations include:
Robert Cowan Collection of photographs relating to his World War I career, 1917-1919. Subjects include a military funeral in Harrisburg, ca. 1917.

Clyde Fisher Motion Picture Films of the Governor's Troop, 1935-1936. Fisher was an officer in the Troop. Scenes show the troop marching in Governor George Earle's inaugural parade. Two reels, 8mm, silent, black and white, 200 feet.

John Putt Motion Picture Films of activities of Troop K, 1938-1941. Views show the cavalry in camp, during mounted reviews, giving demonstrations at a mounted pistol course, at Governor Arthur James's inaugural parade, and induction into federal service for World War II. Five reels, 16mm, silent, black and white, 2,000 feet.

Miscellaneous photographs show the Governor's Troop at various locales; the 104th on and off duty during a 1922 coal strike at Heilwood and the 1936 flood in the Harrisburg area; annual encampments at Colebrook, Indiantown Gap, City Island (Harrisburg), and out of state, 1922-1980; views of Marcay, France, 1943; and various reunion banquets held by the veterans association after 1966.

MG-360
STATE POLICE MEMORABILIA
1906-PRESENT, 1 cu. ft.

A group of acquisitions arranged by donor, usually retired officers, relating to their careers with the State Police. The collections are primarily photographs, but also contain newsclippings, pamphlets, documents and other ephemera.

Collections include:
A.C. Ayers Photographs of a 1936 State Police Rodeo, mounted troopers at a Harrisburg Parade, n.d., and a ca. 1935 silk mill strike in Lancaster, nineteen items.

Philip Doddridge Photograph Albums showing his career with Troop A, Greensburg, 1911-1920, two volumes. Includes scenes of barracks life, leisure activities, drills, parades and Doddridge and fellow officers on assignments, such as a typhoid quarantine, 1912; the 50th Gettysburg Reunion, 1913; strikes in Tarentum, Erie and Wilkes-Barre; floods in Erie and Brownsville; robberies and others.

Lawrence L. Priar Collection relating to his career with various troops and as a deputy state fire marshall, 1908-1961, .3 cu. ft. Includes a photograph of President Theodore Roosevelt with members of Troop B, Wyoming, 1908.

Ray L. Reck Collection relating to his career with Troop A, Greensburg, Pennsylvania Motor Police, 1937-1939, fourteen items. Includes Reck at the 75th Gettysburg Reunion, 1938.

Miscellaneous items include portraits of troopers killed in the line of duty, ca. 1925-1930, five items; and a motion picture film of a parade at the tenth anniversary of the Pennsylvania Highway Patrol, 1933, 16mm, 400 ft.

MG-362
DENISE WEBER PHOTOGRAPHS
1906, 35 items

The Vinton Colliery Company operated bituminous coal mines near Vintondale, Cambria County. In the summer of 1906, it opened #6 mine and constructed coke works and other support facilities. The operations were observed by John Huth, a Vintondale resident who was a mining engineer and later assistant superintendent for the company. Huth either took or acquired photographs of the work in progress.

The photographs are thirty-three 5x7 and two 4x5 glass plate negatives. No original prints are present. PHMC contact reference prints were made in December 1983 and are contained in one loose-leaf binder.

There are no original identifications but captions were supplied by the donors. Huth's granddaughter Denise Weber of Indiana, Pa., and daughter Aileen Michelbacher of Vintondale presented the plates to the State Archives in November 1983 in memory of John and Mabel Huth.

Subjects often are images taken from the same viewpoint before, during and after construction of the entrance to the #6 mine (no interior views), #6 powerhouse and ammonia plant, coal washery and coke ovens. Non-construction views include town views, the Pennsylvania Railroad spur and dinkey, trestles and tipples, company offices, a Vintondale town plan, and a map of the Vinton Colliery Company holdings.

MG-367
LAWRIE AND GREEN COLLECTION
1922-1960, 10 cu. ft.

M. Edwin Green (1897-1985) of Harrisburg and Ritchie Lawrie (1890-1962) of Pittsburgh teamed in 1922 to create the architectural firm of Lawrie and Green. The firm designed several hundred buildings in central Pennsylvania and elsewhere in the state, notable among them the North Office Building and the William Penn Memorial Museum and Archives Building in Harrisburg, and the Hunt Botanical Library in Pittsburgh. Based in Harrisburg, the firm disbanded in 1972. The Green Family donated the collection to the State Archives, 1984-1985, upon M. Edwin Green's death.

The bulk of the collection is the artist's conceptual design boards and schematic layouts for the William Penn Memorial Museum and Archives, ca. 1956-1960 (7.5 cu. ft.). Photographs are primarily 8x10 black and white and color glossy prints and 2x2 color slides (1.5 cu. ft.). Subjects are either artist's designs or the completed building taken by commercial photographers hired by the firm. These often have the photographer's logo stamped on the reverse and include the J. Horace McFarland Company of Harrisburg, Charles E. Burd of Lancaster, Lawrence S. Williams of Pittsburgh, and others.

Other photographs are loosely grouped by type or name of building and include: Harrisburg Area: Camp Curtin Junior High School, Central Y.M.C.A., Dauphin County Courthouse, Dauphin County Prison, Grace United Methodist Church, Harris Ferry Tavern, Harrisburg Hospital, Harrisburger Hotel, North Office Building, Pennsylvania Farm Show Building, Mary Sachs Building and Zembo Temple.

Buildings elsewhere in the state include: elementary, junior and senior high schools in Carlisle, Chambersburg, Coatesville, Columbia, Duncannon, Hazleton, Jersey Shore, Lewisburg, Lewistown, Lock Haven, Muncy, New Cumberland, Saltsburg, Selinsgrove, Warren, Williamsport, and others; hospitals in Lewisburg, Lewistown, Montrose, Sunbury, Wayne, Wellsboro, Williamsport and others; municipal buildings in Lock Haven and Warren; and miscellaneous buildings such as at Bloomsburg State Teachers College; Hunt Library of the University of Pittsburgh, the Lock Haven Bell Telephone Building, the Methodist Children's Home, Shiremanstown, and the Williamsport Y.M.C.A.

MG-376
IRENE BRESSLER PHOTOGRAPHS
1860-1905, .75 cu. ft.

Irene Bressler (1891-1969), lifelong resident of Harrisburg, was an organist for several area churches. Between 1942 and 1969 she donated photographs and other items to the Historical and Museum Commission, including a stereo viewer now in the collections of the State Museum. Little is known of her personal life.

The collection, all prints, is arranged by type of subject. The bulk is seventy unidentified cabinet card portraits of adults, children and family groups. The following photographers, mostly Pennsylvanians, are identified on them: Allen, Pottsville; Bell, Wilkes-Barre; W.S. Capwell, Bloomsburg; Carlin, Atlantic City, N.J.; Clark, Wilkes-Barre; Comwell, Williamsport; R. Dabb, Shenandoah; Dockeweiler, Girardville; E.F. Eaton, Harrisburg; Eisenman, New York, N.Y., Eisinger, no city given; Krigbaum, Shamokin; Lee, Danville; LeRue Lemer, Harrisburg; Lovejoy, Philadelphia; Masters,

Princeton, N.J.; McCollin, Ashland; Miller, Ashland; S.L. Miller, Lykens; Musser, Harrisburg; J.C. Patrick, Williamstown; Porter, Connellsville; Potter, Philadelphia; J.W. Riche, Shamokin; J.F. Ryder, Cleveland, Ohio; Scheirer, Mahanoy City; Smith, Lykens; J.H. Smith, Newark. N.J.; C.H. Snively, Millersburg; Thomas, Shamokin; Trevaskis, Hazleton; and Tyson and Son, Philadelphia.

Identified items are three prints of varying size relating to Frank Durbin, a Lykens lawyer, ca. 1888, including a graduation class at Dickinson Seminary, Williamsport, a Lutheran Sunday School Class at Lykens, and a Durbin Family Portrait by H.E. Gerdom of Lykens; five 3x3 views ca. 1905 of the Dauphin County Courthouse, State Library and Museum and Paxton Church at Harrisburg by an unidentified photographer; one undated cabinet card signed by J.N. Choate of Northern Arapahoe Chiefs at the Carlisle Indian School.

Photographs unrelated to Pennsylvania, but of interest include two undated 4x7 views of Guthrie, Oklahoma, by Mitchell and DeGroff's Pioneer Photo Studio and one 4x7 view of Texado Park in Boulder, Colorado, 1899, by J.B. Sturtevant; and undated series of thirty-three 3x4 views by an unidentified photographer of camps of Apache, Commanche, Sioux, Crow, Shawnee and Umatilla (Oregon) Indians, gold placer mining at Helena, Mont., Old Faithful Geyser at Yellowstone Park, Niagara Falls, N.Y., a waterfall in Wisconsin; six cartes-de-visite of Generals Grant, Sherman, Burnside, Foster, Private James Fisk, Jr. and Italian opera soprano Pauline Lucca; two undated prints ca. 1890 of the cast of an unidentified theatre melodrama, plus other miscellaneous items.

MG-377
JOHN ENMAN COLLECTION
Ca. 1960, .5 cu. ft.

While a geography student at the University of Pittsburgh, John Enman (b. 1921) photographed the dying coal and coke industry in southwestern Pennsylvania. Some views were used to illustrate his 1962 Ph.D. dissertation, "The Relation of Coal Mining and Coke Making to the Distribution of Population Agglomerations in the Connellsville (Pa.) Beehive Coke Region." Dr. Enman thereafter held a teaching position at Bloomsburg State College, Bloomsburg, where he retired in 1984.

The photographs are 454 3x5 prints made from 35mm negatives taken by Dr. Enman, probably between 1959 and 1960. The prints were donated to the State Archives in 1967. Dr. Enman retains the original negatives. The prints are unlabelled, but grouped in envelopes containing identification. All views are towns, mines, or coke ovens in Westmoreland or Fayette Counties and include: Alicia (Southwest #1 & 2 Mines), Alverton, Baggaley, Beatty, Bridgeport Dam and Waterworks, Brinkerton, Butte, Calumet, Carpentertown, Central, Collier, Connellsville, Continental #2 Mine, Davidson, Dorothy, Dunbar, Empire (Drift Mine), Hays, Hecla, Hostetter, Humphrey, Juniata, Laughead, Leisenring, Lemont, Mammoth #1 Mine, Marguerite, Monarch, Mosewood, Mount Braddock, Mount Pleasant, Mutual, Norvelt, Pleasant Unity, Phillips, Oliver, Oliphant Furnace, Owensville, Saint Vincent, Standard Slope, Summit, Tarrs, Trauger, Trotter, United #1 & 2 Mines, Uniontown, West Overton, Whitney, Wynn, Youngstown, York Run, and unidentified.

Also included are seven 16mm 100 ft. color motion picture films taken by Enman in 1967 of the last cokemaking operations at Alicia, Leckrone, Laughead and other areas; and United Mine Workers of America agreements between Districts 3, 4 and 5 and various coal companies, 1934, 1941 and 1945-1948, five pamphlets.

MG-380
MATTIE EDWARDS HEWITT PHOTOGRAPHS
1925-1945, 1.0 cu. ft.

Mattie Edwards Hewitt (?-1956), a St. Louis native, operated a free lance photography business in New York City from the 1920s until her death. She specialized in photographing residences of the wealthy in the eastern United States. Her prints were sold usually directly to the property owners, newspapers or the many domestic and gardening magazines which were becoming popular. Hewitt prints have appeared in *Garden Magazine*, *House and Garden*, *House Beautiful*, the *New York Times*, *New York Evening Post*, and many others. She often collaborated with her nephew Richard Averill Smith, (?-1971), who later became city photographer of New York. Little is known of her early life beyond a marriage to photographer Arthur Hewitt, whom she divorced in 1909, and a partnership with Frances Benjamin Johnston, a Washington, D.C., photographer.

Hewitt's photographs and negatives were donated to the Nassau County (New York) Library and Museum in 1971 by the executors for Richard Averill Smith. Subjects pertaining to Pennsylvania were separated and given to the Historical and Museum Commission shortly thereafter. The photographs are 395 8x10 prints and 154 8x10 film negatives. All subjects are interior or exterior views of buildings and landscaping. Some negatives match the prints. All negative envelopes and prints are identified on the reverse with negative number, subject and whether taken by Hewitt or Smith. Most subjects are undated, but all seem to date between 1925 and 1945. Sometimes the building or landscape architect's name and the publication ordering prints are given. A numerical index to the prints prepared by the State Archives is present.

Structures are arranged alphabetically by name of owner and include: the Baum Family House in Perkasie; Biddle Family "Inver House" near Philadelphia; C. Hugh Blair House in Mt. Lebanon; William Bodine House, Villanova; William Carnill House "Hilltop" in Rydal Meeting; J.H. Clothier, Jr. House "Sunnybrook Farm" in Radnor; A.C. Dyer House in Mt. Lebanon; George W. Elkins' "Chelton House" in Elkins Park; Robert Glendenning House in Chestnut Hill; Frazier Harris House in Chestnut Hill; L.G. Huntley House in Pittsburgh; Henry S. Jeanes House "Langwell" in Devon; O.F. Knight House in Pittsburgh; Horatio G. Lloyd House in Haverford Meeting; Longvue Country Club in Pittsburgh; Granville Montgomery House "Wynnewood" in Montgomery County; H.C. Moran House in Mt. Lebanon; Samuel Morris House in Chestnut Hill; John S. Murray House in

MG-380 Mattie Edwards Hewitt Photographs #21232: Grey Towers, home of Gifford Pinchot, ca. 1935.

Pittsburgh; E.F. Newbold House in Chestnut Hill; Benjamin Franklin Pepper House in Chestnut Hill; Gifford Pinchot House "Grey Towers" in Pike County; Harold F. Pitcairn House in Bryn Athyn; Henry Rea House "Farm Hill" in Sewickley Heights; Wharton Sinkler House in Elkins Park; Edward Stotesbury Houses "Whitemarsh Hall" in Montgomery County, "El Mira Sol" in Palm Beach, Florida and "Wingwood" in Bar Harbor, Maine; Joseph N. Snellenburg House in Philadelphia; C.E. Ufer House in Pittsburgh; Joseph Widener House "Wynnewood Hall" in Elkins Park; George Willing, Jr. House in Chestnut Hill and Alexander Van Rensselaer House "Camp Hill Hall" in Fort Washington.

MG-383
LELAND H. BULL COLLECTION
1955-1974, 2.2 cu. ft.

Leland Hudson Bull (b. 1913), a native of Waterston, New York, graduated from the Pennsylvania State College in 1937 and was for many years a Centre County agricultural agent. Between 1955-1958 he served Governor George Leader as Deputy Secretary of Agriculture. From 1955 to 1963 he was assistant director of the cooperative extension service at Penn State. In January 1963 newly elected Governor William Scranton appointed him Secretary of Agriculture, a post he held until 1970. Now retired, Bull lives in State College.

The collection consists of ten scrapbooks containing newsclippings, letters, proclamations, invitations, photographs, programs and other memorabilia relating to Bull's career between 1955 and 1970. Most photographs are 8x10 publicity stills taken by various news services, especially the Department of Agriculture Press Office. Some items are in color.

Subjects show Bull giving speeches to such organizations as the State Grange, 4-H Clubs, Future Farmers of America, Kiwanis Clubs and others; crowning poultry, livestock, and other agriculture queens; attending bill signing ceremonies of agriculture-related legislation with Governors Leader, Scranton and Shafer; officiating events at the Pennsylvania Farm Show, Penn State's Little International Livestock Exposition, the National Plowing Contest held at Hershey in 1958 and 1968, state plowing contests, and county fairs; posing with Department of Agriculture officials, other state government officials, and with Earl Butz, U.S. Secretary of Agriculture, and many other activities. Also included are signed portrait photographs from William Scranton and Raymond Shafer.

MG-385
WALTER BENSON PHOTOGRAPHS
1955-1985, .5 cu. ft.

Walter Benson (1919-1987), a New York City native, moved to the Harrisburg area in the 1950s. He was for twenty-five years chief of the photography section at Olmsted Air Force Base in Middletown. As part of a project for a University of Oklahoma bachelor's degree in liberal studies, he began around 1960 photographing the Pennsylvania countryside using a Hasselblad camera, often with a super wide lens.

The photographs are nearly 2,000 2x2 negatives of south central Pennsylvania towns, farms and rural areas, usually taken from artistic angles. Some New Jersey locales are included. The negatives are arranged in envelopes bearing descriptive information in Benson's hand. Benson donated the negatives to the State Archives in 1986.

Subjects include rural views in Adams, Berks, Cumberland, Dauphin, Lancaster, Lebanon, Perry and York Counties, especially along U.S. and state routes and the Pennsylvania Turnpike. The views are undated and loosely identified barns, farm houses, churches, cemeteries and other buildings, often abandoned and in ruins. Views of towns or scenic areas include: Amity Hall, Annville, the Daniel Boone Homestead, Dan-D-Orchard Village, Dauphin Narrows, Elizabethtown, Enola Railyards, Ephrata Cloister, Fort Hunter, Gettysburg town and battlefield, Girty's Notch, Grantville, Halifax, Harrisburg, Hershey, Hummelstown, Indiantown Gap, Lancaster, Lebanon, Lewistown, Linglestown, Middletown, Monroe Valley, Olmsted Air Force Base, Pennsylvania Farm Museum, Peters Mountain, Railroad Museum of Pennsylvania, Rockville Bridge, Steelton, Summerdale, Union Deposit, Wellsville, Wertzville, and the William Penn Memorial Museum. Notable items include Amish at Strasburg; scenic views of the Susquehanna and Juniata Rivers, and Conodoguinet Creek near the West Shore Country Club, Camp Hill; the Hershey Chocolate Co. factory; and the State Capitol.

MG-401 Delaware and Hudson Railway Company Collection: #5158 "New Turntable, Carbondale, PA — Moved Under Own Power 10:37 a.m., 3-22-26."

MG-401
DELAWARE AND HUDSON RAILWAY COMPANY COLLECTION
1887-1959, 11.2 cu. ft.

The Delaware and Hudson Railroad grew out of the Delaware and Hudson Canal Company, formed in 1825. By 1829 it was utilizing locomotives to supplement canal travel, the most famous being the "Stourbridge Lion." By the late nineteenth century the D & H had rail lines throughout northeastern Pennsylvania and New York. Today it is part of Guilford Transportation Industries, Inc., of Massachussetts. The Collection is 4 cu. ft. of assessment reports and printed histories, and 7.2 cu. ft. of photographs. These materials were donated in 1970 by the Company's main offices in Albany, N.Y.

The photographs are over 3,800 8x10 prints by staff, ca. 1915-1944, of D & H locomotives and rolling stock. Most are mounted on a card containing the negative number, date, locomotive or car number and other information. Locomotive images are usually builders' photos, showing overall views, and detailed views of important features. Construction views are also present. Rolling stock images are similar. The prints are arranged by locomotive or car number. Not all D & H locomotives and rolling stock are present.

Subjects include steam and electric locomotives, baggage cars, box cars, business cars, dining cars, dump cars, gondolas, hoppers, horse cars, lounge cars, mail cars, milk cars, passenger cars, suburban cars, and miscellaneous rolling stock. Also present are views of a reproduction of the "Stourbridge Lion"; construction of a roundhouse turntable at Carbondale, 1926; explosions and wrecks; a 1915 equipment inventory; and others.

MG-402
CAHILL/UPI PHOTOGRAPHS
1954-1975, 10 cu. ft.

Phadrig "Pat" Cahill of Camp Hill was a photographer for United Press International's central Pennsylvania region, 1954-1975. His prints were sent by UPI telephoto to appropriate newspapers throughout the state and country, dramatizing the news events of the area. The photographs are over 6,000 7x9 and 8x10 prints, each bearing on the front UPI's code, date and an extended typewritten caption by Cahill. The reverse often contains additional information. The prints are arranged by year and thereunder by subject.

The original negatives are retained by UPI. Use of these prints is subject to the U.S. Copyright Law.

Notable topics cover: **1954** - President and Mrs. Eisenhower rehabilitating their Gettysburg farmhouse and receiving visitors; George Leader's gubernatorial campaign; Alger Hiss's release from the federal prison at Lewisburg. **1955** - President Eisenhower at Camp David and his subsequent heart attack; Governor Leader honoring Jonas Salk for his development of a polio vaccine. **1956** - Presidential candidates Adlai Stevenson and Estes Kefauver campaigning; Vice President Richard Nixon campaigning for reelection. **1957** - Governor Leader with Harry S Truman at a Democratic fundraiser. **1959** - Governor David Lawrence's inaugural ceremonies; Poet Carl Sandburg's visit to Gettysburg; the Knox Mine Disaster. **1960** - Presidential candidates John F. Kennedy and Richard Nixon campaigning. **1962**

- President Kennedy attending a Democratic fund raiser with Governor Lawrence; Vice President Lyndon Johnson visiting the Pennsylvania State University; Dwight Eisenhower with Governor-elect William Scranton; the National Governors' Conference at Hershey; the activities of U.S. Senator Hugh Scott. **1963** - a Professional Golf Association tournament at Hershey with Arnold Palmer, Gary Player and Jack Nicklaus; ceremonies at the one hundredth anniversary of the Battle of Gettysburg; President Kennedy dedicating "Grey Towers," Gifford Pinchot's home, as a national landmark. **1964** - Barry Goldwater and Lyndon Johnson campaigning for president; Governor Scranton seeking the Republican nomination for president; Lady Bird Johnson dedicating a building at Wilkes College, Wilkes-Barre. **1965** - the Pennsylvania legislature investigation hearings on State Police corruption; Governor Scranton honoring astronaut Charles "Pete" Conrad; the retirement of Pennsylvania State University football coach "Rip" Engle and his replacement by Joe Paterno; U.S. House Minority Leader Gerald Ford visiting Eisenhower at Gettysburg; reapportioning Pennsylvania House and Senate districts; President Johnson visiting Job Corps Trainees at Catoctin Center, Md.; Chester County Committee for Freedom Now members at a sit-in at the Governor's Office. **1966** - Vice President Hubert Humphrey campaigning for Milton Shapp; activities of the Pennsylvania Council of Republican Women; the Miss America Pageant, Atlantic City, N.J.; President Johnson visiting the Dallastown Centennial celebration; Raymond Shafer and Robert Casey campaigning for governor; President Johnson visiting Fort Campbell, Ky.; the kidnapping of Peggy Ann Bradnick in Shade Gap; groundbreaking for the Hershey Medical Center; activities of U.S. Senator Richard Schweiker. **1967** - the State Constitutional Convention; visits to Pennsylvania by U.S. Senator Edward Kennedy and Michigan Governor George Romney; Teamster President James Hoffa at the Federal Prison in Lewisburg; Governor Raymond Shafer's inaugural ceremonies. **1968** - Governor and Mrs. Shafer moving into the new Governor's Home in Harrisburg; Presidential hopefuls George Wallace, Hubert Humphrey, Richard Nixon and Spiro Agnew campaigning; Senator Edward Kennedy campaigning for his brother, Robert; filming the movie "The Molly Maguires" at Eckley Miners' Village. **1969** - the parents of Mary Jo Kopechne stopping the exhumation of their daughter's body; Vice President Agnew visiting Governor Shafer. **1970** - Pennsylvania State University students protesting campus policies; Governor Shafer dedicating the "Keystone Shortway" (Interstate 80); demonstrations at the State Capitol by the National Welfare Rights Organization; West German Chancellor Willy Brandt visiting Camp David. **1971** - James Hoffa's release from Lewisburg Penitentiary; removing "squatters" from land cleared for the Tocks Island Dam; protests against the erection of a tourist observation tower at Gettysburg; Vietnam War protestors burning draft cards in Bethlehem; convicted Johnson aide Bobby Baker entering the Federal Prison at Lewisburg; Governor Milton Shapp's inaugural activities. **1972** - the Reverends Daniel and Philip Berrigan and the trial of the Harrisburg Seven; the first million dollar winners in the Pennsylvania Lottery; disaster and cleanup from Hurricane Agnes; the presidential election campaign with Hubert Humphrey, Pat Nixon, George McGovern, Sargent Shriver, and Edmund Muskie; Jane Fonda supporting the Indochina Peace Campaign; ratification of the Equal Rights Amendment to the U.S. Constitution by the Pennsylvania legislature; writer Ralph Ginzburg entering the Federal Prison at Lewisburg; the National Governors' Conference at White Sulphur Springs, W.Va. **1973** - Heisman trophy winner John Cappelletti; changing the speed limit to 55 mph; Vice President Gerald Ford speaking to a joint meeting of the Pennsylvania General Assembly; construction of the Gettysburg Battlefield Tower; Pennsylvania House investigations into State Police and Liquor Control Board corruption; boxer Muhammad Ali at his Deer Lake training camp; State workers protesting the legislature's failure to pass a budget. **1974** - Governor Shapp and Drew Lewis running for election; Governor Shapp at a House Committee hearing on State contract policies; Watergate conspirator Jeb Stuart Magruder entering the Federal Prison at Lewisburg. **1975** - Vietnamese refugees arriving for processing at Fort Indiantown Gap; Governor Shapp establishing the Commission for Women; Governor Shapp's second inaugural ceremonies; and George McGovern visiting the State Farm Show.

Subjects common to all years include: airplane, automobile and train accidents; bank and other robberies; beauty pageants, especially the Miss Pennsylvania Pageant; activities of charities and other community organizations; Hershey Bears hockey games; mining disasters; the Little League World Series in Williamsport; the Pennsylvania Farm Show; activities by the Pennsylvania National Guard at Fort Indiantown Gap; the Philadelphia Eagles football team at their Hershey training camp; the Pocono 500 automobile race; Pennsylvania State University basketball, football and wrestling; annual picnics of the Jim Smith Society; and the Washington Redskins football team at its Carlisle training camp.

MG-413
JOHN W. ROSHON PHOTOGRAPHS
Ca. 1865-1920, .5 cu. ft.

John William Roshon (1864-1955) was a leading Harrisburg portrait photographer at the turn of the twentieth century. He was apprenticed to his father Christian S. Roshon, who operated landscape and portrait studios in Harrisburg and many other central Pennsylvania locations ca. 1860-1900.

The bulk of the collection is cabinet card portraits of Roshon Family members made by J.W. Roshon, with a few cartes-de-visite by his father. Most are unidentified. Items of note include Roshon's experiments with naturalistic photography on himself and family members; and photographs of his attempt to build and fly an airplane around 1906.

Also included are letters, school reports, etc., of J.W.'s wife Mary Feehrer and their daughter Dorinda.

The collection was obtained in 1988 from a local antiques dealer.

MG-416
AERO SERVICE COMPANY PHOTOGRAPHS
Ca. 1926-1948, over 4,000 items

Begun in 1919 and based in Philadelphia, the Aero Service Company was a pioneer and world leader in aerial photography and photogrammetry. Its director was Virgil I. Kauffman, a World War I veteran pilot who joined the

MG-416 Aero Service Company Photographs #12227:
"Center City Philadelphia, April 1930."

company in 1924. Under Kauffman's tutelage, the company obtained lucrative government and private contracts, the most notable with the United States Geological Survey and the Tennessee Valley Authority to undertake some of the first aerial surveys of the country. The firm's photographers travelled throughout America and abroad.

Kauffman retained the original negatives until his death in 1985. Thereafter, his survivors permitted the dispersion of the company's negatives to appropriate historical agencies throughout the country. The Pennsylvania State Archives received those pertaining to Pennsylvania in 1988.

The bulk of the collection is nearly 2,200 glass plate and film negatives in varying sizes, usually 8 x 10, 7 1/2 x 9 or 9 x 9, roughly dated between 1926 and 1939. There are very few original prints present. All are oblique aerial views primarily of the Philadelphia area and Pennsylvania, New York and New Jersey towns. They are arranged numerically and feature factories, businesses, individual homes, housing developments, golf courses, sports arenas, etc.

Philadelphia views include: Benjamin Franklin Parkway, Boulevard Airport, Broad Street Station, Byberry Hospital, Center City, Convention Hall, Disston Saw Works, Fairmount Park, Franklin Field, Germantown Hospital, Glenwood Housing Project, Hill Creek Housing Project, Logan Circle, Mount Sinai Cemetery, Patco Field, Philadelphia Museum of Art, Reading Terminal, Richardson Mint Plant, Rittenhouse Square, Roosevelt Boulevard, Sears, Roebuck & Co., Shibe Park, Tasker Housing Project, Temple University, Wanamaker's Department Store, West Philadelphia High School, Westinghouse Electric Company, and many others.

Towns include: Allentown, Ardmore, Bethlehem, Bristol, Bryn Athyn, Bryn Mawr, Buckhill, Chadds Ford, Chambersburg, Chester, Conshohocken, Coatesville, Columbia, Delaware Water Gap, Easton, Exton, Franklin, Hatboro, Jenkintown, Lancaster, Langhorne, Lansdowne, Lebanon, Marcus Hook, Merion, Muncy, New Hope, Norristown, Paoli, Perkasie, Pocono Manor, Pottstown, Plymouth Meeting, Radnor, Reading, Scranton, Skytop, Spring Grove, Stroudsburg, Torresdale, Tullytown, Upper Darby, Valley Forge, Wayne, Washington Crossing, West Chester, Williamsport, Yardley and York.

Notable events include the S.S. *Morro Castle* Fire, 1934, the 1936 Johnstown Flood, the 1938 Army-Navy Game, the inauguration of Governor Arthur James, 1939, and the construction of Graterford Prison.

Out of state views include Camden, Flemington, Princeton, and Trenton, New Jersey; and Staten Island, New York.

Also included is a series of roughly 1,800 6 1/2 x 8 1/2 glass plate negatives of an aerial survey, apparently of areas impacted by the construction of the Pennsylvania Turnpike, ca. 1939-1948. This file is unprocessed.

MG-419
UNITED STATES VIEW COMPANY PHOTOGRAPHS
Ca. 1890-1901, 64 items

The U.S. View Company was an itinerant photography company based in Richfield, Juniata County. It was formed by Henry and Newton Graybill and Ellsworth Garman around 1890 and disbanded in 1901. Company photographers traveled throughout the East and especially Pennsylvania offering to produce views of interesting sites for a fee. Their most common view was a family in front of their home.

The collection is sixty-four photographic prints, mostly 7 1/2 x 9 1/2, fixed on a decorated card mount. Nearly all are unidentified family groups posed in front of a rural farmstead, although school groups are also present. Most have a company negative number on the reverse. Only a few identify family and location, and these are of rural hamlets in Bedford and Somerset Counties.

A numerical listing prepared by State Archives staff is present. The collection was donated to the State Archives in 1989 by Martha Graybill, a descendant. Other U.S. View Company photographs are among the collections of the Library Company of Philadelphia.

MG-425
EBASCO ENVIRONMENTAL AERIAL VIEWS
Ca. 1980-1985

The Ebasco Environmental Company of Sacramento, Calif., conducted an analysis of a utility pipeline project done by the Texas Eastern Corporation in the early 1980s. Part of this analysis included an aerial survey of counties along the southern border of Pennsylvania.

The views are 108 enlarged (22 1/2 x 24) aerial images of Adams, Bedford, Chester, Fayette, Franklin, Fulton, Greene, Lancaster, Somerset and York Counties. The scales is 1:500 ft. The pipeline is delineated on each sheet with black tape. Captions giving mileposts are also affixed to the images. Arrangement is alphabetical by county.

Ebasco donated the images to the State Archives in 1990.

OTHER COLLECTIONS
OF NOTE

These are Manuscript Groups composed primarily of documents. They contain very few photographs or other illustrative materials, but those which are present are worthy of note.

MG-7 Military Manuscripts Collection - includes several cartes-de-visite of Civil War soldiers from Pennsylvania regiments.

MG-8 Pennsylvania Collection (Miscellaneous) - contains photographs of the Keating-Sloan Family of Washington, Pa., area, ca. 1850-1939 (includes some cased photographs); artist Violet Oakley, ca. 1940; the Hocker Family of Carlisle (with allied Brandt and Betz families), 1851-1954; historian Albert Cook Myers, 1911-1946; the Frank S. Brown Family of the Williamsport area, 1882-1896; a pamphlet "Pictorial Carlisle," by the Mooreland Land Company, ca. 1900; a carte-de-visite of Col. T.D. Greenawalt, ca. 1863; and Richard Weiand photographs of activities of a Civilian Conservation Corps Camp near Huntingdon, ca. 1935.

MG-9 Pennsylvania Writers Collection - contains photographs of songwriters Stephen Foster (copy prints) and Harry T. Burleigh, a writer of Negro spirituals, ca. 1920.

MG-11 Map Collection - includes lithographs and engravings, especially "Bird's Eye" or panoramic views of Pennsylvania cities and towns, largely by T.M. Fowler, ca. 1870-1910; maps and atlases sometimes containing engravings or photographs of individual buildings, farms, etc., ca. 1820-present.

MG-16 Francis Asbury Awl Papers - contains photographs relating to Awl's career with the Pennsylvania National Guard, ca. 1880-1918.

MG-17 Samuel Penniman Bates Papers - contains engravings of portraits of Civil War military officers, especially of the Pennsylvania Volunteers; also President Abraham Lincoln and his cabinet; scenes depicting the Battles of Gettysburg, Antietam, Petersburg and Murfreesboro; and Civil War personalities such as Thaddeus Stevens, John Burns and others.

MG-20 Richard Beamish Papers - contains photographs relating to Beamish's career as Secretary of the Commonwealth under Gifford Pinchot, 1931-1935. Items show Beamish with Pinchot, President Herbert Hoover, posing with Pinchot's cabinet, and other scenes.

MG-25 Bloss Family Collection - contains photograph portraits of the William F. Bloss Family of Lackawanna County and their descendants, 1863-1896. Includes Civil War cartes-de-visite of Bloss, Generals Philip Sheridan, T.C. Devin and others.

MG-31 Theodore Burr Covered Bridge Society Collection - includes scrapbooks and a survey of covered bridges throughout the state, and occasionally photographs of the bridges, 1959-1969.

MG-36 Citizen's Fire Company #3 Records - includes a photograph of this Harrisburg company's horse-drawn fire wagon, ca. 1910.

MG-70 Haskell Family Papers - includes a daguerreotype of Franklin A. Haskell of Wisconsin, ca. 1850, and a Civil War photograph portrait of Colonel William A. Haskell of Philadelphia.

MG-73 Liliane Stevens Howard Collection - includes a signed panoramic photograph of participants at a woman's suffrage convention at the Hotel Casey, Scranton, ca. 1915.

MG-80 Samuel C. Lyford Papers - contains one folder of letters from various government officials acknowledging receipt of an album of views of the U.S. Government Building at the Centennial Exhibition in Philadelphia, 1876. Colonel Lyford administered its distribution.

MG-82 Duncan McCallum Collection - includes photographs relating to his career as secretary to Governors Gifford Pinchot, 1931-1935, and John Fine, 1951-1954. Views show McCallum with Pinchot, his wife Cornelia Pinchot, John Fine and other state officials.

MG-94 Morrow-Hittle Collection - includes photographs relating to this Dauphin County family, ca. 1861-1880; especially the Civil War career of William C. Hittle of the 151st Regiment, Pennsylvania Volunteers.

MG-114 Henry W. Shoemaker Collection - includes photographs of Shoemaker posing near the covered bridge at Clarks Ferry before it was razed, ca. 1924.

MG-139 Frank W. Melvin Papers - includes formal portraits of Melvin, and publicity views in his capacity as chairman of the Pennsylvania Historical Commission, ca. 1936-1940, and member of the Brandywine Battlefield Commission, 1947-1961, and others.

MG-145 Daniel H. Hastings Papers - contains photographs pertaining to the career of this state adjutant general, 1887-1894, and governor, 1895-1897; portraits of ancestors and relatives in Ireland; ruins of the State Capitol after the fire of 1897; laying the foundation for the new Capitol, and the Capitol grounds, 1898-1899; riding in the inaugural parade of President Benjamin Harrison with Governor James A. Beaver, 1889; at "Camp Hastings" of Mount Gretna, 1898, and other military encampments, ca. 1890; views of the ruins of Johnstown after the 1889 flood by C.E. Howard of Bedford and E. Walter Histed of Pittsburgh; and President William McKinley, ca. 1898.

MG-146 Ross H. Hickok Papers - includes photographic portraits and other views of this prominent Harrisburg family, owners of the Hickok Manufacturing Company, 1864-1929. Hickok was married to Helen, the daughter of Governor Daniel Hastings (see above) and some Hastings Family items are included.

MG-159 John S. Fisher Papers - includes portraits of this governor, ca. 1928, and Gifford Pinchot, 1922, both by Chandler of Philadelphia; and artists' conceptions of the proposed Education Building, State Street Bridge and Capitol Complex, Harrisburg, by architects Gehron and Ross, ca. 1928.

MG-161 John M. Phillips Collection - includes photographs relating to the career of this Pittsburgh conservationist and member of the State Board of Game Commissioners, ca. 1890-1930. Items show Phillips at Cook Forest; at an Arbor Day parade in Pittsburgh with Governor John Tener, ca. 1912; and a 1914 Boy Scout Encampment in Schenley Park.

MG-163 Hubertis M. Cummings Collection - includes copy photographs by this Historical and Museum Commission historian collected for articles in *Pennsylvania History* and other publications, 1947-1957. Topics cover the covered bridges at Clarks Ferry, Columbia-Wrightsville, and elsewhere; and the State Capitol.

MG-164 Hiram Gilbert Andrews Collection - includes photographs relating to the career of this state representative from Cambria County, ca. 1900-1960. Items include portraits of Andrews and his family; with Governor William Sproul; an unidentified circus parade; scenic views of vacations in Los Angeles and Mexico; and postcards he collected of the United States, Canada, Cuba and Europe.

MG-168 Robert E. Pattison Collection - includes cabinet cards of the relatives of this Pennsylvania governor, ca. 1880-1890; and a view of Pattison in his executive office, ca. 1887.

MG-169 Herman Blum Collection - includes photographs and engravings collected by this historian, ca. 1840-1957, especially of Stephen Girard, James Buchanan, Girard College, William Penn's burial place in England, William Penn's Treaty with the Indians (after Benjamin West) and other scenes of Penn's life in America, a silhouette of President William Henry Harrison, President and Mrs. Eisenhower visiting an Islamic Mosque in Washington, D.C., and others.

MG-190 James H. Duff Collection - includes photographs relating to the career of this state attorney general, governor and U.S. senator, 1943-1957. Notable items include portraits of Duff by Fabian Bachrach and publicity shots of him speaking, campaigning, etc.

MG-191 David L. Lawrence Collection - included among the papers of this governor is a volume of photographs showing the dedication of the National Football Hall of Fame at Canton, Ohio, 1963; and various portraits of Lawrence and images of the Knox Mine Disaster, 1959.

MG-200 Poster Collection - includes posters and broadsides, ca. 1840 - present, relating to the Pennsylvania Canal; balloon ascensions; political campaigns, including Asa Packer for governor, 1862 and George McClellan for president, 1864; Army recruiting posters for the Civil War and World Wars I and II; food rationing and homefront support during World Wars I and II; preventing forest fires with Smokey the Bear; and many others.

MG-201 Gertrude Howard Nauman Collection - includes photographs pertaining to the family and career of this Harrisburg Republican woman, 1899-1972; especially portraits of her, her father Marlin Olmstead, Senator Hugh Scott, President Richard Nixon, Mr. and Mrs. Herbert Hoover, and Nauman with Nelson Rockefeller.

MG-204 State Y.M.C.A. of Pennsylvania Records - includes photographs of statewide conferences, 1914 and 1917; and an album commemorating the Y.M.C.A. centennial, 1944, showing activities of chapters throughout the state.

MG-206 John S. Fine Papers - among the records of this governor's public relations specialist William Wheaton are publicity photographs of Fine's daily activities, 1951-1955. The prints were taken by the Department of Commerce photographic unit, and many matching negatives can be found with the Governor's File of RG-12.

MG-208 William W. Scranton Papers - among the records of this governor are photographs pertaining to his presidential campaign, 1964; and among the records of his press secretary Jack L. Conmy, 1963-1966, are publicity shots pertaining to the Harness Racing Commission, the Council on Business and Industry, the Department of Mines and Mineral Industries and others.

MG-230 David W. Howard Collection - includes a Civil War carte-de-visite of Howard, a member of the Pennsylvania Volunteers, and a cabinet card, ca. 1880, of his son A.K. Howard by John Mather of Titusville.

MG-235 Thomas F. Longaker Collection - includes a photographic portrait of Longaker in uniform by Frederick Gutekunst of Philadelphia, ca. 1863. Longaker was a lieutenant with the 72nd Regiment, Pennsylvania Volunteers.

MG-236 Donald C. Todd Collection - includes a panoramic photograph of Company D, 5th regiment, U.S. Engineers of the American Expeditionary Force, 1917, of which Todd was a member.

MG-242 John P. Wood Collection - includes photographs relating to Wood's career as an officer with the Pennsylvania National Guard, 1912-1918.

MG-243 Jeremiah Rohrer Collection - includes Civil War photograph portraits of Rohrer of Middletown, a major in the 127th Regiment, Pennsylvania Volunteers; of Hiram C. Alleman, ca. 1863; and a lithograph of Camp Boas, Harrisburg.

MG-245 Drake Well Museum Collection - includes original glass negatives and prints by John Mather, a photographer during northwestern Pennsylvania's oil boom, ca. 1860-1880. This collection is housed at the Drake Well Museum, Titusvile.

MG-249 Brady Family Papers - includes photographs relating to the Civil War career of George Keyparts Brady and other members of this Chambersburg family, 1861-1944.

MG-253 Jacob J. Bierer Collection - includes photographs relating to the Civil War career of Bierer with the Pennsylvania Volunteers. Also contains portraits of his Westmoreland County relatives, descendants and members of the Bott Family, ca. 1870-1901; and a carte-de-visite album of Civil War era personalities, including military figures, Queen Victoria, and others.

MG-269 Decorative Arts Collection - contains illustrative items collected by the Decorative Arts Section of the State Museum of Pennsylvania, including holiday greeting cards, 1853-1931; picture postcards, 1896-1917; business trade cards, 1879-1911; and other items.

MG-270 McFarlane-Little Family Papers - contains portraits, ca. 1880-1930 of James McFarlane Little of Gettysburg; and of the family's copper mining properties in Colorado and Mexico, 1905-1911.

MG-271 Frances Toby Schwartz Collection - contains items collected by Mrs. Schwartz including holiday greeting cards and picture postcards, 1903-1954, generally of out-of-state or topical subjects; business trading cards, ca. 1900; and carte-de-visite portraits, most unidentified, by the following photographers: Mechanicsburg: B.W. Matteson, D.W. Boss, A.G. Myers, John B. Brandt, Thomas B. Cardon, Bates and Rupp, G.W. Lachman, and J.H. Keim; Carlisle: H.P. Chapman, J.C. Lesher, C.L. Lochman and Mrs. R.A. Smith; Harrisburg: Burnite and Weldon, R.S. Henderson, A.G. Keet, LeRue Lemer, and J.H. Yeager; and photographers in Philadelphia, Meadville, Erie, Reading, Danville, Columbia, Williamsport and out of state.

MG-279 George N. Wade Collection - includes photographs relating to the political career of this state senator from central Pennsylvania, 1954-1973. Publicity shots, collected from various sources, show Wade with Governors Fine, Leader, Lawrence and Scranton; at ribbon-cutting ceremonies for Interstate 81 near Shippensburg; meeting with various legislators and state officials; attending charity events, etc.

MG-283 Genevieve Blatt Papers - includes photographs relating to her career, especially as secretary of Internal Affairs and judge of Commonwealth Court, 1954-present. Views show Blatt with Presidents Truman, Kennedy and Johnson; with Governors Lawrence and Scranton; and U.S. Senators Hubert Humphrey and Hugh Scott. Also present are items pertaining to her involvement with the Catholic Church.

MG-284 Leroy Horlacher Papers - includes photographs of Horlacher's prison life as a World War I conscientious objector at various camps in the United States, 1917-1920.

MG-297 Mary Sachs Collection - includes photographs showing activities of this Harrisburg businesswoman, department store owner, and supporter of the local Jewish Community Center, 1928-1960.

MG-301 John C. Kunkel Collection - includes photographs pertaining to the career of this Republican U.S. representative from central Pennsylvania, 1943-1966. Views show Kunkel with Presidents Eisenhower, Kennedy and Johnson; political and other celebrities including Barry Goldwater, Virgil "Gus" Grissom, Nelson Rockefeller, Hugh Scott, and others.

MG-302 Bowman's Department Store Collection - includes photographs relating to the operation of this Harrisburg department store, 1895-1954.

MG-303 R. Brognard Okie Collection - includes occasional photographs of buildings interfiled with technical drawings and papers of this eastern Pennsylvania architect. Most prints pertain to his reconstruction of Pennsbury Manor during the 1930s. Use of these materials is restricted by the Okie family.

MG-306 Ernest P. Kline Papers - include photographs of the daily activities of this lieutenant governor under Milton Shapp, 1977-1981.

MG-314 McCalley Family Collection - includes photographs of the military career of aviator James B. McCalley of Pittsburgh, 1916-1925. McCalley, a member of the U.S. Army Air Corps, participated in the Mexican Border Campaign and the Reserve Officers Training Corps at Langley Field, Va. Photographs show him demonstrating a parachute jump at Langley, 1925. Others include portraits of McCalley Family members.

MG-315 William Sellers Company Collection - includes watercolor engineering drawings on linen and paper, ca. 1860-1919, of locomotive mechanical and steam fittings, and hydraulic injectors and tools to service them, manufactured by this Philadelphia firm. Most were drawn by Theodore Bergner, William J. Sellers and Coleman Sellers. Others, of German origin, show the Verbesserter, Gifford and Friedmann injectors.

MG-317 Mary Barnum Bush Hauck Collection - includes photographs and posters relating to Hauck's career as the Works Progress Administration's State Supervisor of Music and organizer of folk festivals in Dauphin County, ca. 1935-1960.

MG-332 Henry Mohn Family Collection - includes photographs of portraits and activities of this Leetsdale family, ca. 1890-1946. Subjects cover the 1907 and 1936 floods in Leetsdale and a family trip to the western United States.

MG-333 George Washington Fenn Papers - contains photograph portraits of Fenn in his Civil War uniform and his wife, Anna Roberts, by Burnite and Weldon of Harrisburg, ca. 1865. Also included are portraits of the allied Dietrich Family, ca. 1865-1912; and unidentified cased photographs.

MG-341 Florence Amelia Linderman Collection - includes photographs of Linderman and her parents, Daniel and Amelia Linderman, of Berks County, ca. 1880-1948. Notable items include a postcard album of State Capitol buildings and an album of yearly portraits of Florence taken by her father from age nine weeks to fifty-three years; and views of her life as a U.S. Navy nurse during World War II.

MG-342 George H. Earle Collection - includes photographs of Earle's career as U.S. Minister Plenipotentiary to Austria, 1932-1934, and as Governor, 1935-1938. Notable items include Governor and Mrs. Earle's trip to Sweden as part of the Swedish Tercentenary, 1937; and at the 1936 Democratic National Convention; President Franklin Roosevelt campaigning in Harrisburg, 1936; and publicity views of the Governor with the Pennsylvania Motor Police, John L. Lewis, at the Allegheny County Fair, etc.

MG-345 M. Lee Goldsmith, Inc. Papers - includes photographs showing activities at Goldsmith's upholstery and furniture store, Harrisburg, 1872-1946.

MG-356 Daniel B. Strickler Collection - includes photographs of Strickler's career as a general with the Pennsylvania National Guard during World War II, and based in Germany during the Korean Conflict.

MG-363 William K. Sowers Collection - includes photographs of Sowers's career with the Reserve Officers Training Corps at Pennsylvania State College, ca. 1925; with the Civilian Conservation Corps Landisburg Camp, 1933; and at Middletown Air Depot, 1949-1956.

MG-373 Richard A. Snyder Collection - includes photographs relating to the career of this state senator from Chester and Lancaster Counties, 1972-1984.

MG-375 Benjamin Franklin Fisher Papers - includes cabinet card portraits of Fisher as a lawyer in Philadelphia, ca. 1880.

MG-379 State Fencibles Collection - contains photographs relating to the history of this military unit, originating in Philadelphia ca. 1850-1950. Notable items include portraits of Civil War soldiers; the Fencibles honoring Theodore Roosevelt, Herbert Hoover, Chiang Kai-Shek and others; and a broadside for a performance of "Uncle Tom's Cabin," 1856.

MG-386 Pennsylvania Federation of Women's Clubs Collection - contains portraits of the Federation's presidents, chairwomen and other officers, 1911-1968; and a scrapbook of photographs of the Wilkins Farm, an area of the proposed Allegheny National Forest purchased by the Federation and given to the public domain, 1927-1931.

MG-388 William A. Schnader Collection - contains photographs of the career of this state attorney general, 1930-1935, and unsuccessful Republican candidate for governor, 1934.

MG-389 James A. Beaver Collection - contains photographs relating to this governor, 1887-1891, including the "old" Capitol, ca. 1880; the Governor's Mansion; and Pennsylvania National Guard activities at Mount Gretna, 1913.

MG-392 Jack A. Bowling Collection - includes photographs of the career of this U.S. Navy admiral and Philadelphia area silversmith, ca. 1930-1978.

MG-393 Pullman-Standard Car Manufacturing Company of Butler, Pa., Records - includes photographs of the production line at the Company's Butler facility, ca. 1942-1981. Employees are shown producing Pullman cars, making shell casings during World War II, and attending retirees' picnics, 1963-1965. Most persons are unidentified.

MG-397 M. Harvey Taylor Collection - contains photographs, 1896-1966, of the career of this state Republican leader from central Pennsylvania. Notable items show Taylor with Governors James Duff and William Scranton, President Richard Nixon and others; the dedication of the Harvey Taylor Bridge at Harrisburg, 1952; and others.

MG-400 W.P.A. Records Collection - contains color plates of costumes through the ages, especially relating to Pennsylvania, made by the Works Progress Administration's Museum Extension Project, ca. 1938.

MG-406 Robert P. Casey Collection - contains copy prints made in 1986 of photographs from Governor Casey's private collection, prepared for a 1987 inaugural exhibit. Views show Casey at various stages of his career, with his wife and family, and with his parents and other ancestors.

MG-415 Ivor D. Fenton Papers - contains photographs relating to the career of this Republican U.S. representative from Mahanoy City, ca. 1939-1962.

MG-422 Herbert Broadbelt Baldwin Locomotive Collection - approximately 14,000 negatives and 3,500 statistical cards of locomotives (builders' photos) manufactured by the Baldwin Locomotive Works at Eddystone, near Philadelphia, 1872-1954. The materials were collected by Herbert Broadbelt, a company employee. This collection is housed at the Railroad Museum of Pennsylvania, Strasburg.

MG-424 Harry Houck Collection - Harry Houck of New Cumberland was an early radio pioneer. The collection is 1.0 cu. ft. of documents and photographs relating to the technological development of radio in Pennsylvania and the United States, ca. 1910-1930. Artifacts relating to Houck are housed at the State Museum of Pennsylvania. This collection is unprocessed.

ADDENDA

RG-1
DEPARTMENT OF AGRICULTURE
Press Office Photograph File, 1954-1984, 12 cu. ft.

This file was created by the Press Office for publicity purposes and contains color and black and white prints and negatives, 8 x 10 and smaller, of the Department's activities. Arranged by topic, and roughly by alphabet, a listing is available for the first five cubic feet only. Subjects include the construction and dedication of the Department of Agriculture Building, 1965; research on animals and animal diseases; bees; the fight against nuisance insects, birds and plants; commodity queens; poultry and egg testing; farm machinery; farm scenes; foods and food chemistry; fruits; Future Farmers of America; the State Harness Racing Commission; livestock; mushrooms; plant diseases; plowing contests; tobacco; trees; vegetables; portraits of Secretaries of Agriculture, 1915-1979 and other Department personnel; the Pennsylvania Farm Show, 1955-1972; the Pennsylvania Livestock Exposition, 1957-1970; the All-American Dairy Show, 1964-1970; and the Junior Dairy Show, 1957-1968.

MG-85
J. HORACE McFARLAND COLLECTION
Ca. 1899-1947, 3.5 cu. ft.

This is a 1990 addition to the collection described elsewhere in this volume and consists of approximately 1,000 glass and film negatives by the McFarland Company. In 1991 the Pennsylvania Historical and Museum Commission produced contact prints of these negatives. Arranged numerically, an in-house listing is available. Subjects include images of flowers, fruits and vegetables created for catalog sales for such companies as W. Atlee Burpee and B.H. Farr Nurseries; views of Ephrata Cloister, 1899; Admiral Dewey Day in New York City, October 6, 1899; the construction and dedication of the State Capitol, including the 'interim' capitol, 1899-1906; placing of the George Barnard Statuary on the Capitol steps, 1911; the Dauphin County Courthouse; Harrisburg city government and business buildings; the Executive Mansion; the Eagles Mere Hotel; and an ostrich farm in Jacksonville, Fla. Views taken of slums to illustrate McFarland's

"City Beautiful" Movement speeches include Harrisburg, Homestead, Mechanicsburg, Philadelphia, Pittsburgh, Vandergrift and Wilkes-Barre, Pa.; Albany, Buffalo, and Niagara Falls, N.Y.; Cincinnati, Ohio; New Haven, Conn.; Trenton, N.J.; and Atlanta, Ga.

There is also a file of approximately 2,000 lantern slides and autochromes, many of which match the negatives listed above. This file is currently unprocessed.

MG-432
RATHMELL COVERED BRIDGE COLLECTION
ca. 1950-1960, 1.5 cu. ft.

This collection contains several hundred black and white images, 8 x 10 and smaller, of covered bridges throughout Pennsylvania taken during the 1950s by James and Virginia Rathmell, of Lansdale. Arranged alphabetically by county, most photographs are accompanied by a data sheet giving length, dates of construction, historical facts, and in some cases date of removal or destruction. Some images are copies of older historical photographs. Also included are 76 2 x 2 color slides by the Rathmells of ferries, trolleys, train stations, steam traction and locomotive engines throughout Pennsylvania.

GLOSSARY OF PHOTOGRAPHIC TERMS

Ambrotype: a negative image on glass. The glass, placed against a dark background, made the negative image appear as a positive. Subjects were usually portraits. Popular in America ca. 1855-1865.

Autochrome: a positive color image on glass. The autochrome, introduced in 1907 by the Lumiere Brothers of France, was the first commercially successful color photograph process.

Builder's photo: an image of a railroad locomotive, sometimes rolling stock, usually taken from the right side. The background is often masked out. The photographs were primarily taken by the manufacturer for record keeping and sales purposes.

Cabinet card: an image on thin photographic paper mounted on a card 4 1/2 x 6 1/2. It was introduced in America in 1866 and remained a popular Victorian item until about 1910. Subjects were usually portraits.

Carte-de-visite: literally French for "visiting card," it was an image on thin photographic paper mounted on a card 2 1/2 x 4. The format was patented in France in 1854 and remained popular until the turn of the century. Subjects were usually portraits.

Contact print: a photographic print made by exposure through direct contact with its negative, and therefore the same size as the negative.

Daguerreotype: a positive image on a silver-coated copper plate. The process was announced by Frenchman Louis Daguerre in 1839 and was popular until about 1860.

Lantern slide: a 3 1/4 x 4 positive transparency on glass, either black and white, tinted or hand colored. These were intended for screen projection and viewing by an audience. The first standardized slides were introduced about 1870 and widely used until the 1950s.

Nitrate film: roll or sheet negative film with the base made from cellulose nitrate. It was developed by George Eastman in the 1880s and was used until the availability of safety-base film in the 1930s. Cellulose nitrate is an unstable medium, and if conditions are right can be highly combustible.

Panoramic print: a print made with a negative from a panoramic view camera having a wide-angle lens, or a print made as a composite from several different negatives joined together. Prints made from these were popular between 1900 and 1940. They are usually less than ten inches wide but may vary in length from twenty inches to several feet.

Stereographs or stereoviews: a double image appearing as three dimensional when viewed through a special apparatus called a stereoscope. Stereographs have been made with a variety of processes, including da-

167

guerreotypes and glass slides, but more familiarly on a thin photographic paper glued to a cardboard mount. Early paper stereographs measure 3 1/2 x 7 and later ones 4 x 7 and larger. They were popular from around 1850 to the 1920s.

Tintype: also known as a ferrotype, a photographic image on a thin sheet of iron. Is was popular from 1856, when they were introduced in America, to the turn of the century.

Wirephoto: a thin photographic print usually 7 x 9 or 8 x 10 made for sending by telephone or telegraph wire. The method is used by news agencies to send to newspapers, magazines and other information sources around the world.

INDEX

170

Bank of North America (Phila.), 95
Banks, 35, 132
  robberies, 151
Banks, Nathaniel P., 114
Banquet rooms, hotel, 121
Banquets, 135, 140
Barber shops, 120, 121, 135
Barbour Flax Spinning Co., 96
Bare Mill, 52
Barges, 101
  coal, 34
Bar Harbor, ME, 146
Barkley, Alben W., 114, 138
Barkley Family, 105
Bark peeling, 8, 12
Bark, tree, 14
Barnard, George Grey, 66
  State Capitol statues, 22, 41, 66, 165
  statues by, 69
Barnegat Point, NJ, 111
Barnesboro, 79
Barns, 9, 64, 120. See also: Farms
Barnum, P. T., 84
  circus, 87
Barracks, state police, 140. See also: Police,
  State
Barrelmaking, 13, 122
Barrington, C., 126
Bars, barrooms. See: Saloons
Bartram, John, house of, 130
Bartram's Gardens, Society of, 63
Baseball, 135, 151
Baseballs, manufacture of, 97
Basie, Count, 85
Basketball, 65, 86, 135, 151
Basketmakers, gypsy, 12
Baskets, fruit & vegetable, 13
Bass, 30
Bates & Rupp, 160
Bates, Samuel Penniman, Papers, 156
Bathing, 107. See also: Beaches, Swimming
Baton Rouge, LA, 40, 115
Batteries, storage, 36
Battlefields, 13, 22, 25, 40, 53, 78, 79, 80, 89,
  92, 157
Battles, sham, 68
Baum Family House, 145
Bauxite mining, 97
Bayless Paper and Pulp Co., 132
Beach Lake, 82
Beaches, bathing, 94, 107
Beal, G. S., 9
Beamish, Richard, Papers, 156
Beans, bean picking, 96
Bear hunting, 53
Bear Rocks, 112

Bears, black, 4
Bear Valley Public Camp, 11
Beary, Frank, Coll., 115
"Beatrice," 89
Beatty, 144
Beatty, Clyde, 101
Beauty pageants, 117, 151. See also:
  Commodity queens
Beauty salons, 105, 135
Beaver, James A., 86, 87, 157, 163
  Administration, 86
  Collection, 163
  Photograph Album, 86
Beaver (town), 17, 79
Beaver County, 21, 23, 24, 34, 51, 79, 94, 139
Beaver Creek, 104
Beaver Dam Marble Co., 99
Beaver Falls, 79, 94
Beaver Meadows, coal breakers at, 118
Beaver River, 7, 23
Beavers, 11
Beaver Springs, 81
Becker Family, 105
Beckley College, 123
Bedford (city), 52, 79, 122
  photographers, 157
Bedford County, 13, 14, 20, 21, 23, 24, 25,
  36, 51, 53, 63, 64, 79, 154
  Courthouse, 52
Bedford Springs, 71, 79
Beef cattle, 96
Bees, beekeeping, 4, 102, 165
Beetles, 4
Behavioral science, 18
Beidel, H. Frank, 91
Belgium, 117
  King Albert of, 131
Bell (photographer), 142
Bell, Alexander Graham, 82
Bell, Edwin, stave mill, 13
Bell, John C., 24, 57, 71
Bell, Martin, Mansion, 133
Bellanca aircraft, 123
Bell, Book, and Candle, 107
Bellefonte, 79, 122
Bell Telephone Co., 101
  buildings, 142
Belle Vernon, 80
Belleville, 8
Bellevue, 78
Bellevue-Stratford Hotel, 95
Bellows, furnace. See: Furnace bellows
Bells Are Ringing, 107-108
Bellwood, 79
Belmont (estate), 130
Beltzhoover House, 130

Ben Avon, 78
Benjamin Franklin Parkway, 95. See also:
  Philadelphia
Benson, Walter, Photographs, 147
Bensonville Railyards, 111
Bentleyville, 82
Berger, Anna, 89
Bergner, Theodore, 161
Berks County, 13, 21, 23, 24, 25, 34, 49, 51,
  52, 53, 61, 73, 79, 94, 99, 147, 162
Berlin (Somerset Co.), 81
Bernville, 112
Berrier Family, 105
Berrigan, Revs. Daniel & Philip, 151
Berry pickers, immigrant, 14
Bertolet Mennonite Graveyard, 73
Berwick, 79
Berwyn, 127
Bethlehem, 17, 35, 52, 81, 98, 110, 112, 130,
  151, 153
Bethlehem Steel Co.
  Bethlehem, 98, 110
  Cambria Co., 22
  Coatesville, 99
  Northampton Co., 35, 62
  Pittsburgh, 32
  Steelton, 34
Betula, 12
Betz Family, 156
Beverly, NJ, 100
Bible classes, 135
Bicentennial Celebration, U.S., 109, 113
Bicentennial Commission, State, 50
"Bicentennial Raft and the Rafting Era in
  Pennsylvania, The," 109
Bicentennial Wagon Train, 51
Bicycle clubs. See: Wheel clubs
Bicycles and bicycling, 53, 83, 103, 105
Biddle Family House, 145
Biglerville, 78
Big Run, 80
Big Spring Public Camp, 11
"Big Trees," 10
Bikini Atoll, 116
Billiard parlor, 121
Bining, Arthur C., 61-62
Biology, 44
Birch Run Dam, 11
Bird Mansion, 61
Birds, 4, 102, 165
Birdsboro, 7
Birmingham, AL, 68
Birmingham (Greene Co.), 80
Birmingham Meeting House, 73
Birthday celebrations, 135
Bishop, Francis, 89

Bison, 11
Bitterns, 4
Bitumen, 12
Bituminous coal mining, industry, culture.
  See: Coal, Mines & mining
Bixler Run, 23
Blackberries, harvesting, 96
Black Hills, SD, 111
Black Moshannon State Park, 11
Blacks, 36, 47, 84, 91, 156
  churches, 36
  housing for, 36
  migrant, 18
  spirituals, 156
Blacksmiths, 105, 120, 121, 122
Blackwell House, 130
Blain, 122
Blaine, Ephraim, House, 130
Blaine, James G., 114
  birthplace, 71
Blair, C. Hugh, House, 145
Blair, Frank P., 114
Blair County, 13, 20, 21, 23, 25, 36, 51, 52,
  53, 79, 94, 133
Blairsville, 80
Blandon, 120
Blandon House Saloon, 120
Blank & Stoller, 48
Blast furnaces, open hearth, 99
Blatt, Genevieve, 27, 45, 85, 160
  Papers, 160
Blight, chestnut. See: Chestnut blight
Blimps, 123
Blind Boy Scouts, 102
Blister, white pine, 4
Bloom, George I., 85
Bloomsburg, 79, 122
Bloomsburg, photographers, 142
Bloomsburg State College, 15, 142, 143
Blossburg, 81
Blossburg, state hospital at, 15, 42
Bloss Family Coll., 156
Blossoms. See: Flowers
Blouch, Herbert K., Coll., 115
Blue Hole Spring, 11
Blue Knob State Park, 53
Blue Mountains, 112
Blueprints, 15, 61, 66, 125
"Blue Ridge Mountain Was A Fortified
  Frontier, When The," 113
Bluestone Quarry, 88
Blum, Herman, Coll., 158
Blythe Spirit, 108
B'nai B'rith, 27
Boak Family, 105
Boalsburg, 8, 70

176

177

197

200

Main File, Dept. of Highways. See:
 Highways, Dept. of
Main Line, PRR. See: Penna. Railroad
Mallard ducks, 30
"Malolo," SS, 100
Mammal fossils, 102
Mammoth #1 Mine, 144
Man of La Mancha, 108
Man Who Came to Dinner, The, 108
Manada Gap, 123
Manassas, VA, PNG maneuvers at, 72
Manayunk, 8
Mancini, Henry, 86
Mann Farm, John, 130
Manns Run, 104
Manor, 82
Manser, Edward, 30
Mansfield, 81
 State Teachers College, 15, 42
Map Collection, 156
"Maple Sugar Industry in Penna., The," 14
Maple sugar or syrup, gathering, 12, 64, 96
Mapleton Depot, 91
Maps, 14, 48, 51, 73, 115, 156
 aerial, 51
 forest, state, 14
Marble quarrying, 99
Marble works, 120
Marcay, France, 140
March, William Allen, Coll., 88, 116
Marching, military, 116
March of Dimes, 27
Marcus Hook, NJ, 53, 94, 100, 153
Marguerite, 144
Marianna, 56
Marietta, 80
Marietta Centennial Celebration, 74
Marine Corps, National Day, 138
Marine Depot, U.S., Phila., 32
Marion Center, 80
Marion, OH, Steam Shovel Co., 101
Maritime Academy, Penna., 55
Markers, 12-13, 14, 34, 53. See also:
 Monuments
Marketing, agriculture, 96
Marketing, commerical product, 97
Markets, farmers or curb, 5, 17, 34, 35, 85,
 96, 131
Markleton, 81
Mars (town), 79
Marshall, George C., 71
Marshall, Thomas Riley, 46, 108
Marshall Arboretum, 12
Marsh Creek, 23
Marsh Run, 123
Martic Forge, 61

Martin, Edward M., 17, 24, 29, 69-72, 88,
 115, 117, 138
 Collection, 88
 Papers, 69-72
 Trophy, 70
 with Mrs., 70
Martin aircraft, 101
Martin, Park, 27
Mary Ann Furnace, stove plates from, 62
Maryland, 62, 67, 73, 96, 97, 98, 99, 101, 102,
 105, 112, 117, 123, 126, 150
Marysville, 123
Mason & Dixon Line Marker, 13
Masons, 95, 135
Masontown, 80
Massachusetts, 62, 99, 101, 111, 148
Massacres, monuments to, 22
Masters (photographer), 142-143
Matamoras, 95, 123
Maternal health programs, 17, 18
Mather, John, 99, 159
Matteson, B. W., 160
Mauch Chunk, 8, 22, 52, 75, 79, 94, 134
"Mauretania," SS, 101
Maytown, 74
Meade, George G., 89, 92
 monument, 41
Meadville, 79, 109, 160
 photographers, 160
Meat packing industry, 96
Mechanical engineering, 110, 161
Mechanicsburg, 80, 123, 134, 160, 166
Media, 80
Medical Field Service School, U.S. Army,
 32, 134, 135. See also:
 Carlisle Barracks
Medical social work, 18
Medical societies, 85-86
Medicare services, 18
Medicine, disaster. See: Disaster medicine
Meetinghouses, religious, 52, 73, 94, 95, 130,
 145
Meetings, club. See: Clubs
"Meet the Press," 138
Melhuish, Camp, 68
Melvin, Frank W., 28, 31, 157
Memorials, 34, 115, 131. See also: Cemeter
 ies, Markers, Monuments
Mennonite Graveyard, Bertolet, 73
Mennonite meetinghouses, 52, 73
Mennonites, 73
Men's clubs, 121
Mensuration, forest, 14
Mental health films, 45
Mental Health, Office of, 45
Mental Health Week, 45

211

Rye, 96

219

Ward, J. W., 77
War History Commission, Penna. See:
Penna. War History Commission
War History Program. See: Penna.
Historical & Museum Comm.
War Manpower Commission, U.S., 39
Warren, Earl, 114
Warren, Gen., statue at Gettysburg, 92
Warren (city), 8, 15, 18, 42, 82, 91
Warren (county), 12, 20, 21, 23, 36, 51, 52, 81
Courthouse, 52
state hospital at, 15, 42
Warrior Ridge, 8, 133
Warriors Mark, 133
War, U.S. Secy. & Asst. Secy. of, 135
Warwick, 130
Warwick Furnace, 61
Warwick Iron and Steel Co., 62
Washington, George, 84, 114
at Ft. LeBoeuf, 29
Braddocks Field monument, 22
letter, 73
Washington & Jefferson College, 36
Washington Boro, 74
Washington (PA city), 22, 70, 72, 77, 82, 97,
156
Washington County, 4, 21, 23, 36, 51, 53, 62,
71, 82
Agricultural Fair of 1920, 4
Washington Crossing, 33
monument at, 22, 53
State Park, 11, 22, 53
Washington, DC, 19, 49, 63, 72, 97, 158
photographers, 136, 144
Redskins, 151
Washington House Hotel, 122
Washington, NJ, 119
Washingtons Headquarters, Valley Forge,
61, 130
Waste. See: Garbage
Waste drains, 18
Watches, historical, 102
Water
pollution, 9, 18, 19
power plants. See: Hydroelectric plants
quality, 18, 19
sports, 53
supply, 11, 18
wheels, 132
Waterfalls, 7, 12, 21, 24, 35, 54, 67, 94, 95,
104, 129, 143. See also name
of waterfall
Waterford, 33, 37, 80
Waterfronts. See: docks
Watergate Scandal, 151
Waterman, John, grave, 73

Watermelons, 96
"Water Power, 1913-1916," 7
Waterston, NY, 146
Water Street, 133
Waterway, Intercoastal. See: Intercoastal
Waterway
Waterworks, 105, 130, 131
Waterworks, Fairmount. See: Fairmount
Waterworks
Watrous, 133
Waukegan, IL, 97
WAVES, U.S. Navy, 70-71
Way, B. G., Lantern Slides, 138
Waymart, 82
Wayne, 80, 127, 142, 153
Wayne, Anthony
grave, 89
statue, 73
Wayne County, 21, 23, 36, 51, 64, 82, 95
Wayne Inn, Gen. Anthony, 89
Waynesboro, 80
Natl. Guard Armory at, 15
Waynesburg, 22, 69, 70, 72, 80
WCAU radio, 35
WDAB radio, 100
Weasels, 4
Weather instruments, 14
Weatherly, 5
Weaver Family, 105
Weber, Denise, Photographs, 141
Weber, Francis, Coll., 117
Weber Family, 105
Webster, Daniel, 114
Wedding anniversaries, 135
Weddings, 135
Weest, Harry, 71
Weiand, Richard, 156
Weinrich Sanitarium, 94
Weiser, Conrad, Park & Monument, 11, 22,
23, 25, 52
Weissport, 134
We-Klothe-U Outfitting Co., 122
Welding, machines for, 99
Weldon. See: Burnite & Weldon
Welfare Rights Organization, Natl., 150
Welfare, Secretary of, 24
Wellsboro, 81, 142
Wellsville, 123, 147
Wentz, Peter, house, 73
Wernersville, 79, 94
state hospital at, 13, 15, 42
Wertzville, 123
Wesleyville Archeological Site, 33
West, Benjamin, 158
Westbay, James H., Coll., 76
West Branch, Susquehanna River. See: